THE BEST OF Charles E. Jefferson

THE BEST OF
Charles E. Jefferson

SELECTED AND WITH AN INTRODUCTION BY

FREDERICK KELLER STAMM

Thomas Y. Crowell Company New York

Established 1834

COPYRIGHT © 1960 BY THOMAS Y. CROWELL COMPANY
ALL RIGHTS RESERVED
DESIGNED BY EDWIN H. KAPLIN
MANUFACTURED IN THE UNITED STATES OF AMERICA
BY THE VAIL-BALLOU PRESS, INC., BINGHAMTON, N.Y.
LIBRARY OF CONGRESS CATALOG CARD NO. 60-9216

PREFACE

If I could carve a statue of Charles Edward Jefferson, I should like to do it after the manner of one that stands outside Trinity Church, Boston, where Jesus stands behind with his hand on the shoulder of Phillips Brooks. The history of great American preaching could not be written without including in its pages the preaching of Charles Edward Jefferson. Sitting at his feet and reading what he said over a period of thirty-one years as the minister of the Broadway Tabernacle, New York, was indeed a rich experience for me.

This editor does not claim that he has selected *all* the best of Dr. Jefferson. As someone has said, "He was always at his best." He never preached a poor sermon. Some who read this book will wonder why a certain sermon they heard him preach or have read has not been included. Then, too, nothing is included here from *The Character of Jesus* or *The Character of Paul,* two of his greatest works, which should be read in their entirety in order to gain a true understanding of Jefferson's view of these two personalities.

Suffice it to say that what is set down here seemed to appeal to the editor as he again read the many volumes of sermons, lectures, and talks. When a congregation hears a sermon, not all the people will think alike about it. One Sunday's sermon will make its deep appeal to some, while next Sunday's will lift others to a higher peak of resolve and action. What is chosen here, however, was characteristic of Dr. Jefferson's preaching. He had many strings to his fiddle, and here are some of them.

My thanks are due to David H. Scott, Editor of the Religious Book Division of the Thomas Y. Crowell Company, for asking me to edit this book, and for his help in finding all of Dr. Jefferson's published works; and to Mrs. Ina Clements, long-time member of the Tabernacle, who sent me a pamphlet by Dr. Jefferson which put me in the way of learning precisely the influence which Phillips Brooks had on the young Jefferson's decision to become a minister.

FREDERICK KELLER STAMM

Plumsteadville, Pennsylvania

CONTENTS

II LECTURES

III CONVERSATIONS

THE BEST OF Charles E. Jefferson

INTRODUCTION

There is no biography and no autobiography of Dr. Charles Edward Jefferson, who stood as a light set on a hill in the pulpit of the Broadway Tabernacle Church—now the Broadway Congregational Church—for thirty-one years. The material which is set down here comes from the writer's own personal acquaintance with him, hearing him preach on many occasions, and reading again his many books of sermons, lectures, and talks.

My first contact with Dr. Jefferson occurred in the very early years of my ministry when he came to the small city in the hinterlands of Pennsylvania where I was preaching. He was there to lecture on "Peace" in the first years of the First World War, before the United States entered that conflict. I was asked to introduce him that night, and had the privilege of a half hour's chat with him before the lecture. He was in the heyday of his power as the minister of the Broadway Tabernacle; and as I talked with him and heard him speak, I was not a little conscious that I was in the presence of a modern prophet of God.

Aside from the possibility of hearing him preach in the Tabernacle if ever I should travel to New York, I thought my meeting him was like ships passing in the night. I would never again feel the touch of his hand nor the warmth of his friendship. I would know him through his books, but I would not know *him*. But about fifteen years later my path led me to the Clinton Avenue Congregational Church in Brooklyn, in the spring of 1929.

Evening services were still being held in the Tabernacle, so one evening my wife and I went to hear him. We arrived a bit early and were seated near the front of the sanctuary. Hardly had we been seated when the door of the vestry opened and a man looked out—whom I came to know later as the superintendent—and presently walked straight to our pew.

1

"Are you a preacher?" he inquired.

"Yes," I replied.

"Well, come with me, please," he said. "Dr. Jefferson wishes to see you."

Stepping into the vestry, I was surprised to be greeted by Dr. Jefferson by name. He said, "My foot is broken; it was put in a cast just yesterday, and I have difficulty standing. My assistant is away, and there is no one to help me in the service. I can stand long enough to preach the sermon, and would be pleased if you would take the other part of the service."

Thus my second personal contact with Dr. Jefferson, and the beginning of the privilege of standing in that pulpit one or two Sundays every summer for a long period of years. At my installation as minister of the Clinton Avenue Church some months later, he came over to Brooklyn to give the charge. I remember clearly only part of what he said that night: "A church is here to do a *work,* not to make a *show.* A preacher is here to do a *work,* not to make a *show.*" It was characteristic of Dr. Jefferson to be a workman that needeth not to be ashamed, and not to be a showman.

My last contact with him was a year or two before his death. His powers had waned, and the one-time Jefferson was no more. I picked him up at the close of a meeting of the New York City Congregational Association at Mt. Vernon, and dropped him off at his home in New York. On the way I said to him, "I think I have read most, or all, of your books."

"Which one do you like best?" he asked.

"The Building of the Church," I replied.

"Everyone says the same thing," he remarked. "Which one do you like next?"

"Well, you have a great book in *Things Fundamental,*" I said.

"Everyone says the same thing," he again remarked.

"Are you doing any preaching these days?" I asked.

"No," he said.

"Doing any writing?"

"No. I wrote all I knew long ago."

"What do you do?"

"Oh, sit around the house reading the newspapers and listening to the radio all day."

Like Emerson, his mental processes were no longer keen, and the vibrant, vigorous "Greatest American Preacher"—as someone called him—was no more. He was seventy-six when he died in 1936. They laid him away in a New England cemetery with a few people present, and a memorial service was held in the Broadway Tabernacle.

The memory of my contacts with Charles Edward Jefferson will live with me to the end. Preaching to him was more than a profession. It was a commission from God. He was Isaiah, Jeremiah, and Paul, all wrapped up in one personality, and always with the words in his heart and on his lips, "Thus saith the Lord." He never regretted, after hearing Phillips Brooks, that he became a preacher. He regarded his ministry, not as a task, but as a privilege. He never faltered in his devotion to Jesus Christ, whether Man or God, and he looked upon Paul, not as the theologians look upon him, but as a man with the peace and love of God in his heart and mind.

Dr. Jefferson was born August 29, 1860, at Cambridge, Ohio, the son of Dr. Milton Jefferson, a native Virginian, and his wife Ella Sachet, born in the Isle of Guernsey. It was a Methodist family, and Charles was graduated from Ohio Wesleyan University in 1882, and from the Boston School of Theology in 1887. He was called that September to the Congregational Church, Chelsea, Massachusetts. A little sketch in *The History of the Broadway Tabernacle* says that he was greatly admired by the people in Chelsea, and was known as one of the brilliant young men in Boston who were friends of Bishop Brooks. When he left the Chelsea church to become the minister of the Tabernacle in 1898, a public reception was given for him and Mrs. Jefferson at which more than 1200 persons passed in the receiving line. He preached his first sermon in the Tabernacle, then located on Thirty-fourth Street, on the first Sunday in March. In 1905 the present church was erected at the corner of Broadway and Fifty-sixth Street.

But Jefferson's path into the ministry had not been a direct one. When he went to Boston, it was not to matriculate at the theological seminary, but to study law at Harvard University. His heritage was not that of a long line of preachers. Indeed, the church held little interest for him during his college days. In Ohio he found no preacher who made him want to preach. He looked down on preachers. They were an inferior set. He looked down on the church. It was a belated institution. He looked down on Christianity. It was, he thought, becoming obsolete. His idols were Huxley and Herbert Spencer. He found no inspiration in the pulpit. He found it in Emerson and Carlyle.

His life plans were settled, and he knew what he was going to do and be. His classmates looked upon him as a coming prominent lawyer, perhaps a statesman.

Then one evening in Boston he went to hear Phillips Brooks, at the suggestion of Dr. Frank W. Gunsaulus, pastor of the Congregational Church in Newtonville. Boston was rich in famous preachers—James Freeman Clarke, Edward Everett Hale, Brooke Hereford, Bernard Carpenter, Minot J. Savage, John L. Withrow, and Joseph T. Duryea. He heard all of them. He was a sermon taster. He soon learned, however, that Phillips Brooks surpassed them all. He was in a class by himself—richer, deeper, mightier. He was more piercing, more searching, more vitalizing, than all the others. It was Jefferson's custom to hear three sermons every Sunday, and it was seldom that a Brooks sermon was not one of them. "At last," he said, "I had discovered a preacher. I wanted all my friends in the West to hear him. I felt sorry for them because they could not live in Boston. I longed to tell everybody about him. Like the woman of Samaria, I wanted to cry out, 'Come, see a man, which told me all things that ever I did.' "

His description of Phillips Brooks's personality, preaching, and breadth of view, as he gave it in a sermon on January 13, 1931, in Trinity Church, Boston, is fascinating and ought to fire the imagination and soul of every young minister as he sets out to preach. It would be rewarding study in every class in homiletics in every theological seminary in the land. "Every sermon," he said, "was baptized in the spirit of Christ. No matter what his text, one could always feel certain that before he got done with us, we should all be standing before the judgment seat of Christ."

Not many weeks passed before he began to wish he might be a preacher. Now that he had found out what preaching was, he felt sure that preaching was what the world most needed. He had never had that wish before. Old things were gradually passing away, all things were presenting themselves in a new light. Interest in law books was waning. In the midst of his law studies he could hear the voice of Phillips Brooks above the voices of his professors. The church was irresistibly crowding out the courtroom. He wanted to be a preacher, but he was a bundle of doubts. He was a skeptic. He believed in God and immortality, and that was about all. He had never had a call. But he wished he could preach.

So one day he spoke to Dr. Gunsaulus about it, who said, "Why not have a talk with Brooks? I will arrange an appointment for you at his home."

The thing was done, and for an hour and a half they talked. When he rose to leave, Brooks asked him to come again. But Jefferson never did. He felt he had no further claim on the Bishop's time and strength. But after a week of meditation he decided to enter the ministry. Through three years of his seminary course he heard Brooks again and again. Brooks was his seminary. He said he learned more from him than from his professors. "He kindled a fire in me. He made me believe in God, in man, and in myself. Nothing could induce me to leave Trinity. Through three years I received Communion there. I was not an Episcopalian, but he received me into the family. I have now been preaching forty-four years, just twice as many years as he preached in Trinity, and through all of these years his face has been in my eyes, and his voice has been in my ears."

To anyone who loves preaching and who is interested in great preaching, there is much more that could be said about Dr. Jefferson than space permits in this book. All I can do is to sketch briefly the characteristics of his ministry and hope that the younger and older preachers of today will catch some of the fire from the same altar that kindled his mind and heart; his voice was stilled a quarter of a century ago, and though dead, yet speaks.

First of all, the mainspring of Charles Edward Jefferson's preaching was found in his high regard for the ministry as *the greatest work in which one can engage.* "I would rather," he declared, "be the pastor of the Broadway Tabernacle than hold any other position on earth." His first sermon in the Tabernacle was preached on the text, "For other foundation can no man lay than that is laid, which is Jesus Christ," and every year thereafter on the occasion of his anniversary, he preached from the same text. It was the inspiration in all his preaching, for he believed implicitly that Jesus is the cure for all of humanity's ills.

When he built the Tabernacle, he said, "Do not let us build an institutional church, a church which concerns itself with amusements and gymnastics. That is good, but let other institutions do it. Let us have an inspirational church, a church which shall put the emphasis on the Spirit; a church that shall inspire men and women to think, to use their minds, to reason and think God's thoughts after him; a church that shall expand and beautify the heart, developing the affections and widening the sympathies, creating friendship which shall add a new fragrance to the life of the city; a church which shall concern itself supremely with the building of character after the pattern of Jesus Christ." One could wish that this would be the aim of every young man as he starts out to preach, and of all the older preachers, instead of succumbing to the externals of their environment, making the church big business, and measuring the success of the church by how many buildings there are, how many members are received, and how much the budget has been increased.

Dr. Jefferson also stood for the *freedom of the pulpit*. "I have aimed," he said after twenty-five years, "to keep the torch of liberty burning. It is often asserted that a minister is not free; that he is a mouthpiece of his congregation. But it is not true that a minister is certain to lose his place as soon as he begins to think for himself. I have always done my own thinking and always shall. I have been free all my ministerial life. I have never trimmed a sentence to suit anybody. I have never held back an idea which I thought was my duty to express. I have never had mental reservations. I have never looked to any man or to any group of men to find out what I ought to say. Every man in this church has always known that I would not turn my hand to retain my position. It has never made the slightest difference to me whether I remained the pastor of the Tabernacle or not. The world is big and there are many fields in which an honest man can do a fine work for God. No man nor any group of men have ever tried to intimidate me or to induce me to say something other than I wanted to say. I make this statement with great boldness and deep pride, for the encouragement of all young men now studying for the ministry, and for the inspiration of all the boys who may be looking toward the ministry as their life work. In an age of controversy and intense feeling, when good men have been divided on nearly all important matters, I have gone on year after year expressing my convictions with great positiveness and clearness, though many times these conclusions did not agree with the conclusions arrived at by many members of the church. But you allowed me to go on expressing the truth as I saw it. This is the best thing you have ever done for me."

In this connection, any present-day preacher who sets himself up as an authority in all things, and who wishes to impose his ideas and will upon the congregation, has missed the spirit of Charles Edward

Jefferson. He believed that a church ought to be broad enough to hold all sorts of opinions, different viewpoints, and diverse theological positions. "Each one," he said, "is under Christ and must answer to Him. Each one must be free to follow the direction in which the Spirit seems to lead." The Tabernacle congregation repeated the Apostles' Creed at every Sunday morning service, but no one was compelled to do so. Every one was left to put his own interpretation upon every phrase. The church had a creed of its own, but no one was asked to subscribe to it. It was not a condition of church membership. He wanted people to be led by the Spirit into all truth. He did not want people to believe in the doctrine about Jesus, but rather to be willing to follow his way of life. A free pulpit for free men was what he wanted for the Tabernacle.

Then too, he was an *intellectual and a scholar*. He spoke to the mind as well as to the heart. From the time he attended public school, through college and seminary, books were his meat and drink. He played a little tennis, and now and then a round of golf, but only because he knew that a bit of exercise was good for his bodily health. But delving into all sorts of books was his chief recreation. He knew the masters in literature, art, science, nature, philosophy, and religion. And he knew the Bible. No one knew it better. As I read his books again, I marvel at how he could reel off one name after another of men and women who were leaders of thought down through the ages. His congregations were made up of many professors in universities, colleges, and seminaries. Students in New York and visiting ministers were found in his church every Sunday, morning and evening. No one ever went away from hearing him without knowing he was listening to a master of thought and diction.

When he wrote his book *The Character of Paul,* he referred to it as "a book of sermons which have never been preached." As he grew older in years, he added, he had more sermons to preach than Sundays to preach them. But for thirty years Paul had been one of his favorite heroes, and for thirty successive summers he made one of Paul's epistles his daily study. He read the letter again and again, "meditated on its contents, pondered the problems it presented, and communed with the spirit of the man who wrote it." He read every book on Paul he could find. Is it any wonder that as one picks up his book on Paul, one gets an entirely different conception of the great apostle from that usually presented by seminary professors? "Theologians," he said, "had so hedged him in by piles of learned rubbish that a layman can hardly get at him. Even the biographers of Paul become so learnedly prolix that the average reader can do little with them."

However, Dr. Jefferson was wrong when he said, "The reign of the Calvinist Paul is coming to an end." Ever since the First World War it has taken on new life, and Calvinism has been in the ascendancy in the teaching of our theological seminaries. One may imagine Dr. Jefferson, with his keen mental and spiritual insight, today in the Tabernacle pulpit, thundering away at our present theological fashions, as he did against the evils of government, politics, international diplomacy, and vice in the city of his day.

Moreover, Dr. Jefferson was a *higher critic*. What else could he be, with his incisive mind and his devotion to the truth of things? Long before the Fundamentalist-Modernist controversy of the twenties he was talking about the historical approach to the Old and New Testaments, and calling the literalists ignoramuses. Along with his prophecy in the pulpit he was a teacher, and instructed his people in religion. Time and again—in sermons, in his midweek services, and in private conversation—he told his people how to read the Bible.

As one contemplates his fearlessness in dealing with controversial issues, and his honesty of mind and heart, as he sought to make the Bible intelligible, one wishes that those who are responsible for giving us new translations of the Scriptures would be as concerned about having people read them with an understanding mind as they are about making the Bible a best seller. Unity of all the religious forces will come only when all preachers exchange their literalism for an intelligent and historical approach to the Bible.

Dr. Jefferson likewise was a preacher of the *Social Gospel*. The only gospel he knew was the gospel which covered all departments of human life. He said that Isaiah, Jeremiah, Jesus, and Paul all preached the Social Gospel. He did more than mouth the petition in the Lord's Prayer: "Thy Kingdom come, thy will be done, in earth as it is in heaven." "I have meddled," he said, "year after year with business, with industry, with politics, with diplomacy. I have repudiated the monastic conception of life, and have urged you to work with all your might for the extension of the way of love. I have spoken to you in trumpet notes on the sacredness of political duty. Unless a man is a good citizen, he cannot be a good Christian. A man to be good must do his duty. I have struck with all my might at the gigantic evils of our time. There has never been a wrong that I have been afraid to hit. Social injustice, the twelve-hour day, the seven-day work week, I have denounced with passionate reiteration. The Ku Klux Klan and all other oath-bound societies, organized for the purpose of setting class against class or races against races, I have denounced as un-American and un-christian and stupid worldliness, extravagance, and sloth. Unfairness, unbrotherliness, prejudice, race hatred, cruelty, these are abominations you have been warned against time and again."

If he had been here during the past twenty-five years, one could hardly think of him as capitulating to the theology of defeatism which has characterized much of our preaching during these years. One could hardly think of him as shutting himself up in a gospel that cared little for the welfare of mankind. "People . . . talk," he proclaimed in his sermon, "The Social Vision of Isaiah," "of the 'Old Gospel.' That is the very gospel I am speaking about. The 'Old Gospel' is the 'Social Gospel.' . . . This individualist gospel is no gospel at all. Dip down into the teaching of Jesus anywhere you please, and you will find him preaching the Social Gospel. . . . This is indeed the gospel that we all want. The Simple Gospel is the Social Gospel. . . . Your worship of God is meaningless and offensive until you are in right relations with your neighbors." One time after the other he rang the changes on honesty, justice, love, in all man's relationships with his fellows. One cannot think of him as repudiating that gospel in any day or in any age.

Then again, he was a *lover of peace and a hater of war*. In his lectures at Vanderbilt University he seems to betray a bitterness against Germany. He doesn't sound like the real Jefferson. But who can criticize him with good conscience? As with many another man before the First World War, he had hoped the world had come to a long era of peace. The war broke suddenly, and he felt Germany must take the guilt of it all. The war startled Dr. Jefferson and wounded his spirit. It wasn't easy to preach in a day he had hoped would never come. His mind and heart, however, were always in the direction of a peaceful world.

One Sunday morning he said to his large Tabernacle congregation: "I am going to preach sixty minutes on Peace, and I do not want anyone to leave during the preaching of the sermon. You are at liberty of leave, but if you must go, please do so during the singing of the hymn before the sermon." No one left.

"The Broadway Tabernacle pulpit," he told some preachers at an informal gathering, "is a place where the preacher preaches as long as is necessary to develop his subject."

At any rate, peace was a consuming fire in Dr. Jefferson's breast. "A nation is doomed," he declared in his sermon "Christianity and War," "as soon as it gives itself up to the leading of military experts. It is because the nations of Europe have so largely followed the advice of their military experts that all Europe is in such a deplorable condition. The blind have led the blind, and they are all in the ditch. As Huxley says in one of his letters, 'Directly a man gets the smallest repute in any branch of science, the world immediately credits him with knowing about ten times as much as he really does.' How large an army and navy a nation should have is not a question of military experts. That is a question for scholars and men of wide experience and sound practical judgment. It is for the men of learning and large outlook and clear vision, who know the history of the world from the settlement of Greece to the capture of Aguinaldo, who are acquainted with the age and know the currents of its manifold life, who believe in the principles of the Son of God and desire to give them the fullest embodiment in the lives and institutions of men."

If space permitted I could give a hundred instances of how he lashed at war with scorching indignation; how he tore to shreds the accursed philosophy of militarism; how he kept saying that our nation was headed for perdition; and how he denounced the doctrine of preparedness as fallacious and fatal. As I read again his fierce denunciation of war, the only conclusion I can come to is that if all the preachers and the church in general had been as forthright in this matter as was Dr. Jefferson, we would not now be in danger of annihilation from the atom and hydrogen bomb. The church has listened, not to its Lord, but to the politicians and military experts who say, "We must be so strong that if we are knocked down we can get up again and retaliate." Charles Jefferson thundered against war and all its evils.

Last but not least, Dr. Jefferson was *a simple preacher*. By that I mean that no one ever went away from hearing him not knowing what he was talking about. He said to the preachers in *Quiet Hints to Growing Preachers,* "Always remember that there is a little boy in your congregation." When he preached of Isaiah's idea of the remnant, he started his sermon with the words, "If there is any boy or girl in the congregation who is wondering what is meant by 'remnant,' I must begin by an explanation of that word." By the time he had finished the explanation, he had the whole congregation at his feet. When he preached to boys and girls, as instanced in his volume, *My Father's Business,* he preached, not little junior sermons, but full-length sermons, from which adults, too, could gather information about the great truths of the Gospel.

A friend once told Aneurin Bevan, a leader of the British Labor Party, "If you can't say it, you don't know it." Thereafter Mr. Bevan could speak without stammering. It was so with Dr. Jefferson. He knew his subject and he could talk about it in lucid language. His ideas were clear, and consequently he could speak in clear and simple language. He could use long words when he had to, for he was a master of English, but he generally used short words and short sentences. He preached extemporaneously and often dictated his sermons on Monday morning exactly as he had preached them on Sunday. He had little patience with the intellectually lazy preacher. He told preachers that as a man grows older, he ought to be able to prepare a sermon in a half hour. He didn't mean that a man could waste the precious hours during the week running about here and there and engaging in extracurricular work, and then expect to preach a sermon on Sunday that would speak to the minds and hearts of his congregation. Preaching, he held, is the preacher's main business, and only after he studied day after day, week after week, year after year, could he stand in the pulpit and feed a hungry flock.

Perhaps the rank and file of preachers will not reach the heights which Dr. Jefferson attained, but they can emulate his studiousness, his consecration, his wholesome respect for his high calling, his insight into truth, and his fearlessness and honesty. It is a great privilege to gather together in one volume the things he said over a long and successful ministry, and to present in this fashion a truly great American preacher.

Would to God that some young man sitting in our congregation would, through long years, see our face and hear our voice!

I

SERMONS

I

Two Views of the Bible

In the first chapter of his Second Letter to the Corinthians, the Apostle Paul uses an expression which to me seems an admirable statement of the function of a Christian minister. He says to his Corinthian friends, "Not for that we have dominion over your faith, but are helpers of your joy. . . ." He had written somewhat positively, as was his custom, and on reading it over, what he has written sounded a trifle dogmatic, and so he threw in this apologetic sentence—"we"— that is, Silas, Timothy, and I—"do not want to lord it over your faith, we are simply helpers of your joy. You stand fast in your own faith." In other words, every man must have a faith of his own. No other man can give it to him, but another man may be able to help him clarify his faith, strengthen it, and defend it. That is the function I hope to perform in these sermons. I shall not attempt to dictate to anybody what he is under obligation to believe, but I should like to assist him in arriving at conclusions which will contribute to his freedom and peace and joy.

We begin with the Bible. The Bible is the storm center of the religious world in our generation. All the great religious controversies which are now raging are rooted in the Scriptures. There are two views of the Bible contending for supremacy, or, in other words, two views of inspiration. No body of men in the Christian Church is denying the inspiration of the Bible. That point is not up for discussion. All members of our evangelical churches are agreed that the Bible is inspired— that it is the greatest book in the world, the best book, and the most useful—the immeasurably precious treasure of the Christian church. The only question which is stirring the minds of thoughtful men to-day is the question of *how* the Bible is inspired. What is the nature of the inspiration, and to what extent does it go? Before one plunges into any controversy, it is desirable that he should see clearly just what the point at issue is. The question before us is: "What theory of inspiration shall we hold?"

The first theory about which we are to think may be called the "dictation" theory. According to this theory, the Bible is a dictated book. It was dictated by God. God wanted to deliver a message to mankind, and so He chose certain men to whom He dictated His message, and the men have written down His message in documents which constitute our present Bible. This view of the Bible is clear, and easily understood. We know what *dictation* means. When a man dictates a message, he makes use of an amanuensis. The amanuensis does not supply any of the ideas or any of the words. The message belongs entirely to the man who does the dictating, and the message is his from beginning to end. If a man does not have an amanuensis, he uses his own pen. The pen is an instrument in his hand—not at all responsible for what he says. And just so is an amanuensis an instrument which the dictator makes use of. He is a "pen man." According to one view of the Bible, the men who wrote the Bible were "pen men." God dictated the message, and these men wrote it down.

According to this theory, the Bible is God's Book. It is not man's book. It is a divine book and not a human book. It is the "Word of God." That is a title which has been applied to it for hundreds of years. Many persons still make use of it. It is an appropriate title to use if you hold the dictation theory. If the Bible is a dictated book, the whole Bible belongs to God. Every book of the sixty-six books is His, and every paragraph and every sentence in every book. They are all His, and because they are His, they are equally authoritative. In a book which God has dictated, there can be no errors. Infinite Wisdom could not dictate mistakes. If God dictated the Bible, then the Bible is infallible. It is the final authority. You cannot go beyond the Bible for the reason that you cannot go beyond God. God, in the Scriptures, has given the world His final message. This is the dictation theory stated in the baldest terms. Very few persons probably hold it in that extreme form. Whenever a large number of people hold any theory, they hold it with different degrees of tenacity and strictness. The dictation theory has many modifications. Almost everyone is willing to admit that there are errors in the Bible which is in our possession.

For many hundred years the Bible was transcribed from one skin to another by copyists, and it was impossible to keep errors from creeping in. There are errors in the Bible due to the carelessness of copyists. Moreover, the Bible has been translated from two languages into English, and the translators were not infallible. They have here and there made mistakes. Everyone is willing to grant that there are errors in the Scripture due to the fallibility of translators. And then many persons are willing to admit that it was ideas and not words which God dictated. God gave an idea, and allowed His amanuensis to clothe it as he chose. Every Bible writer was at liberty to make use of his own vocabulary, and to employ his own individual style. In this way we can account for the fact that Isaiah writes in one way, Jeremiah in another, and that both of them differ widely from Amos and Hosea. We all know that Paul does not write like John, nor John like Peter, from which we may infer that God did not dictate words. His dictation was confined to the ideas. The old doctrine of verbal dictation has well-nigh disappeared. But after all these modifications have been made, this theory remains—the dictation theory. The Bible is the "Word of God"—authoritative in its every part—the infallible guide of mankind.

This is the traditional view of that part of the Christian world in which we have grown up. This was the view, if not of our fathers and mothers, at least of our grandparents. Nearly every one of us can remember some saintly grandfather or grandmother, or uncle or aunt, who made a practice of reading the Bible through every year, beginning always with the Book of Genesis, and never halting until arriving at the end of Revelation. To be sure, it was hard reading in many places, but this did not deter the brave-hearted Bible reader. It was very dull in Leviticus, and very dry in Numbers. There were long stretches of desert in the Books of the Chronicles, but the reader plodded patiently forward, feeling that God must be pleased because such reverence was being shown to His Word.

These good people of the earlier day read the Bible after this fashion because the preachers held the dictation theory. They believed the whole Bible to be the Word of God, and had no hesitation in dipping into the Scriptures at any point for a sentence by which to establish any idea which they wished to lodge in the minds of their hearers. Many of the sermons preached a hundred and two hundred years ago are insufferably dull to us because they are little more than a string of Biblical quotations. The minister started out with something he wished to prove, and he proved it by making a miscellaneous collection of quotations taken from all ports of the Bible. Esther was just as authoritative as Isaiah, and the First Book of the Kings was as reliable as Hosea. The earliest portions of the Old Testament stood on the same level as the latest portions of the New Testament, because all alike were the Word of God. The preacher used the Bible in this way because this was the way in which the theologians used it. When you pick up the confessions of the sixteenth and seventeenth centuries, you find that every article in them is supported by quotations from the Scriptures. It is interesting to note that no distinction whatever is made between the Old Testament and the New, or between one book of the Old Testament and another book. The theologians made no distinction when it came to quoting the Scriptures, for the reason that it was their conviction that all the books of the Bible were the Word of God.

This, then, is the traditional view, and it survives to the present hour. There are many people in all parts of the country who hold the dictation theory of inspiration, and in some parts of the country it is the dominant view. Whenever you hear a person say he "believes the Bible from cover to cover," or that he "always takes the Bible as it reads," you may confidently infer that that person holds the dictation theory of inspiration. When you hear any one say that the Bible which was good enough for his mother and his grandmother is good enough for him, you may conclude that that person believes that the whole Bible is the authoritative and infallible Word of God.

Over against this dictation theory of inspiration there is another theory, and for lack of a better word I am going to call it the "illumination theory." According to this theory, God is Light, and since God is Light, the Holy Spirit is Light, and when the Holy Spirit comes into a human mind, that mind is lighted up, or, as we usually say, "inspired." A man is inspired when he sees things more clearly than other men see them, or when he sees some things which other men do not see at all. If a man sees more or less clearly spiritual realities and spiritual distinctions and spiritual relations which escape the attention of the average man, we call that man inspired. The men who wrote the Bible were inspired because their minds were lighted up by the indwelling of the Holy Spirit.

According to this theory there must be degrees of inspiration, just as there are degrees of illumination. You can illumine a room brilliantly, or you can illumine a room partially, or you can illumine a room very dimly. You may let all the gas jets burn, or you may turn half the gas jets out, or you may allow only one gas jet to burn. In the first case, you will see everything in the room with great distinctness. In the second case you will see many things clearly while other things lie in shadow. In the last case many things will escape your eyes. And so if we accept the theory of illumination, we are not reluctant to admit that some Bible writers were more illumined than others. Some saw distinctly, and some saw only dimly. And because of this difference in the degree of illumination, we cannot put all the Bible books on the same level. They are not all equally authoritative. They are not equally binding on the conscience of living men. There was some light in the minds of the patriarchs, but not sufficient for them to be greatly troubled because they were polygamists or because, when it served their purpose, they could tell lies. There was more light in the minds of the judges, especially Samuel, and there was still more light in the minds of the prophets, while the illumination became far more intense in the minds of the apostles. And when we come to Jesus of Nazareth, we find his whole mind so flooded with light that he could say, "I am the light of the world."

If we hold the theory of illumination, we are to conceive that inspiration must be progressive. Truth comes into the minds of men as the sun comes into the eyes of the world. The dawn begins with only the faintest tinge of light low down in the eastern sky, but little by little the sun climbs, crowning first the hills with glory, and later on filling the deepest valleys with light. Thus came the Sun of Righteousness into the consciousness of the human race. At first the light was faint and uncertain, but little by little it grew until things that could not be seen at all at first became later on clear as the sun at noon.

If inspiration is indeed progressive, we shall not be surprised to find that in the earlier stages of Hebrew history there were many crudenesses of conception, and many rudenesses of conduct, which have long since been left behind. Because the Jews believed a certain thing in the morning of their national life, it does not follow that that idea is still binding on us; and because good men did certain things three or four thousand years ago, it does not follow that they are examples for men of our own generation. Many things in the Bible have long since been outgrown. Many ideas have been exploded, and many practices have been discarded. We all see, without difficulty, that the great mass of Levitical ritualistic legislation does not belong to us. The civil legislation of the Jews has also been left behind, the political ideas are antiquated, all of the science of the Bible has been outgrown, many of the moral ideas of the Scriptures have been left far behind. This is because inspiration is progressive, and the Spirit is guiding humanity into wider ranges of truth. According to this theory of inspiration, we are not to consider the Bible as the "Word of God," but rather the literary record of the progressive revelation of the character and purposes of the Eternal.

Possibly, at this point, someone may ask, What difference does it make which of these two theories a man holds? The answer is that up to a certain point it makes no difference whether a man believes in the Ptolemaic astronomy or the Copernican astronomy. He may believe that the earth is flat or he may believe that it is round, and in both cases he can live a happy and successful life. In my boyhood I knew a farmer in Western Pennsylvania who held the Ptolemaic theory. He was a sensible man, and a noble man—a member of the Christian church, and respected and honored by all who knew him. But he steadfastly maintained that the earth was flat, and that the sun and moon and stars revolved around it. He believed all this because the Bible said so. The Bible, to him, was the "Word of God," and he was unwilling to accept the opinions of the astronomers when they set up their opinions against the opinions expressed in the Scriptures.

And what harm did this do him? He sheared his sheep and fed his pigs just like all the other farmers, and got just as much pork and wool as any of them got. He sowed his grain and reaped his grain just as his neighbors did, and his barns were just as full as theirs. The seasons came and went for him, as they did for other men—summer following spring and spring coming after winter, and winter following autumn. Spring laid her blossoms at his feet; summer filled his lap with fruits; autumn stored his barns with grain; and winter spread over his fields a blanket of spotless white. The sun rose and set for him; the moon waxed and waned for him; and the constellations—cohorts in the shining army of the Lord of hosts—marched nightly across the fields of blue for him.

And so it is with one's view of inspiration. One man may believe that the Bible is a dictated book, and the other man believe that it is an illumined book; and both men will find it a lamp to their feet and a light to their path. To each man it will be meat and drink. To each man it will give comfort, strength, and joy—both men, by reading it, will be able to go down into the valley of the shadow of death saying, ". . . I will fear no evil: for thou art with me. . . ." Both men will be able, because they have feasted on this book, to say to the king of terrors, "O death, where is thy sting? O grave, where is thy victory?" Up to a certain point it makes no difference to which of these two theories you subscribe.

But if you wish to explain the phenomena presented by the Bible —if you wish to account for certain things which are to be found in the Bible—then the dictation theory will not serve you. So long as a man simply feeds his pigs and shears his sheep, sows his fields and reaps them, it does not matter whether he follows Ptolemy or Copernicus. But if he wishes to understand why there are eclipses of the sun and why there are eclipses of the moon; if he wants to explain the motions of the planets; if he wishes to know why the constellations hold one position in midsummer and a different position in midwinter, then he must let the Ptolemaic theory go. He cannot satisfy his mind, if he wishes to use his mind upon the stars, with the theory of Ptolemy. It was the astronomers who first protested against the Ptolemaic theory, and decreed that it must go. It *had* to go because it crumbled in the presence of the facts. It made no difference to the common masses of men whether Ptolemy was right or Copernicus. They could marry, and give in marriage; they could eat, drink, and make merry. They could buy and sell and get gain just as readily under the Ptolemaic astronomy as under the Copernican astronomy; but every man who became a student of the stars had to surrender the Ptolemaic theory. He was forced to become a disciple of Copernicus.

So it is with the Bible. The average man is not a student of the Bible. The things he finds in it do not disturb him. He gives his life to certain forms of work, and after working hours he gives himself up to certain forms of pleasure. The difficulties and mysteries of the Bible do not trouble him. But if a man becomes a student of the Bible and tries to explain it to his own mind, he is obliged to surrender the dictation theory of the Scriptures, and look around for another theory which will fit the facts. That is why the protest against the dictation theory came, first of all, from the Bible scholars in our theological seminaries. Here were groups of men whose business it was to make a study of the Scriptures, and when they studied them earnestly and thoroughly, they discovered that the dictation theory was not tenable.

It is stated in the Scriptures that God made the earth in six days. We are sure He did not dictate that. We are told, once in Exodus and once in Deuteronomy, that He wrote the Ten Commandments with

His own finger on two tables of stone. We are convinced that He did not dictate that. It is written by a Hebrew historian in the tenth chapter of the Book of Joshua that in answer to a prayer of Joshua's, ". . . the sun . . . hasted not to go down about a whole day." It is not likely that God ever dictated that. When you turn to the New Testament, you will find Paul in the fourth chapter of his First Epistle to the Thessalonians saying that the Lord is going to come down out of heaven with a shout, and that when He comes, the Christians who are dead are going to come out of their graves first; that these risen Christians, along with the Christians who have not died, are going to be caught up in the clouds where they will meet the Lord in the air. Nothing like that ever happened, and therefore we are very sure God did not dictate that. In the last book of the New Testament, we find at the very beginning of it these words: "The Revelation of Jesus Christ, which God gave unto him, to shew unto his servants things which must shortly come to pass. . . ." Now, many of the things written in the Book of the Revelation did not come to pass, nor have they come to pass yet, nor will some of them ever come to pass, and therefore we may be sure that God did not dictate the last book in the New Testament. It is difficult to believe that He dictated any of them, and therefore it is our duty to let the dictation theory of the Scriptures go.

But there is still another reason why we must discard the dictation theory, and that is because if we carry it out, it leads to scandal and tragedy. Nearly all the scandal and tragedy of Christian history can be traced to the dictation theory of the Bible. Anybody who takes the Bible as the Word of God, and attempts to carry out literally everything that it says, brings mischief upon the world. For instance, in the twenty-second chapter of the Book of Exodus, God is said to have told Moses not to "suffer a witch to live." Many men, reading that, concluded that this was a command to them, and so through the centuries there were perpetrated the most horrible cruelties upon people who were accused of witchcraft. It is estimated that in a single century a hundred thousand innocent men and women suffered death on the charge of witchcraft. The executioners were not heartless and cruel men, but conscientious men, heroically doing their duty, believing that they were carrying out the will of God.

In the eighteenth chapter of the First Book of the Kings, it is written that Elijah, the prophet, brought four hundred and fifty priests of Baal ". . . down to the brook Kishon, and slew them there." The medieval Church kept the Bible open at that page, and when men led people away from belief in God, the medieval Church believed that it was its duty to follow the example of Elijah. Elijah was a prophet of God—one of the greatest and most honored of the prophets—so beloved that at the end of his life, he was taken to heaven in a chariot of fire. If God told Elijah to kill four hundred and fifty priests to Baal, why should not leaders of the Church put to death every man who was discovered destroying the faith of men in God?

The age-long conflict between science and the Church, so discreditable and shameful, is the result of a wrong conception of inspiration. Ever since the days of Galileo, church leaders and scientists have been arrayed against each other, and in every conflict the leaders of the Church have been routed. They have been wrong every time. If you want to read the disgraceful story, read Andrew D. White's great volumes on *The Conflict between Science and Theology*. One of the reasons why so many young men are biased against Christianity is because of the record which church leaders have made. Their blunders have been due to a false conception of inspiration.

In the days of Shakespeare these literalists were making infinite mischief, causing Shakespeare to say in one of his plays:

> . . . In religion
> What damned error, but some sober brow
> Will bless it, and approve it with a text.

All through the first half of the nineteenth century there were Christian men in America proving that slavery was right by quoting from the Bible. Many of the Southern slaveholders were sincere and noblehearted men, as sincere and noble as any of the Christians of the North, but they held the dictation theory of inspiration, and it was not difficult for them to gather sentences from Holy Writ to prove that slavery was a divine institution, and that owning slaves was not contrary to the will of Christ. During the Great War, there were theologians and ministers in Germany, and also in this country, who published pamphlets defining war as "an ordinance of God," and they clinched their arguments always with quotations from the Bible. One would have said that it was incredible that in the twentieth century such an atrocious and damnable thing as war could ever be defended by any Christian man by quoting from the Scriptures.

Eighty years ago there was a fanatic in the State of New York by the name of William Miller who was an enthusiastic student of the Scriptures. He believed that the Bible is the Word of God from cover to cover, and by concentrating his attention largely on the Book of Ezekiel and the Book of Revelation, he came to the conclusion that the end of the world was coming on April 23, 1843. He was so confident and so enthusiastic that he stirred the hearts of men near and far. Men and women became wild over the words he uttered, and enormous meetings were held in New York and throughout New England. Many men gave up their farms. Other men closed their businesses. In the city of New York the crowds were sometimes so great that passage through the streets was impossible. Shops were closed and placards placed in the windows which read: "This shop is closed in honour of the King of kings, who will appear about the 20th of April. Get ready, friends, to crown Him Lord of All."

The Lord did not come on April 23, 1843, as William Miller had confidently proclaimed, and on revising his figures, he discovered that he had made a slight mistake, and that the day which ought to have been announced was October 20, 1844. Of course the Lord did not come either in 1843 or in 1844, and He has not come yet in any such spectacular and miraculous manner as William Miller expected by a literal reading of the Scriptures.

The Miller fanaticism died down, but it flares up again here and there, and just now there are in New York and in many cities throughout the country ministers of the Christian gospel—earnest men, educated men, high-minded and noble-hearted men, who are enthusiastically declaring that "the Lord is coming within the lifetime of men who are now alive"; and the pity is that tens of thousands of people are believing what they say. What induces these men to talk such nonsense? It is because they have a false idea of inspiration. Why are people found who are ready to accept such preaching? It is because they hold the dictation theory of the Bible. We shall never have peace in the Christian church until we get rid of that mistaken theory.

If so much can be said against the dictation theory of inspiration, someone might reasonably ask: "Why, then, are people unwilling to accept a theory that is better? Why is it that the illumination theory does not win universal acceptance? How does it come that any considerable number of people will go on holding a theory which is demonstrably false?" The answer to this question is that the illumination theory is not an easy theory to manage. The dictation theory is clear and definite, and anyone can easily get hold of it. The illumination theory is vague and indefinite, and you hardly know what it may lead you into. If, for instance, there are errors in the Bible, how are you going to tell what is error and what is truth? Who will pick out the errors, and who will pick out the truths? If you can be certain of some of the Bible and not of all of the Bible, who will instruct you where to find the paragraphs that are certain and the paragraphs that are uncertain? If a part of the Bible is reliable and another part is unreliable, it would seem that you have no guide at all. Unless your guide is free from error, it would seem to be better not to have any guide. It is because of this feeling that one loses the Bible altogether unless he holds on to it from cover to cover that many people cling to the dictation theory, notwithstanding all that can be said against it.

In answer to this difficulty, it may be said, in the first place, that the illumination theory is no more difficult to manage than is the dictation theory. The fact is, the dictation theory cannot be managed at all. You cannot do anything with it in the presence of the facts. The theory crumbles to pieces in the light of the open Bible. It must be admitted that it is difficult to manage the illumination theory, the theory which teaches that the books are on different levels, and that some voices are from heaven, and other voices are from earth. It sounds quite final to say that "if there are errors in the Bible, then you have no guide at all." But this is an instance of what one of my teachers long ago was in the habit of calling "verbal intimidation." We are often intimidated by words. They sound formidable and unanswerable, and we take to our heels and run. If someone asks you if your senses sometimes deceive you, you are obliged to say, "Yes." And if someone goes on to say, "How do you know that your senses do not always deceive you?" you are obliged to answer that you do not know. The logical consequence is that you cannot depend on your senses at all. But at that point we refuse to be logical. After we have admitted that our senses sometimes deceive us, and that they might possibly deceive us all the time, we go right on making use of our senses. That is the only sane thing to do.

There are some problems that have no theoretical solution. They are solved only in action. There is an abstract argument against the possibility of motion. You cannot move where you are, and you cannot move where you are not, and therefore you cannot move at all. That was the way in which Plato was arguing one day, and Diogenes did not attempt any theoretical answer. He answered Plato by walking up and down before him. Many of the problems of life must be solved not by arguments, but by walking. When, therefore, someone says, "Does the Bible ever mislead you?" your answer is, "Yes." And if that person further asks, "How do you know that the Bible does not *always* mislead you?" the proper answer is, "I do not know." The logical consequence would be to have nothing to do with the Bible, but the sensible thing is to go on and use it. You learn the value of it by using it. You learn the principles of it which you need by using it. If you will only use it faithfully, it will guide you to God. If you will only use it as it ought to be used, it will put your feet on the path that leads to life, and your path will grow brighter and brighter "unto the perfect day."

One of the causes of our trouble is that we think we must have an infallible guide. This is a false assumption. We have never had any infallible guides, and there are no infallible guides anywhere in the world, and yet humanity gets on. Our parents were guides, but they were not infallible. We got on very well under their leadership. There are no infallible professors of science, or philosophy, or history, or language in any of the universities of the world. There have never been infallible teachers in any of the centers of learning. There never has been an infallible book in any of the great world libraries, but the world of education gets on without any infallible guides. We do not need an infallible guide in religion. The Roman Catholics thought they did, and so, in the year 1870, they made it a dogma of their church that the Pope is infallible. That is an opinion that had been held by individual Catholics for a long time, but not until 1870 was it proclaimed as a dogma. Many of the wise men of the Church strenuously opposed its passage, but the Italian and Spanish Jesuits pushed it through. Some men were greatly elated, feeling that the Roman Catholic Church would now speak with new power. Others were greatly depressed, feeling that the Catholic Church had discredited itself in the eyes of the most thoughtful. But for fifty-four years, strange to say, the Pope has never once made use of his powers of infallible utterance.

According to the Roman Catholic dogma a Pope speaks infallibly only under these three conditions: (1) He must speak *ex cathedra;* (2) he must speak on a question of faith or morals; (3) he must speak for the guidance of the whole Church. Not once in all these fifty-four years have these three conditions been met. There have been five Popes in this period, and they have issued encyclicals and syllabuses and allocutions, but these are not counted infallible. These can all be modified by future Popes. Pius IX was on the papal throne seven years and never spoke once infallibly. Leo XIII was on the throne twenty-six years, Pius X was Pope eleven years, Benedictus XV was on the throne eight years, and Pius XI has been Pope for over a year, and not one of these five has ever seized the opportunity of making use of his infallible authority.

The Roman Catholic Church gets on very well without any infallible utterances. Nor do we need an infallible Bible. We need the kind of Bible that we have. There are errors in it, but they are only minor errors. They do not quench the light that shines in the Book. If any one twits you on the fact that you do not have an infallible Book, the reply is, "I do not need one. The infallible guide is the Spirit of God." And the spirit of God is given to everyone who asks for His guidance. We are assured that He will guide us into all truth that it is necessary for us to know in order to fulfill our obligations to our fellow men, and to honor our Father who is in heaven.

And so we come around to a position which all of us can confidently hold. We can all be sure that the Bible is a useful book. Paul in his letter to Timothy says: "Every scripture inspired of God is also profitable for teaching, for reproof, for correction, for instruction which is in righteousness: that the man of God may be complete, furnished completely unto every good work." We can all be sure of that. We can also be certain that it is a reliable book. It is not a book of falsehoods. It is not a book of fables and myths. This book was written by honest men. They expressed truth as they saw it. They had no intention to deceive or mislead. They walked by the light that they had. They tell us the best that they knew. It is a trustworthy book. And you can read it with great confidence that you are listening to the words of honest men. You can be sure that it is an inspired book. When someone says that the Bible is no more inspired than Shakespeare, he does not know either Shakespeare or the Bible. That is one of the stupidest things that a man can say. We can be sure that it is an authoritative book. It speaks as one having authority, and not as other books speak. For instance, when we read in this book, "Go, and do thou likewise. . . ." we know that we are listening to the voice of God. When we read, ". . . Whatsoever ye would that men should do to you, do ye even so to them," we know that that is a voice from heaven. When we read, "Thou shalt love the Lord thy God with all thy heart, and with all thy soul, and with all thy strength, and with all thy mind, and thy neighbour as thyself. . . ." we do not quibble, we do not argue, we know that an authoritative message has come from God.

We all agree that it is a unique book. There is no other book like it in all the world. There are other sacred books, but none so sacred as this one. There are other holy books, but none so holy as this. The Koran is a Bible, but it is not like this Bible. Wherever it goes, it blights and withers. Wherever the Bible goes, the skies brighten and the flowers begin to blossom. There is no book like this one. "Read to me from the Book," said the dying Sir Walter Scott to his son-in-law, Lockhart.

And Lockhart, somewhat perplexed, asked, "Which book?"

Whereupon the dying man said, "There is but one."

That is what we all say. The man who holds the dictation theory of inspiration says, "There is but one!" And the man who holds the illumination theory of inspiration also says, "There is but one!"

2

Evolution and the Book of Genesis

By evolution I mean a theory put forward to account for the earth in its present shape, and for all existing forms of life upon it—vegetable, animal, and human. The fundamental idea in evolution is the idea of development. The evolutionary hypothesis assumes that all life as we know it has come from a few simple organisms—possibly from one organism—by a process of continuous modification extending through immeasurable periods of time. Evolution is a theory of the method of creation.

The question about which we are to think is not whether evolution is true or not. That is a scientific question, and scientists must deal with it, and answer it. Vast masses of evidence must be sifted, analyzed, classified, and evaluated, and only a scientist can do this work. He must be an expert in anthropology and morphology and geology and physics and paleontology and zoology and a dozen other sciences. Within the last sixty-five years an enormous literature has been created around this subject, and a man who would start out either to prove or disprove the theory of evolution in a single sermon could touch only lightly on the outermost fringes of the subject. Fortunately, our task is a far simpler one.

The question which concerns us is this: Is evolution anti-Christian? Can a man be an evolutionist and at the same time be a Christian? Does Christianity leave it open for a man to accept the theory of evolution provided the evidence in favor of it, in his judgment, is ample? If evolution comes in at the door, must Christianity fly out through the window? Can a person believe that man has come up from the amoeba and still be a consistent follower of Jesus Christ? There are many people who say "No"—honest people, good people, high-minded people, devoted people, and devout people. They are convinced that evolution is anti-Christian in that it is a repudiation of the Book of Genesis, and therefore of the whole Bible. They think that it is a denial of God, at least of a personal God, and a rejection of the whole spiritual interpretation of the universe. They claim that it degrades man to link him with the beasts instead of with his Maker. They assert that it explodes the doctrine of the Fall, and topples over the whole Christian scheme of redemption.

There are many people who think this. Already in two states of our nation, laws have been passed prohibiting the teaching of evolution in the public schools, and such legislation has almost been passed in several other states. It is frequently asserted that the reason why so many young men and young women become skeptics in college is because of the teaching of evolution. Forty-seven years ago the Pope declared that Darwinism was repugnant to history, to tradition, to exact science, to observed facts, and to reason itself. There are many Protestants who agree with him.

Let us begin our discussion with the Book of Genesis. It is the only book in the Bible that deals with origins. No other book of the Old Testament is concerned with the beginning of the world or the human race, and the only part of this book which deals with such matters is the first three chapters. It is with the eighty verses of these three chapters, then, that we have to deal. The first question is: What is this that we are reading in these three chapters? Is it history, or is it science, or is it philosophical speculation? Is it poetry, or legend, or fable, or myth? Every man must find out for himself. This is not a matter to be left to experts. The ordinary man, whoever he may be, is capable of answering the question.

One might not be able, at the end of the first chapter, to give a positive answer to the question as to whether Genesis is science, or history, or myth. But when we reach the ninth verse of the second chapter, we come to a sentence which gives a clue. We are there told that in the midst of the garden there was ". . . the tree of knowledge of good and evil." No one has ever seen that kind of tree in an orchard, nor has any one found such a tree in the woods. All parts of the world have been visited and studied, and on no continent or island has such a tree as that been found. That sentence sounds like a story. When we come to the twenty-first verse, we are arrested again by a sentence that throws light upon our question. "And the Lord God caused a deep sleep to fall upon Adam, and he slept: and he took one of his ribs, and closed up the flesh instead thereof; And the rib, which the Lord God had taken from man, made he a woman, and brought her unto the man." That sounds very much like a story; women are not made that way now, nor is it at all likely that any woman was ever made that way. We are probably reading a story.

When we come to the beginning of the third chapter, we are absolutely convinced that it is a story, for we read of a woman and a snake holding an animated and serious conversation on a spiritual subject. This is conclusive proof that we are not reading either science or history, we are reading a story. How do we know that? What right have we to say so positively that this is a story? How do you know when you open Aesop's fables and hear the animals talking to one another that you are reading a story? How do you know when you open La Fontaine and hear the birds talking that you are reading a story? How do you know when you open Bunyan's *Pilgrim's Progress* and see Pilgrim fighting with Apollyon that you are reading a story? Your own common sense tells you. You do not need the advice of any expert. Why should not one use his common sense when he reads the Bible? There is no doubt that the first three chapters of Genesis are a story.

It is possible that someone may be shocked or surprised by hearing a preacher say that the first chapters of the Bible are a story. But why should anyone be shocked at that? Why should not the Bible begin with a story? It is the very way in which one would expect the Bible to begin. It could not possibly begin in any better way. If it is indeed God's Book, a book intended for the education of the human race, there is every reason why it ought to begin with a story. Mothers are the ordained teachers of humanity in the earliest stages of its development, and mothers are all born story tellers. They educate their children by the stories which they tell them. Even if a girl has no talent for telling stories, the talent comes to her when she has her first baby. She is instructed by the Holy Ghost as soon as she becomes a mother to tell stories. She feeds her baby's body with milk, and as soon as it has a mind, she feeds its mind on stories. The first books she buys for it are storybooks. No woman who has not fallen into the clutches of some faddist who does not understand children at all would ever think of giving her little children books of history or science. A child's library is made up of storybooks. Every child comes into this world with an insatiable hunger for stories. You never can tell him enough of them. He is always saying, "Tell me another one." You cannot offer him a more tempting prize than a story. Tell him to be good and you will tell him another story, and he will make a desperate effort to be good. Not only do we come into the world with a great liking for stories, but we never outgrow this juvenile hunger. We belong to a story-loving race.

All over the world men and women are hungry for stories. When you glance over the books on sale in the bookstalls at the street corners and in railway stations, you find that nearly all of the books are novels. When you pick up a popular magazine, you find it is largely filled with stories. There *are* magazines which do not run to stories, but they are not popular—their circulation is small. No magazine can have a circulation of a million subscribers which is not filled with stories. Even the newspapers in many parts of the country carry serial stories. One would suppose that the narration of passing events would be sufficiently fascinating and thrilling, but such is not the case. There are millions of human beings who feel that a day is lost in which they do not read at least one chapter of a story. When you read the statistics of the public libraries of this country, you have a demonstration of the fact that we are a nation of novel readers. The New York City Public Library reports that in 1923, 5,568,646 novels were called for. That is more than twice as many as all other books, of all other kinds, put together. Sixteen times as many novels were called for as books of history. Only a few people are interested in history enough to read it. Nearly thirty-two times as many novels were asked for as books on science. We call this a scientific age, and imagine everybody is interested in science. Only a few people, comparatively, care to read scientific books. Nearly fifty times as many novels were taken out of the library as books on philosophy. Only a handful of human beings are at all interested in philosophy. The masses are interested in storybooks. Why should not the Bible begin with a story?

One of the reasons why the Bible has such a grip upon the mind of the race is because it has in it so many stories. The Book of Esther is a story. So is the Book of Daniel. So is the Book of Jonah. The Book of Job is a story in verse, and the Book of the Song of Solomon is a story in metrical form. The Bible is God's Book, and because it is His Book, it has in it many fascinating stories. When you open your New Testament, you stand in the presence of the Man of men, and He is the

Supreme Storyteller of all time. What are His parables but little stories? What stories are better known than the story of "The Foolish Virgins," the story of "The Talents," the story of "The Prodigal Son," the story of "The Good Samaritan"? Matthew says that at a certain period of Jesus's life, He did not do anything at all but tell stories. Every time He opened His mouth, a story came out. That period was the period in which He was popular, and made the deepest impression on the minds of the people. Why should anyone, then, look askance at stories, and feel that they are not worthy of a place in the Bible?

There are different kinds of stories. Many are told for amusement or entertainment, but this Genesis-story is not that kind. This is a religious story, and is told for the purpose of teaching certain religious ideas. It is a serious story. The ideas which it sets out to teach are very few and easily caught. The first idea is that God made everything. The story begins with "In the beginning God . . ." and from that sentence onward we are told that God made everything that you can see. He made the heavens and He made the earth. He made the land and He made the water. He made the grass and herbs and trees. He made the fish and birds and animals. He made man. He made everything. Nothing came by chance. Everything came out of the mind of God. Nothing happened by accident. Everything came into existence out of the heart of God. Nothing came as the result of blind force acting on senseless matter, but everything came by the will of God. "And God said, Let there be light: and there was light." No sublimer sentence has ever been written by the pen of man, and here is another one like unto it: "And God saw every thing that he had made, and, behold, it was very good." How vivid and graphic and unforgettable it all is. Read it once and you never can forget it. And how simple it is—a child can grasp it, a dullard can take it in, a man without any education can catch the point. Even barbarians and savages when the story is read to them are possessed of the idea that God made the heavens and the earth.

The second idea is equally simple and clear. It is the idea that man is the crown of creation. He is the lord of the world. That idea is expressed with great vividness and force. The story says that God made man in His own image. He created him after His own likeness, and He gave him dominion over all vegetable life, and over all animal life. God breathed into him His own breath, and made him a living personality. God gave man authority to give names to every creature on the earth. Whatsoever name he gives to a fish or a bird or an animal, that is its name forever. The story says that after man was created, God created nothing further. He is the climax of the whole creative process. How vividly and beautifully and impressively it is all said! It can never be said better. A child catches the idea at once. So does everyone. A child never forgets it. Neither can anyone. It is a perfect specimen of storytelling.

The third idea is that man did wrong. He did something he knew he ought not to do. Because he did wrong, shame and sorrow came into the world. He did wrong because the thing he did was pleasant to the senses. He did what was wrong and had to pay the penalty. He disobeyed God, and the result of his disobedience was sweat and pain. The writer of the story is especially impressive on this point. He wants everybody to hate the spirit of disobedience, and so he puts that spirit into a snake—the most hated and loathsome of all creatures. He knows that everyone hates a snake, and therefore he links a snake and the spirit of disobedience together. This is the story, then, with which the Bible opens. It will never be surpassed in majesty, in impressiveness, or effectiveness by any storyteller to the end of time. It is the greatest religious story ever written.

Someone asks, "Does this story teach science?" The answer is, "No." The man who wrote the story was not a scientist. He did not know anything about science as we understand that word today. The age of science had not yet arrived. His countrymen were ignorant of science, and so was he. He was not interested in science, and therefore he did not set himself up to teach it. He did not possess the scientific mind. He was not interested in structure as the scientific mind always is, or in processes, or in methods, or in sequences, or in chronology. All these things were outside the circle of his concern. He was a religious teacher, and his scientific ideas have no weight whatsoever.

How do we know that he ignored all science, or that he did not care for it? Everyone can find that out for himself. At the very beginning of the story we are told that "God made the firmament, and divided the waters which were under the firmament from the waters which were above the firmament. . . ." The early Jews believed that the sky is solid, and that there is an ocean above it, and that is what this writer of the Book of Genesis believed. This is what he says: "God separated the ocean above from the ocean below by means of a firmament." But this is not one of the ideas which he is attempting to teach.

He is not interested in the structure of the universe. His only concern is making it clear that the universe, no matter what its structure may be, is the creation of God. He accepted the popular view of the firmament as holding above it an ocean, but that is no part of his message. A little later he says that the grass and herbs and trees were made on the third day, and that the sun and moon were made on the fourth day. That would be a strange thing for a scientist to say. How could a tree grow without the sun? This man, however, is not a scientist, and cares nothing for science. It matters nothing to him whether the trees were made first, or the sun and the moon. God made them, no matter when they were made. The idea which be makes emphatic is not the sequence of the creative acts, but the fact that everything was created by God.

Later on he tells us that everything was created in six days. There, again, he is stating something that science cannot accept, but this is not a part of his teaching. This man is not interested in the clock. He cares nothing for chronology. It makes no difference to him how long it took God to make the world and everything in it. His only concern is that God was the Creator, and that the universe was not all made at once. There were stages in the creation, first inorganic life, then vegetable life, then animal life and then human life, and all the stages were carried forward by God. A preacher can say "firstly," and "secondly," and "thirdly," and "fourthly," but a storyteller cannot do that. A storyteller must be picturesque. He must put things in a way which will catch and hold and delight the mind. And so this storyteller says that one day God made the sun and moon. Another day He made the grass and herbs and trees. Another day He made the fish and the birds. Another day He made the animals and man. There were six different kinds of things which he wished to embrace in his story of creation, and therefore he put them all in six days. But his object is not to teach science, but religion. He cares nothing whatever for the facts and details of physical creation; his ambition is to make clear great truths about God and man.

It is not necessary, therefore, for us to reconcile science and the Book of Genesis. It has often been attempted, but it is a foolish thing to try to do. You can ever reconcile science and the Book of Genesis without twisting language out of its shape, and cramming into words meanings which they never had. You cannot be honest with human speech and reconcile Genesis and science. It is a futile thing to attempt to do, and, moreover, it is a mischievous thing. When you try to reconcile science and Genesis, you give the impression that science and religion are opposed to each other, and that is not true. Muddle-headed scientists and muddle-headed theologians have often fought one another, but there is no hostility between science and religion. How could there be? They move in different spheres. Science is concerned with structure, with processes, and sequences, and what does religion care about these? Religion accepts these as rapidly as science finds out what they are. But if you try to reconcile the Book of Genesis with the latest science and it turns out that the Book of Genesis is mistaken in regard to structure and to sequence, then many people draw the inference that religion has been worsted. The science in the Book of Genesis is absolutely worthless, and it is a waste of time to try to do anything with it with the hope of bringing it into harmony with the science of our day.

Right here we are confronted by another question: Can a man be an authoritative teacher and make mistakes in his scientific thinking? Can he be a reliable teacher in the realm of religion and be ignorant of science? Of course he can. It is not necessary for a religious teacher to be an expert in scientific knowledge. A religious teacher makes use of the scientific knowledge of his generation. That is what the writer of the Book of Genesis did. He simply used the scientific knowledge of his time as a vehicle for the presentation of great religious truths which he wished to teach. St. Paul was one of the greatest religious teachers the world has ever known. His insight into spiritual life was amazing, but what did he know of science? He knew absolutely nothing of astronomy, of biology, of chemistry, or physiology, or medicine. There is not a boy twelve years of age who does not know more of science than Paul knew at the end of his life. Paul was an ignoramus in the realm of science, but one of the mightiest of all religious teachers.

Can a man be an authoritative teacher of religion and still be ignorant of history? Of course he can. Shakespeare was one of the greatest teachers of the human heart that the human race has yet produced, but what did he know of history? He had only a smattering of it. He knew nothing of it as compared with Grote, Gibbon, Freeman, or Froude. Moreover, Shakespeare cared nothing for history. It did not matter to him when or where an event occurred. His plays are filled with historical blunders. But who cares for that? Shakespeare was interested in something far more important than the sequence of events or the geography of the earth. He was interested in the human heart—in its aspirations and despairs, its raptures and agonies of remorse. He understood its appetites and passions. He was an expert in the ideals and movements of the soul. He knew very little history, but that does not discredit him as one of the greatest masters of the secrets of the human heart.

And, therefore, while the man who wrote the story of creation knew nothing of science, he was a matchless teacher of religion. If any of you should ask me do I believe this story, my answer is, "Of course I do." If you should ask me if it is true, I should reply, "It certainly is." If you should ask me if it is reliable, my answer would be, "Yes." If you should say, "Is it authoritative?" my answer would be, "Yes." If you should say, "Is it inspired?" I should say, "If any story in the world was ever inspired, then this one surely is." Its science is mistaken, its history is of no account, but in the realm of religion it is incomparable and final.

Let us compare the three great religious ideas of the writer of the Book of Genesis with the ideas put forth by the doctrine of evolution. In the Book of Genesis a constantly recurring phrase is, "God said . . ." "God said . . ." "God said . . ." He said, and the thing which He said was done. Nothing whatever is said about the method by which the thing was done. No attention is paid to processes. All of that is left open. We can fill in the gaps as best we may. The evolutionist comes and offers to fill in the gaps. He says that the thing was done by a process of development. Things came to be what they are by a long process of unfolding. There is no contradiction between Genesis and evolution. At this point the doctrine of evolution supplies something which the Book of Genesis omits.

Some persons feel that evolution is atheistic, but in thinking this, they are mistaken. To be sure, a man may be an atheist and hold the doctrine of evolution, but he is not an atheist because of the doctrine. Henry Drummond was not an atheist, but he was a confirmed believer in evolution. There are many atheists who are evolutionists, and many evolutionists believe in God—a personal God, the Father of our Lord Jesus Christ. The doctrine of evolution does not render God unnessary. If you want to account for the process of evolution, then you must fall back on God. It is not enough to say the universe evolved. I want to know why it evolved—what made it evolve? The only answer which satisfies my mind is God. It is not enough to say, "The universe climbs." I want to know why it climbs—what makes it climb? The only answer, I think, is God. Why did man come out of this process? He could not have come out of it had he not been in it; and he could not have been in it unless somebody put him in it. Who put him in it? Who could have put him in it but God?

According to the doctrine of evolution, God creates gradually and not instantaneously, and in this, science would seem to be correct. How does God create a rose? He is able to create it instantaneously, but He does not do it. It takes several weeks to make a rose, even after the bud is created. Did you ever sit down in the presence of a rosebud and watch God in the process of creating a rose? If you ever did, you did not see anything happen. You watched it, it may be, for fifteen minutes, and at the end of the fifteen minutes, it was still a bud. You waited a half hour, and still it was not a rose. You waited an hour, and it continued as it was. You went back the next morning and you possibly detected a slight change. A day later you came again, and the change was more marked. Day after day you watched it, and in the fullness of time the rose was full-blown.

How did the rose come to be? It is possible to say that God mixed up some material elements and a few forces and set them to work, and then allowed the living forces and elements to work as they could. That explanation does not satisfy me. I like to think of God being present in the rose. He is not far off. He is there. It is He who is making the colors, and bringing the colors out. It is He who is weaving the pattern—that exquisite pattern, surpassing the patterns of all earthly artistries. It is He who cuts the shape of the sepals and petals. It is He who determines the perfume and texture of the flower. God creates a rose, and He creates it gradually by the process of evolution. It may be that the whole universe is a rose, and that it is unfolded by a process extending through periods of immeasurable time. The Book of Genesis allows you to believe that.

The Book of Genesis says that man is the crown of creation, he is the lord of the world, and that the universe has not produced anything higher. And this is just what evolution declares. Evolution and the Book of Genesis are beautifully at one when it comes to putting the crown on man's head. According to Genesis, man was made in the image of God. God breathed into him the breath of life, so that he was different from all other creatures. God gave him dominion over all creatures. According to evolution, man is the climax of creation. The movement of life was always upward and toward him. The lower forms of life were anticipatory of him—they pointed the way to him. When he appeared, the highest form of life which we know had arrived, and beyond him we do not know anything nobler or mightier. This is the teaching of evolution. It is likewise the teaching of Jesus.

According to the Book of Genesis, man is a fallen creature. And according to the doctrine of evolution, man is an ascending creature. But the two things are not contradictory. The Book of Genesis does not state that man started perfect. We have read altogether too much into the Old Testament text. All that is claimed in the Book of Genesis is that man started innocent. He was free from the sense of guilt. His conscience did not torture him. Genesis says that he started in the woods, and was naked as the animals were. The Book of Genesis says that the time came when he did what he knew to be wrong, and because he chose the worse when he might have chosen the better, and decided to take the lower when he might have taken the higher, he brought sorrow and misery into the world. And there is nothing in that which is contradicted by science. We are members of a fallen race. We have fallen short of the ideal. We do not come up to what we know we ought to be. I know I am a fallen creature, and so also do you. Every man knows that we have fallen from the place which we might have held.

Evolutionary science has written no more awe-inspiring chapter than the chapter which it has written on "degeneration." There is a development up, but there is also a development down. It is possible to lose one's footing and fall. Science tells us of the tragedy of the evolutionary process: species have fallen, and genera have fallen, and races have dropped out of existence altogether. Science assures us that it is possible to be lost. There is nothing in evolutionary science then to contradict the idea of the fall, or to do away with the need of redemption.

Why is evolution so repulsive to many Christian men? It is because they cannot help feeling that it degrades man by linking him with the animal creation. Many persons do not know any more about the doctrine of evolution than that it teaches that we are descended from monkeys. A distinguished professor in a college one day asked his class of thirty students to write down a definition of "evolution," and twelve out of the thirty wrote down this: "Evolution teaches that men came from monkeys." In a discussion of the evolutionary hypothesis, somebody is, of course, sure to bring in the word *monkey*. But all such talk is cheap and thin. It throws no light whatsoever on the subject. What difference does it make whether God made man in an instant, or whether He spent a million years in His creation, so far as man's dignity is concerned? In both cases he could be the son of God. The evolutionary hypothesis has been obliged to fight against human prejudice, as the Copernican theory of astronomy was obliged to fight. Men would not accept it because it disparaged man. For centuries men had believed the earth to be the center of the universe, and that the sun, moon, and stars revolved around it. This gave man great dignity and glory. When Copernicus took the earth out of the central place and put it in an obscure corner, he thereby knocked the crown from man's head. That is what the people of the sixteenth century thought. What would they have thought if they had known the full truth? For after Copernicus, a farther-sighted astronomer came, who took our sun out of the central place and put it in an obscure corner, substituting a still larger sun, in comparison with which our sun is only a tallow dip. And within the last few years new depths of space have been explored, and new nebulae have been brought to the eye, in comparison with which our whole solar system is but a speck of dust in the ether.

But what has all this to do with the dignity of man? The earth has shrunk. Man is greater than ever. The universe is big, but man is great. And today, as in the sixteenth century, we can still say: "What a piece of work is a man! How noble in reason! how infinite in faculty! in form and moving, how express and admirable! in action, how like an angel! in apprehension, how like a god! the beauty of the world! the paragon of animals!"

There are those who believe that you increase the dignity and majesty of man by considering him the climax of an immeasurable evolutionary process. What of the upward movement of life? Look down the illimitable vista of time and see the long climb—the heroic climb—life struggling, mounting, conquering, pushing up, that mysterious, unaccountable *"élan vital"* of which Bergson speaks so much. See life climbing, unfolding, becoming more and more mysterious, powerful, beautiful, glorious, and you can repeat with a new meaning the words of a poet of long ago, "For thou has made him but a little lower than God, and crownest him with glory and honour."

Does evolution do away with the need of a Redeemer? No. According to the doctrine of evolution, we are free to think of Christ, the Son of God, coming down to meet a baffled but ascending race. Man, because of his sin, has lost his way, but the Good Shepherd comes to find him. Man, by his transgression, has become sick in body and in mind, but the Great Physician comes to heal him. Man, by his violation of law, has become bewildered, and the Supreme Teacher comes to teach him. Man, because of his remorse, is heavy laden, but the Great Burden-Bearer comes to give him rest. Man, because of his wandering from God, has become the victim of forces which he cannot overcome. He is met in his impotency and despair by the all-sufficient Saviour. No scientific theory will ever be able to extinguish the music of the words: ". . . come to me; . . . and him that cometh to me I will in no wise cast out."

3

The Unrecognized God

"I girded thee, though thou hast not known me. . . ." ISAIAH 45:5.

"I girded thee, though thou hast not known me." God is the speaker, and Cyrus, king of Persia, is the person spoken to. Cyrus is the greatest man in the sixth century before the Christian era, one of the greatest of all the men who have figured in human history. Xenophon makes him the ideal prince of the ancient world. His career of conquest has been unbroken and glorious. He has conquered Media and added it to his kingdom. He has taken Lydia with all her wealth and made her his own. Great Babylon has fallen before his irresistible arms, and now God is calling him to a service greater still, the liberation of the Hebrews. They are to be sent back to Jerusalem. The temple is to be rebuilt. The fire is to be rekindled on the altar. The sacred utensils which Nebuchadnezzar stole are to be restored to their former uses. For this work of emancipation Cyrus is raised up. He is God's anointed; he is God's shepherd. To him God gives assurance of support and victory, saying: "I have even called thee by thy name: I have surnamed thee, though thou hast not known me: . . . I girded thee, though thou hast not known me."

Strange language, this, for a Hebrew prophet to put into the mouth of God! Cyrus is not a Jew. He is a Gentile. He has no part in the convenant made by God with the chosen people. He is not a monotheist. He is a polytheist and reverences Merodach and all the other Babylonian gods. And yet to this heathen polytheist God is represented as saying, ". . . [thy] right hand I have holden. . . . I have even called thee by thy name. . . . I girded thee, though thou hast not known me." Surely this is a great prophet. He has grasped the truth that God endows men with wisdom and grace and power, though the men themselves may be ignorant of the source whence come their gifts, and that he uses men for the carrying out of his vast plans, though these men do not know the end for which they were born, or for what purpose they came into the world. The unknown God in spiritual life —that is our theme this morning.

The physiologists tell us that in the body there are two forms of life, the conscious and the unconscious. There are two nervous systems, the cerebrospinal and the sympathetic. A large part of our life is carried forward without any volition on our part, and even without our knowledge. The heart beats day and night without waiting for our orders. The lungs expand and contract on their own initiative and impulse. The processes of digestion are carried forward from stage to stage without our attention or direction. The foundation movements of our life are conducted below the level of our conscious thought, and on this unconscious life are built the activities of the life we know. The activities which lie beyond the reach of will and even outside the realm of conscious life are more essential to our welfare than the activities which have been placed within our knowledge and control.

The psychologists are telling us that the soul, like the body, has its unconscious life. A large part of personality is as yet submerged. The greater part of us never comes into the field of consciousness. What personality is, we shall never know until death has let life out to its completion. There are subliminal regions, dark and mysterious, filled with forces which weave the texture of our life. Out of these abysmal depths come our intuitions, convictions not born of the reason and yet able to sway and to mold our lives. Up from these depths feelings now and again surge, feelings for which reason can find no satisfactory explanation, and yet which constitute a "heat of inward evidence" which compels us to doubt against the sense. There are forces outside our conscious self that bring redemption. The heart has reasons which the reason cannot understand. The sources of our spiritual life lie in a region which cannot be explored. It would seem that down below the level of conscious thought God feeds the springs of feeling and carries on the processes of spiritual reconstruction. In him we live and move and have our being, and he does for us constantly more than we ask or think. He girds us, though we do not know him.

This throws light upon experiences which often perplex us. Life is filled with surprises. We find ourselves doing things we never imagined we could do, enduring things which we were sure would completely crush us, overcoming difficulties which we had no strength to meet. We are surprised at ourself. People say, "I don't know how I did it!" "I can't see how I lived through it." "That I am alive today is to me a mystery!" We measure our resources, and then in imagination call up some awful calamity whose coming would blot the sun from heaven and make life unendurable; and then on some terrible day the dreaded calamity arrives, and, strange to say, we do not die; we are borne up by forces of whose existence we were not aware, and in spite of our unspeakable misfortune we are by and by able to laugh, and even sing. We are perplexed, but not in despair; cast down, but not destroyed. No visible hand from heaven is outstretched to hold us; no angel comes in the hour of bloody sweat to sustain us, and yet we are sustained. He helps us, though we do not see Him; He guides us, though we do not know Him.

Light is also thrown upon a phenomenon which has caused perplexity to many thoughtful minds, the appearance in heathen countries of truths and graces which were once supposed to be the exclusive possession of Christianity. There was a time when Christian men, in painting the pagan world, painted it black. There was not one sunbeam in all the terrible picture. The darkness was total. The degradation was complete. The religions of the people were a mass of error, fraud, and falsehood. But within fifty years the heathen world has been opened up to the eyes of Christendom. The sacred books of the East have been translated into English. The study of comparative religion has gone forward until scholars know the contents and spirit of all the world's great faiths. Much that we formerly thought of heathendom has been found to be untrue. The darkness is great, but it is not total; the degradation is terrible, but it is not complete. Outside of Christendom all is not midnight. The Christian religion is not the only religion which contains truth. There are in other literatures passages of poetry like unto the Hebrew psalms. There are in every country ethical maxims similar to some of those contained in the Sermon on the Mount. In every religion there are lofty sentiments, sublime conceptions, sound and wholesome moral precepts; and among the followers of every great religious teacher there are saints who manifest many of the graces of the disciple whom Jesus loved. Fragments of Christianity are found everywhere.

How are we to account for this? Some men have satisfied themselves by saying that these outcroppings of Christianity in pagan lands are accidental. Ethical coincidences have come about by chance. These beautiful sayings of pagan poets are happy hits, fortunate guesses, a play of heat lightning in a sullen sky. Others have claimed that every good thing in pagan lands is borrowed from the Jews. The truths in non-Christian religions all had their home in Palestine. The truth flowing from the mouth of prophet and apostle fell upon the earth, made its way eastward through mysterious subterranean channels, and bubbled up in life-giving springs in the midst of heathendom. Or else it was carried from country to country by faithful missionaries whose names have been lost to history. But why contrive an explanation so cumbersome and difficult, when an easier one is far more reasonable? Why not go for an explanation to the first chapter of the fourth Gospel? "All things were made by him; and without him was not any thing made that was made. In him was life; and the life was the light of men. . . . That was the true Light, which lighteth every man that cometh into the world. He was in the world, and the world was made by him, and the world knew him not. He came unto his own, and his own received him not. But as many as received him, to them gave he power to become the sons of God. . . ."

Put a great God over the world and in it, over man and in him, and you will be prepared to find truth everywhere, and Christian graces blooming in all the lands. It is because God is everywhere that there are pearls in all the seas and stars in all the skies. Men had spiritual life before Jesus of Nazareth taught in Galilee. He taught that men might have life more abundantly. There was wine in all the goblets; He simply filled them to the brim. There were dreams of immortality in many a sensitive heart: He brought them to the light. Men tell us that part of our Bible came from Egypt, a part from Babylon, a part from Persia, and that much of it was not original with the Jews. What of it? If God girds men with wisdom and with strength, even though they misconceive His nature and His will, why should we not expect great empires like Egypt and Babylon and Persia to make contributions to the religious textbook of the world? If there is a wideness in God's mercy like the wideness of the sea, we should expect it to wash the shores of all the world.

When Confucius brings his common sense, and Buddha his doctrine of self-abnegation, and Zoroaster his conception of the conflict between good and evil, and Epictetus his teaching of humble submission, we need not say that these men have borrowed from the wise men of Palestine, but can easily believe that they have all sat at the feet of the invisible and omnipresent Christ; and if our ears be sensitive, we can hear Christ saying, "I girded them, although they did not know me." Since God is wise and also sovereign over all His works, we may feel assured that not one nation has ever walked with aimless feet, and that the moral achievements of no tribe or people will ever be destroyed or cast as rubbish to the void when God hath made His pile complete.

There is another problem which perplexes many: How are we to account for so many good people outside the Christian church? Each one of us has acquaintances and friends of whose moral integrity we are certain and whose Christian graces and virtues are many, and yet who are not professedly religious people. They do not read the Bible, so far as we know they do not pray, they do not partake of the Lord's Supper, and some of them do not even attend public worship. Some of them do not believe in Christ in any such sense as the church desires that men should believe in him; and yet, strange to say, many of these persons are undoubtedly good, honest, kind, generous, and self-sacrificing, and a few of them are far superior in moral worth and spiritual attainment to many of the members of the church.

How can we account for this? The easiest thing to do is to deny that such persons are good. We may say that their virtues are only so much dead morality, that their graces are nothing more than the product of training in politeness, and that however decorous in deportment, they lack the spirit of God in their hearts and are therefore dead in sin, even when they seem to be alive. This was once the favorite method of dealing with the outside saints, but it is a method which has long since been discarded. Christians are no longer willing to deny indisputable and conspicuous facts. A flower is still a flower, even though it blossoms all alone in the depths of the vast forest or grows amidst the weeds beside the dusty road. It will not do to say that a flower is not a flower because it is not growing in our garden. God delights in producing lovely things in the most unexpected and surprising places, and when we get our eyes upon them, it is not for us to deny that they exist.

Honesty is honesty, and kindness is kindness, and purity is purity, and generosity is generosity, and self-sacrifice is self-sacrifice, no matter where you find them; and instead of weaving arguments by which to prove that apparent virtue must be something else, let us thank God for every evidence of His presence, no matter when or where the evidence is presented. Moreover, it is a hazardous thing to say that a man is not good because he does not fit into our program. That was the fearful blunder made by the Pharisees in dealing with Christ. They had a narrow inclosure all finely hedged in with rules and regulations, inside of which every man acceptable to God was sure to be found. They had a schedule of pious actions which every genuine saint was expected to follow. Jesus came, and the first thing He did was to step over the hedge. He would not stay inside. He refused to follow the schedule.

The Pharisees were shocked, alarmed, enraged. Jesus seemed to be a good man—at least He spoke gracious words and performed gentle deeds—but He would not stay inside the inclosure! He had a beautiful spirit and lived a beautiful life, but He would not follow the program! And so the Pharisees began to suspect Him. They doubted His goodness. They tried to get Him back inside the hedge. When He refused to go, they were sure He was bad. His beautiful life counted for nothing. They began to jeer at Him. He went about doing good, but they hated Him. "He is a glutton and a winebibber," they sneered, "a friend of publicans and sinners," which, being interpreted, meant, "Birds of a feather flock together." Later on someone ventured to suggest that He had a devil in Him; and the final conclusion was, after He had lived for years a life without a flaw and without a stain, that He was in league with the monarch of the infernal world. Think of that! Absolute goodness, perfect wisdom, supreme kindness, immeasurable self-sacrifice, all ascribed to the Devil, and for no other reason than that Jesus did not fit into the church program, and refused to stay inside of the ecclesiastical inclosure. May God save us from committing so heinous a sin!

What shall we say then? Shall we say that religion is unnecessary and that the church can be dispensed with and that it makes slight difference whether a man believes in Christ or not? Some have said just that, but in this they have greatly erred. It is not difficult to account for all the goodness which exists outside the Christian church if we bear in mind certain facts. First of all, let us remember that there is such a thing as heredity. Every man is in part the product of the past. What he is depends in a measure on what his ancestors have been. Now, wherever in a Christian country you find a person with a beautiful face, and by a beautiful face I mean a face in which there are spiritual lines, and with a life which is fragrant with Christian graces, if you will take up the history of that man or woman and trace it back to the earlier chapters, you will come sooner or later upon a Christian —a Christian father or mother, or grandfather or grandmother, or great-grandfather or great-grandmother—some true saint of God who loved the place of prayer and who spoke the name of Jesus with reverence and love. This saint held in check his impulses, subdued his lawless inclinations, bridled his appetites and passions, brought his life into beautiful submission to the law of heaven; and just as the iniquities of the fathers are visited on the children down to the third and fourth generations, so also are the virtues and graces, and many a man has on him today the mark of Christ, although he takes no interest in the Bible and is never seen in the house of God. Of such a man God says, "I girded him, although he does not know me."

Moreover, environment is a factor in every human life. No man can live isolated or in a vacuum. We are all modified by our surroundings. The fiber of our being is in part determined by the atmosphere we breathe. It is not necessary for a man to read the Bible, to get the Bible; nor to pray, in order to get some of the effects of prayer; nor to go to church, in order to receive the aroma of the gospel. The church floods the world with light. This light falls on the reflecting surfaces of Christian institutions, and is thrown into the eyes and lives of men who imagine themselves independent of Christianity. It falls on the pages of magazine and book and is reflected into the hearts of thousands who never hear a preacher preach. It falls on every side of our complex civilization as on the myriad facets of a gem, and the whole atmosphere is so saturated with the glory of the Eternal Son of God that every eye is a partaker of that glory and every heart illuminated by a light which cannot be escaped.

Suppose that a rose in a foolish moment should say: "I will have nothing to do with the sun. I do not like him. I will not reverence him. I will not even turn my face his way." And so, all in a pet, the little flower turns its face toward the dull and unresponsive earth to escape the influences of the sun, which it is determined to despise. But the great sun, sorry that a flower should be so foolish, carries on his ministries of love. The air, with the warm kisses of the sun upon it, steals down under the petals of the rose, wooing them to fuller form and brighter color. The sunlight, falling now on this object and now on that, is reflected into the downcast countenance of the drooping flower. And the industrious sun, the steadfast friend of all flowers, both wise and foolish, keeps right on pumping water from the sea, and sends it in gentle showers upon the land, the raindrops trickling down through the sullen earth until they find the rootlets of the rosebush, and then mount upward through stalk and stem, until in the tips of the petals the water becomes the red blood of the rose! And over the rose the great good-natured sun keeps saying, "I girded you, although you did not know me."

When a man turns his back upon the Sun of Righteousness and says, I will not look at Him nor believe in Him, nor pray to Him, nor praise Him, will the great Sun cease His shining, will He cut off the foolish man and allow him to fade and perish? Not so have we learned of Christ. Our God is a God who causes His sun to shine on the evil as well as on the good; He sends the rain on the just and the unjust also. No matter how determinedly a man endeavors to escape the power and love of Christ, he fails completely in the end. For the compassionate Son of God floods the world with light, pours all round the man a sea of glory, steals into his heart through the love of wife, of child, of friend, glides into his soul through picture, song, and printed page. And as the man grows in the elements of manhood, if he could only hear what Christ is saying, he would catch these words: "I am girding you, although you do not know me!" Let no man think that because he has cast off God, therefore God has let him go. He works with us and deals with us most wondrously, even when we are least conscious of His presence.

Whither shall I go from thy spirit? or whither shall I flee from Thy presence?

If I ascend up into heaven, thou art there: if I make my bed in hell, behold, thou are there.

If I take the wings of the morning, and dwell in the uttermost parts of the sea;

Even there shall thy hand lead me, and thy right hand shall hold me.

If I say, Surely the darkness shall cover me; even the night shall be light about me.

Yea, the darkness hideth not from thee; but the night shineth as the day: the darkness and the light are both alike to thee.

We do injustice to the ways of God unless we remember that He is our Father, and not only our Father, but the Father of all. He is working in Christendom and outside of Christendom, in the church and outside of it, in Christians and in those who are not Christians, in those who pray and in those who never pray. We sometimes speak of the means of grace, meaning prayer and Bible study, the Lord's Supper, and church attendance. Rather a meager list of means of grace for a God so great and a world so needy! Why not go on and name other means of grace—fatherhood, motherhood, friendship, literature, art, music, business, work, suffering—all these are channels through which the good God comes to men. God does not confine His work with human souls to Sunday. He works with us straight through every day of every week. In every experience He is present, endeavoring to enlarge our heart.

And what He does with us, He is doing, so far as human wills will let Him, with all men everywhere. He is a Saviour, and He goes forth to seek and to save those who are lost. He does not confine Himself to church members. He mingles with the publicans and sinners. If He were working only inside the church, then well might we despair; but because He is working everywhere, sovereign of all the forces which are or are to be, we can hold up our heads in hope, knowing that at last every knee shall bow. He goes everywhere, convincing men of their sins. When a girl takes her first step downward, her cheeks burn with shame. Why? Because the eyes of Christ are on her. It is His gaze which causes the burning in the cheek. The cheek would never burn if there were no God. The young man who surrenders to his lower self feels an awful sense of degradation. This is because Christ has condemned him.

There would be no remorse if there were no God. The businessman who stoops to do a mean or dishonest thing has planted a thorn in his memory which pricks him and causes him to bleed. This, too, is nothing but the condemnation of the Lord. And if God is present in every soul to chide and warn and rebuke, so He is present in every soul to soothe and cheer and bless. Before every man, high and low, rich and poor, saint and sinner, Christ is standing, saying: "Behold, I stand at the door and knock. If any man hear my voice and will open the door, I will come in." No one makes a right choice without receiving the blessing of heaven; no one takes a step upward without a "well done" from the lips of the King.

Along the avenues and the alleys, in the garrets and cellars, in the mansions and slums, the unsleeping God is at work ministering to men and relieving them in the midst of their distresses. Poor tired

women, who do all their work and all their sewing, and bear the burdens
and anxieties which children bring, and who, because of household
cares, never go to church and never hear an anthem and never sing a
hymn, are not forsaken by Him. They grow in grace, learning patience
and tenderness and self-sacrifice all the time. They may not be
familiar with pious phrases, they may know little of Isaiah or even of
St. John, but God is with them, and at the last great day many of them
will be found at His right hand. A poor woman in a miserable tene-
ment, who makes a bed in a corner of her shabby room for some poor
wretched creature poorer than herself, has a strange glow in her wearied
heart which is nothing less than the voice of Christ saying, "My peace
be unto thee." Such a woman may with surprise say in the other
world, "When saw I thee?"

There is nothing more interesting, I think, in the New Testament
than its account of people who were surprised. The woman at Jacob's
well talked with Jesus and did not know that she talked with the
Messiah. He helped her, and her heart burned within her before she
knew Him. On the morning of the Resurrection Jesus met Mary, but
she did not know Him. In the afternoon two sad-hearted men walked
with Jesus from Jerusalem to Emmaus, and though their hearts kindled
and glowed as He talked, they did not know Him. The blind man,
blind from his birth, whose eyes Jesus opened, did not know Him
even when he looked into His face. To the question of Jesus, "Dost
thou believe on the Son of God?" the pathetic answer came, "Who is
he, Lord, that I might believe on him?" Many a sad-hearted man on
his way to Emmaus feels his heart burn within him and finds life becoming tolerable again who does not realize that he is in the presence
of the Son of God; and many a man whose eyes have been opened to
spiritual values, and who sees that only the things which are invisible
and eternal are of worth and beauty, does not know the name of Him
by whom his blindness has been changed to sight. Christ girds men
constantly who do not know Him.

Ages ago the sun built up mighty forests on our earth, which
forests, moldering down, became buried deep and were transformed
gradually into beds of coal. We dig it out and cut it up and throw it
into the grate, all black and cheerless; it does not look like sunshine.
But once kindled, its ancient memories are revived, and it burns and
glows and lights up all the room, exerting a witchery over the heart
which causes it to dream of sunny days of yore or golden ages yet to

come. While seated before the blazing grate, we do not think of the sun; but the coal fire is nothing but sunbeams let out of prison, and if we had ears to hear, we should hear the old sun saying, "I am girding you, although you do not know me." Mrs. Browning, in her greatest poem, says that earth is crammed with heaven, and that every common bush is aflame with God. If that be true of bushes, much truer is it of men. Souls are crammed with heaven, and every loving heart is afire with God. God has deposited His love in human beings—in lover, maiden, wife, mother, friend—and their love warms us, thrills us, cheers and charms us, lights up with glory this old drab world until it glistens like a palace, and life becomes so supremely blessed we wish we might live here forever. We call it human love, forgetting that all love comes out of the sky. Had we ears to hear, we should hear Christ saying, "I am loving you, although you do not know me."

> We may not climb the heavenly steeps
>   To bring the Lord Christ down;
> In vain we search the lowest deeps,
>   For Him no depths can drown.
>
> But warm, sweet, tender, even yet
>   A present help is He;
> And faith has yet its Olivet,
>   And love its Galilee.
>
> The healing of the seamless dress
>   Is by our beds of pain;
> We touch Him in life's throng and press,
>   And we are whole again.
>
> O Lord and Master of us all,
>   Whate'er our name or sign,
> We own Thy sway, we hear Thy call,
>   We test our lives by Thine.

4

Expectancy

"Maran-atha." I CORINTHIANS 16:22

"Maran-atha" was a common salutation. When one Christian met another Christian, he greeted him with "Maran-atha." He lit up the day by the declaration that the Lord was coming. When a Christian wrote a letter to his friends, he often wrote at the end of the last page, "Maran-atha." That was a benediction. He wanted his friends to know that he was still rejoicing in the expectation that the Lord was coming. "Maran-atha" was a slogan which the soldiers of Jesus Christ repeated to one another as they went forth to the conquest of the world. They braced their hearts for the great battle by reminding them that the Lord was coming. "Maran-atha" was a password which Christians in the early times made use of. When they went into their meetings, when they met before day in sequestered places, that was the word which gained them immediate admittance, "Maran-atha." It was a word that was used at the celebration of the Lord's Supper. We have a volume, entitled *The Teaching of the Twelve,* which was written not far from the middle of the second century. In that book we are told that it was the custom, in the celebration of the Lord's Supper, to offer a prayer of thanksgiving, ending with the word "Maran-atha." And so the celebration of the Lord's Supper came to have a triumphant tone by the repetition of the word "Maran-atha."

It is not to be wondered at, then, that all the translators have shrunk from tampering with the word. It is the same with this word "Maran-atha" as it is with the Hebrew words repeated by our Lord on the cross, "Eloi, Eloi, lama sabachthani?" These words occur in the first two Gospels as they were spoken. There was a sanctity, an awfulness attached to them which made the early Christians reluctant to put them into any other tongue. But whether this conjecture is correct or not, the fact remains that all the translators through nineteen hundred years have refused to blot out the word "Maran-atha" and substitute in its place any other word.

What a difference there is between the Apostolic Church and the church of our day. In externals, of course, they are worlds apart. The people in the New Testament all wore turbans on their heads and sandals on their feet. When they traveled, they either walked or they rode on the backs of donkeys and camels. They had none of the comforts and luxuries which we enjoy. They had no telegraphs, no telephones, no railroads, no automobiles, no airships, no radios. Heaven and earth have passed away, all things have become new. Look at the pictures of Tissot, and you look upon a world entirely different from the world in which we are living. But the interior world of the Apostolic Church was also entirely different from the mood of the church today. There was a spirit of expectancy in that church which we do not possess. There was a hope then which we have lost. There was a mood of anticipation to which we are strangers. We do not say to one another, "Maran-atha." We seldom think of His coming.

That will account in large measure for the difference in spirit between the first-century church and our own. Their belief in the early coming of Christ gave an intensity to their life which ours does not possess. We are intense about certain things, but not about our religion. There was an other-worldliness in the church of the apostles which has vanished. The early Christians kept their thoughts upon the other world into which Christ had vanished and from which He was soon to emerge again. We do not think much about the other world. The present world is amazingly attractive, and it absorbs all our strength and time. It is a difficult world to manage, and we have no time for any other. The Apostolic Church was a radiant church. A distinguished British scholar of Oxford University not long ago wrote a book entitled *The Lost Radiance.* He notes a vivid contrast between the early church and our own. That church was jubilant, and ours is not. The face of that church shone. Our face does not shine. One of the reasons why the jubilant tone has vanished is because we have lost the expectancy which the apostles possessed.

Why have we given up our belief in the coming of Jesus? It is very largely because the apostles were mistaken about the manner of His coming. They supposed He was coming dramatically, spectacularly,

miraculously. They thought He would drop down out of heaven. Not
only did one of them think that. They all thought it. Let me read you
just two quotations. Luke, about thirty years after our Lord's death,
went down into Palestine to get data from which to write his volume
of church history. He talked with all the leading Christians he could
meet. He got from their lips the important things which they believed.
This was one of them: "Ye men of Galilee, why stand ye looking into
heaven? This Jesus, who was received up from you into heaven, shall
so come in like manner as ye beheld him going into heaven."

That was what Christians believed throughout Palestine thirty
years after the Crucifixion. Let us see what Paul believed about the
same time. We have his belief recorded in I Thessalonians 4:16–18:
"For the Lord himself shall descend from heaven with a shout, with the
voice of the archangel, and with the trump of God: and the dead in
Christ shall rise first; then we that are alive, that are left, shall together
with them be caught up in the clouds, to meet the Lord in the air:
and so shall we ever be with the Lord." That is very clear and very
positive. The Lord is coming out of the sky with a shout. An archangel
is going to speak. The trumpet of God is going to blow. All the Christians then alive, and Paul will be among the number, will be caught
up in the clouds to meet the Lord in the air. That was Paul's joyful
belief. Of that he had no doubt. That is the doctrine which he taught
his converts. He told them to comfort one another by repeating the
words which he had written. But in regard to the manner of the Lord's
appearance, Paul was mistaken, so were all the apostles. Every one
of them was mistaken. There mistake is recorded in our New Testament. That mistake cannot be gotten rid of. It was a huge mistake,
and it forms a part of the New Testament forever.

At this point let me inject into my sermon an extended parenthesis.
Let me explain what has caused the commotion in our generation concerning the Bible. Why do we have so much controversy over the
Scriptures? Why are Christians divided into hostile camps when it
comes to a conception of the Bible? Many of you already know. Some
of you do not yet know. I speak to those who do not know. It is very
important that everybody should know just what has caused the controversies which have swept in recent years across the Christian world.
We inherited from the seventeenth century a doctrine of inspiration,
according to which the Bible is a dictated book. Inspiration, our fathers
thought, meant dictation. God dictated his ideas to the apostles, and

they, as amanuenses, wrote down exactly what he said. The New Testament was a dictated book, and because it had been dictated by the Almighty, it could contain no mistakes. Every sentence was true. Every idea was correct. God cannot be mistaken, and therefore in God's Book, no mistake can occur. The Almighty cannot be in error, and therefore it is absurd to look for errors in the Word of God.

That was the belief of the majority of Protestant Christians fifty years ago, and then the world entered upon a new era. Groups of men began to study the Bible scientifically, that is, they began to search it with scrutinizing eyes. They observed it closely. They compared sentence with sentence. They weighed the sentences. They even pondered the syllables. They studied the New Testament precisely as Herschel studied the stars, and as Charles Darwin studied the plants and the birds. As the result of this scientific study of the Scriptures, men saw that the dictated theory of inspiration is not correct. The Bible is not a dictated book for the reason that the Bible has errors in it. Here is one error that nobody can dispute—the opinion that Jesus was going to drop down out of the sky and that Christians were going to meet Him in the air, and that all this was going to take place in the lifetime of the Apostle Paul.

Paul was the most learned of all the apostles, the ablest of them all, the mightiest of all; but he was mistaken, and all the other apostles were mistaken with him. When the fact became know in wider church circles that the New Testament contains errors, there followed a series of explosions. They occurred first in the theological seminaries because there the scientific study of the Scriptures had been carried forward with more thoroughness and boldness. The people outside the seminaries who did not know what was going on began to say that the seminaries were hotbeds of infidelity, that theological professors had been beguiled by the devil, and that all our young men were being led astray. Later on there were explosions in various churches. When a church had a scholar in the pulpit and he announced what scholarship had discovered, there was in many cases a great uproar in the pews. Some people left the church; others felt that the pulpit had been captured by the Evil One. A great many people outside the churches, hearing the explosions and not knowing the cause of them, began to be troubled. The report went abroad that Christianity had been undermined, that the New Testament, after all, was a book of falsehoods, that the Christian creed was no longer reliable, and that the religion of Jesus was destined to pass away. That, in a few words, is the cause of the explosions which have attracted the attention of our modern world.

When you find that the New Testament is not a dictated book because there are errors in it, what are you going to do? The sensible thing is to modify your theory. You cannot change the New Testament. It remains what it has been, and what it is, and what it always will be. The only sensible thing is to modify your theory. Make your theory wide enough to take in all the facts. Somebody suggests that it is dangerous. I do not think so. Why should it be considered dangerous to acknowledge a fact? The universe must be a poor ramshackle affair if it will tumble down on you when you acknowledge a fact. The Christian religion must be exceedingly flimsy if it will topple over when you acknowledge a fact. Why should anybody be afraid to acknowledge a fact? It is a fact that there is this error in the New Testament. Why not face it and confess it? Why not let the whole world know that you know it is there? It is not at all dangerous to confess a fact. It is dangerous not to confess it. It is dangerous to play fast and loose with truth. It is dangerous to shut your eyes and re-fuse to stare into the face of an unwelcome fact. The only safe thing to do is to face all the facts without wincing and without running.

Somebody suggests that it is very difficult to hold this new theory of inspiration, one wide enough to take in all the facts. That is all very true, but the difficulty is no objection to it. Everything is difficult in a world like this. The corpuscular theory of light is difficult to man-age. So is the undulatory theory of light, so is the theory of luminiferous ether, and so is the theory of relativity. The fact is that life itself is difficult to manage. We who have lived it the longest know that the best, but we have to manage difficult theories. The only thing for us to do is to believe that the men who wrote the New Testament were inspired. They certainly got light from heaven. They certainly were assisted by the Spirit of the Eternal. There is no doubt of that. It is equally clear that their inspiration did not preclude all possibility of error in opinion.

Little by little the early church sloughed off the mistaken concep-tion of the manner of Jesus's coming. They came to see that He was not coming dramatically or spectacularly or miraculously. He was coming in another manner. That manner is described for us in the fourth Gospel. The fourth Gospel is the latest of all the Gospels. It gives us the maturest thought of Apostolic Christianity. There is a passage in the fourteenth chapter of the Gospel according to St. John which you ought to read and mark and digest. There our Lord is represented as saying: "I will not leave you desolate. I will come to you. . . . At that day ye shall know that I am in my Father, and ye in me, and I in you." In other words, the coming of Jesus is to be invisible, spiritual, progressive. He is to come and dwell in the hearts of his followers, and through them is to save the world. Therefore it is a mistake to talk about the Second Coming of Christ. The proper expression is the "continuous" coming of Christ. He has already come many times. He is coming many times. In the present hour He will come and keep on coming. He is occupying the mind and heart of his people throughout the world. All this language in the New Testament concerning the coming of our Lord is capable of a higher and truer interpretation. When Paul told the Corinthians that the "Lord is at hand," he spoke the truth. He was at hand. He is at hand today. He will always be at hand. When John said, "Behold, I come quickly," he expressed words that are true. That is what Christ said, and what He says, and what He will forever say. He is coming quickly. The proper response for us to make is, "Come, Lord!"

There are two serious errors by which the church is handicapped at the present hour. There are groups of zealous men, sincere and conscientious, who are so deeply impressed by what the New Testament says concerning the coming of Christ, they make it the cardinal and crowning doctrine of the Christian creed. They are literalists, and cling to the ancient opinion that the Lord is coming dramatically, spectacularly, and miraculously. He is coming out of the sky with the voice of the archangel and the trump of God. He is going to interfere in some mighty and overwhelming way, overturning the world that now is and setting up another. They say He is coming soon. They used to name the date. They missed it so many times, they dare not do it any more. Only a fanatic of unusual stature ventures any longer to specify the day on which the Lord will bring the world to an end. They now use ambiguous adverbs. They declare He is coming "soon." Some throw all discretion to the wind and boldly assert He is coming "in the lifetime of men now living." The startling announcement is made sometimes in newspaper advertisements, and sometimes by posters on the billboard, and sometimes by flaming orators on the platform. Men and women of a certain type of mind and of a particular grade of culture are in considerable numbers powerfully impressed and swept away.

These advocates of the Second Coming use the Bible with great agility, and hold up the present unhappy condition of the world as evidence that the last days have come. St. Paul told Timothy that in the last days perilous times would come, and that evil men and seducers would wax worse and worse, and such a time, these prophets say, has evidently arrived. It is this combination of Scripture and present-day darkness which renders these modern apostles so persuasive and influential. According to their teaching, there is no hope for the world through anything which mortals can do. They take no interest in social-betterment work, and upon all efforts for cummunity uplift they pour the vials of their scorn. They denounce all international machinery for the establishment of world peace as devices of the Devil. Arbitration treaties and world courts and leagues of nations have all been conceived in hell and are tricks to deceive the elect. Some of the more radical of these zealots are too advanced to take any interest in the ballot. What is the use? Only God Almighty can make the world better. They denounce all movements which aim at better laws. Legislation is of the Evil One. You cannot make society better by laws. Nothing can be accomplished by statesmen. Only the Lord God Almighty can cope with the evil of the human heart, and we can expect no improvement until he lays bare his strong right arm. Things must grow worse and worse. The more rapidly they get worse, the happier we ought to be. It is not till they get as bad as possible that the end will come!

What a pity that conscientious and well-meaning men should be so deceived. What a travesty of the Christian religion such teaching is! What a caricature of the gospel of salvation is a message like that! An interpretation of life and God which reduces the soul to impotency must be false. A reading of the Bible which cuts the nerve of action is certainly a deadly superstition which all open-eyed lovers of the truth must resist and overcome.

But there is also another error against which we must be on our guard. You to whom I am speaking are in little danger of being captured by the error to which I have referred. Your danger lies in the opposite direction. You know the Lord is not going to drop from heaven with a shout. You do not believe that the end of the world is at hand. You do not believe that Christ is coming in the manner so vividly pictured by traveling evangelists, and therefore you do not believe He is coming at all. You do not look for Him soon or late. There is no expectancy in your eyes. There is no leaping hope in your heart. "Maran-atha" is not in your vocabulary. You do not rejoice in an anticipated fresh disclosure of God's power. You think that men must do everything alone. No reliance can be put upon the Almighty. If the world is to become a better world, it will become better solely through human effort. God will have nothing to do with it. It is for men to devise new schemes and lay out new programs. They should not count on any help from heaven. Whatever progress may be made will be the result of human cleverness and genius.

Such is the opinion of many. This is a blighting error. This error, like the former one, cuts the nerve of action. It leaves us dubious and doleful. We are not sure whether our hopes will ever be realized, or whether our dreams will ever come true. We are not certain what man may be able to accomplish. As for God, he is a mystery. Christ has come and died and gone, and now we must struggle on alone. If Christ is not at the door, then the spirit of expectation dies. If we cannot say "Maran-atha," there is no radiancy of hope. Alas for those who cannot face tomorrow with beating hearts eager to see some fresh unfolding of the power of God!

There is nothing more wonderful in modern science than its spirit of expectancy. The great scientists are all alike in expecting greater things tomorrow than anything known today. They do not prophesy small things, but great things; not common things, but wonderful things. No matter what marvels have already been achieved, still greater marvels are coming. In laboratories all around the world eager groups of men are working, all of them expecting some new manifestation of the power of nature. They are looking, among other things, for a cure for cancer. They will find it because they are expecting it. The spirit of expectancy is the very breath of the nostrils of the scientific world. The church must catch that spirit if it is to conquer.

What do you expect for your church? What new thing are you looking for? What great thing are you counting on? Are you really expecting any fresh disclosure of God's power and love in your church? Or do you rather expect that the church will continue to travel along the old drowsy, routine ways, learning nothing wonderfully new and doing nothing startlingly great? What do you expect for your city? Can any new thing take place in your city? What great thing can come to pass by God's help in your city? Or must your city continue to trudge along the old dusty road, repeating endlessly experiences which are monotonous and tame?

What do you expect? In what new form will God appear? What new work do you expect him to perform? With what fresh miracles will He crown this year? "Maran-atha!" There is tragic sadness in St. Mark's description of Jesus's experience on His return to His own city of Nazareth: ". . . he could there do no mighty work. . . ." And why not? They expected nothing.

5

The Miracles

Let us think this morning about the miracles of Jesus. The Christian religion is incredible to a large number of people in our day because of the miraculous element which runs through the New Testament. The miracles are everywhere spoken against. Men are saying that Christianity would make a stronger appeal to the heart and conscience of the twentieth century if in some way the miraculous element could be dropped. Let us hold fast, these people say, to the ethical element and the Golden Rule, the Beatitudes, and all of the parables and discourses which inculcate reverence toward God and love toward men; but let us lay aside all miraculous stories as the creations of a credulous and superstitious age.

Now it is not difficult to understand how this state of mind has come to be. It has been created in large measure by the emphasis which science has placed upon the fact that the universe is governed by unchanging law. Everything, says science, in the heavens above and in the earth beneath, is in the grip of laws which know neither variableness nor shadow of turning. In a universe in which everything is thus ordered, and in which all processes go forward, advancing from step to step in a sequence which is invariable, a miracle seems to be an interloper. It is an eruption into the realm of ordered harmony. It seems to be an impertinence which ought to be rejected by the mind forthwith. And the scientific spirit is being reinforced by the spirit of historical investigation. It has become clear to all students of history that a broad stream of miraculous pretension flows down the centuries. Herodotus has his miraculous tales and Livy has his prodigies, and when we pass into Christian history, the centuries are simply weighted down with legends and traditions of the miraculous. So many of these tales are absurd and incredible that men look with suspicion upon all stories of the miraculous, no matter where the stories are found. If the miracles of the fifteenth and tenth and fifth and fourth and third and second centuries are the creation of the religious imagination, why not throw the miracles of the New Testament into the same class and pitch them all behind us?

No member of the Christian Church can go far into the modern world without finding himself face to face with people who look upon the New Testament miracles as fables, and who look down upon a person who accepts these stories as authentic history with a smile half of pity and half of scorn. In the presence of such persons, what is a Christian to do? If a man accepts the miracles of the Gospel, he ought to have good reasons for so doing, and if these reasons are clear to his own mind, he ought to be able to state them to those who look upon the New Testament as a book filled with outgrown superstitions.

It is not possible for me in a single hour to take up the problem of the miracles in all its various relations and implications, nor is it possible for me to bring out all the evidences which can be adduced in favor of the reality of the miracles ascribed by the evangelists to Jesus. All I can do is throw out a few suggestions indicating to you the direction in which the sanest modern scholarship is moving, and to lay down a few simple propositions upon which a man may stand if he wants to beat back the attack of those who ridicule belief in miracles as the action of a belated mind.

It should be borne in mind at the start that the question of the miracles is not closed. Many people speak as though this whole question were closed, as though there were not two sides to it in the opinion of any sensible man, as though the door had been shut and locked, and the key thrown away. Now all this is pure assumption. It is not a closed question which we are considering. If a man says, "You cannot prove that Jesus worked miracles," we may say with equal confidence, "You cannot prove that he did not." Not a man on this earth, be he scholar, philosopher, explorer, or scientist, can ever prove that these miraculous deeds ascribed to Jesus were never done. If it cannot be demonstrated that Jesus worked miracles, neither can it be demonstrated that he did not work them. So that we are all on the same footing, and there is room for the discussion of the question whether or not it is probable that these things took place in the manner in which the evangelists say they did.

Nor should it be forgotten that it is not indubitable proof of extraordinary mental acumen to toss the miracles aside as unworthy of study. Nothing is easier intellectually than to cut out of the New Testament the miraculous element. It requires no mental effort to do this, and after it is once done, there are no perplexing problems remaining. It causes no more mental exertion to rub out these miracles than it does to rub out figures written on a slate. If a teacher hands to a boy a slate on which he has written down a few sets of figures, there are two courses open to that boy. He can rub the figures out. This requires no intellectual effort, and for that reason a boy is sometimes tempted to do it. Or he can do the other thing: he can work at those figures, endeavoring to get out of them a solution. It may be he will cry before he gets through with them, and possibly he will have a headache before a solution has been reached; but if he is a boy intellectually in earnest, he will hold fast to those figures until the problem is solved. It takes more intellectual effort to keep the figures on the slate than to rub them off.

Now if any man wants to do the thing that is intellectually easy, by all means let him rub the miracles out. If he wants intellectual work, let him hold fast to the miracles, and say, "Climb, O my soul, to the heights of these great stories, and see if they are not windows opening out upon God and nature and man!" For if these miracles are things which really happened, then they throw fresh light upon the nature of man as well as upon the heart of God. New problems at once come before us, and we must go to work afresh to think out the relations of God and man and nature to one another.

If one hears it said that the miracles are impossible, a proper reply to offer is that the word "impossible" is rather a hazardous word to use. It was once safe to use it, but the advance of modern science has taken it from our lips. It will not do at this date in the world's history to be dogmatic in regard to what is possible in the realm of fact. The meekest men on the earth today are the great scientists—not the little men who rush into the morning newspapers and tell you that they have discovered something which they have not discovered at all, but the great scientists who understand most fully the immeasurable range of nature and the tiny reach of man's mind. Men who live close to nature become exceedingly modest. They realize they are simply children standing on the shore of a tiny island, and that at their feet there break the waves of an immeasurable and unexplored sea.

In a former age scientists dared to say what could happen and what could not. The great Laplace once declared that it is impossible that stones should fall out of the heavens on the earth. Only about sixty years ago Auguste Comte declared it to be impossible for man by any means to determine the chemical composition of any of the heavenly bodies. The illustrious Stephenson asserted it to be impossible for the Mediterranean to be connected with the Red Sea. Did we not say, all of us, only the other day, that it was impossible to see through an oak plank six inches thick? We once thought we could tell what could be and what could not be, but fuller knowledge has made us modest. A man has more presumption than wisdom who asserts with confidence that these New Testament miracles could not have happened.

And if one should say that he must reject the miracles because he cannot believe that the laws of nature were ever violated, our reply is that a miracle is no violation of the laws of nature. Miracles are neither a violation of the laws of nature, nor a suspension of them, nor a modification of them. Every miracle known to the New Testament was undoubtedly done in accordance with the laws of nature. When we talk about the laws of nature, we refer simply to the laws of nature which we ourselves have some knowledge of; but what are these laws? Name them. How many have you? Have you named them all? Until you are sure that you know all the laws of nature, you cannot say that a miracle is a violation of natural law. Many laws of nature have been discovered only recently. It was yesterday that Marconi got hold of a law by means of which he has been able to perform what seems to me the most wonderful miracle wrought within the last hundred years.

Now if the great scientists can thrust their hands into the soft walls of the temple which we call the universe far enough to touch forces by means of which they are able to work the miracles of the modern world, why should it be thought a thing incredible that God's only begotten Son should thrust His hand down deep enough into the universe to touch forces by means of which He could accomplish all the wondrous things spoken of in the Gospels? If we could see the universe as it is, we should undoubtedly see that everything which Jesus did was done according to law. No law was ever violated by Him in any work He did.

But here the question may arise: Can the course of nature be changed? Is it likely that once in Palestine the course of nature was really changed? In reply to such inquiries, we may fairly say that we ordinary men are able to change the course of nature, and that, indeed, to an extent quite surprising. In the course of nature this book lies here before me on the desk. It is natural for it to lie there. But I can pick it up and hold it above my head. In doing this, I am not violating the law of gravitation, nor am I suspending it, for the force of gravitation to my certain knowledge is still at work. I am not interfering with the law of gravity in any manner, but am simply working the force of my will into the force of gravitation in such a way as to get an outcome that would never have been obtained except for the exercise of my will. Now if an ordinary man can work his will into this complex of forces which we call nature in such a way as to get out of nature products which nature if left to herself would never produce, why should not the Son of God be able to work His will into the winds and the waves, into blind eyes and shriveled nerves, to such an extent as to bring forth results at which the world marvels?

I have a little piece of land in New Hampshire, and the land for all I know has been lying there for hundreds of thousands of years. In all that time it has never brought forth one single potato. The course of nature has had freedom through all the hundred thousand years, and if that land were not interfered with, it might lie there a hundred million years without bringing forth a potato. But if I scratch the soil a little and toss into it a few pieces of potato (just enough to give the soil an idea of what a potato is like) nature immediately takes the hint and brings forth a whole basketful of potatoes. I have changed the course of nature. God has made it possible for man thus to change nature's course. To a potato bug sitting on the fence, I am a worker of miracles. Now if a man can change the course of nature and compel nature to do what nature would never do if left to itself, why should it be deemed a thing incredible for God's only begotten Son so to change the course of nature as to bring forth the products narrated by the evangelists? It will be safer, then, to give up the use of that word "impossible" altogether. With God all things are possible.

The strongest thing which any man can say against the miracles is that they are to him incredible. But no man has a right to use that word until he has studied the evidence and found out whether the miracles are credible or not. The credibility of the miracles is simply a question of evidence. The evidence must be sifted and weighed before any verdict is given. No man is fit to sit on a jury who decides the case before he has heard a word of evidence. Whether it is credible or not, the evidence for the miracles of the New Testament is voluminous. A man cannot set himself up in this field as a judge before he has done some hard and honest work. A bookkeeper cannot look up from his books and say in a careless way, "Ah, those things are all preposterous!" A merchant has no right to say while he is eating his lunch, "I think those stories are incredible." A man cannot jump in from the street and say, "I will give you an opinion regarding this matter; those stories are all discredited." The wise man will wait until the evidence is in before he gives his answer. When, therefore, you hear a man talking about the incredibility of the miraculous stories of the New Testament, simply ask him whether or not he has sifted and weighed the evidence. If he tells you he has never given any time or thought to the evidence, it might be suggested to him that, all things considered, it would be well for him to ascertain what can be said in their support.

But suppose a man says he does not care to study the subject at all? He reminds you that nothing is so common as stories of the marvelous. John says Jesus worked miracles; Tacitus says Vespasian worked miracles. As Tacitus was evidently mistaken, so John must have been mistaken also. This is a kind of argument which is common. Oh, the superficiality of many men and women who imagine themselves to be wise! The Christian church has a Bible, and we are told that every religion has a Bible, and if every religion has a Bible, then, of course, all Bibles are alike. They are all good, and all helpful, and our Bible differs in only minor points from the Bibles of the other great religions of the world. That is the fashion of much of our modern reasoning. A man who has gotten all his knowledge of the Bibles of the world from the headlines of newspapers and from a half dozen articles in some magazine finds no difficulty in throwing all the Bibles of the world into the same class; but scholars who have given thought to the subject, and who have studied all the sacred writings of the world, place the Bible in a class by itself. There is no other book in all the world like our Scriptures.

The same sort of reasoning is often heard from men who talk about the Trinity. The Christian religion has a Trinity, and so also, they say, has Buddhism, and so also had the old Egyptian religions, and so have many other religions. Of course the trinities are all alike, and all of them to be discarded! But the man who tosses the doctrine of the Trinity as taught by the Christian church into a class along with the trinities of other religions proves by his action that he knows nothing of the subject concerning which he is speaking. The doctrine of the Trinity as taught by the Christian church is not like any trinity known to any other religion under heaven.

When we come then to the subject of miracles, we must learn how to discriminate. Because there were miracles in the Middle Ages, it does not follow that those miracles were like the miracles recorded in the New Testament. The name is the same, the differences are world-wide. The New Testament miracles are sane; the medieval miracles are nearly all wild, extravagant, absurd, crazy. There is evidence for the miracles of the New Testament; for most of the miracles of the medieval ages, there is little or none. There was a cause for the miracles of the New Testament; for most of the medieval miracles, there was none. There is a person in the New Testament around which the miracles gather. There is no such personality in the Middle Ages. There are no miraculous stories in the world like those in the New Testament.

Some people speak as though it were a very easy thing for the human imagination to create miraculous stories. It is indeed easy to construct stories of a certain sort, but not easy to construct such stories as those of the evangelists. After Jesus's death various stories sprang up concerning miraculous deeds which He did when He was a child. All these stories are ridiculous and disgusting. He made birds out of clay and bade them fly. He turned boys who ran away from Him into kids. He struck dead a teacher who scolded Him. He caused a tree to bend over that He might get the fruit which grew on it. That is the sort of stories which the imagination can create. Or if we go into the Middle Ages, we read of pieces of gold falling from heaven; of a mighty serpent ascending a pyre in order to be burned in the presence of the people; of floods rising to the roofs of churches, but not entering the doors; of robbers being held up by the white hands of the Virgin Mary, and being saved from merited death. The medieval stories are violent and abnormal. We have no right to class them with the miracles of the Gospels.

Now because one of two things is false, does it follow that both must be false? I hold in my hands two greenbacks. One greenback is a counterfeit. The authorities at Washington City have passed judgment on it. Shall I, therefore, say that the other greenback is counterfeit? "O judgment, thou art fled to brutish beasts!" and men have lost their reason if they argue after that fashion. There are, indeed, in the literature of every people, spurious miracles in abundance, but because this is so, we shall not surrender the miracles of the Gospels.

But someone says, If things narrated in the Gospels were reported to have happened somewhere on the earth today, would you believe the report? Our reply is that we should not be likely to believe any such report, for the reason that no miracle is credible unless there are good reasons for its occurrence. Isolated marvels must always be looked at with suspicion. An isolated miracle is a sort of monster. The miracles of the New Testament, however, are a part of a great historic movement. They are not isolated wonders. They are clustered round one supreme person. They belong to one vast historic movement which starts in Abraham and culminates in Jesus of Nazareth. There is a great mountain range of spiritual achievement running across the expanse of two thousand years, its mountain peaks glistening in the light of heaven, all the peaks leading up at last to one colossal summit that overtops them all.

About the existence of this mountain range there is no dispute. It is something unique in the history of the world. Nowhere else is there such spiritual devotion, spiritual character, or spiritual achievement. In the presence of such a colossal moral miracle, why should it be wondered at if we find in connection with it physical miracles too? The New Testament miracles are credible because they are attributed to Jesus of Nazareth. It is not hard to believe that He worked miracles. Great things were natural and easy to Him. He never strained in the doing of them. He never spoke of His acts as though they were wonderful. The most miraculous things He ever did were as natural to Him as our most ordinary acts are to us. A person who has molded the heart-life of races and created new civilizations, as Jesus undoubtedly has done, may reasonably be believed to have said to the wind and to the sea, "Peace, be still!"

In studying the evidences for the miracles of the New Testament, it is wise to begin with study of the greatest miracle of them all—the Resurrection of Jesus. St. Paul stakes all his teaching on the truth of the Resurrection. We can afford to do the same. For the Resurrection of Jesus there is stronger proof than can be adduced in support of any other event in ancient history. Paul was converted four years after the death of Jesus. A few years later he went to Jerusalem to have a talk with Peter. You can imagine the conversation. Peter was a great talker. Even in the presence of Jesus himself, he could hardly be restrained. How he must have talked to a man whom he recognized as his equal! Nor was Paul slow of speech. His mind was marvelously alert. He was a man who knew how to see difficulties and to ask questions. What a stream of talk must have flowed through those days in which Peter and Paul were together. Cannot you imagine you hear Paul saying, "Now, Peter, tell me, did Jesus do this? Did Jesus do that? Did he say this? Did he say that? What did he tell you by the sea? What did he say in the upper Chamber? What did you find in the open tomb? What happened on the day of Pentecost?"

Paul never left Peter until Peter had told the whole story from beginning to end. A few years later Paul in the course of his work had occasion to write to the church which he had founded in Corinth. That letter has been preserved. It is a part of our New Testament. It was written within twenty-five years of the death of Jesus. That it was written by Paul is admitted by every sane critic. Men who have cut other parts of the New Testament to shreds have stayed their hands on coming to this first letter to the Corinthians. If this letter is not genuine, then we can give credence to no historical document whatsoever. In this letter Paul takes up the Resurrection of Jesus. Among other things he says: ". . . I delivered unto you first of all that which I also received, how that Christ died for our sins according to the scriptures; And that he was buried, and raised the third day according to the scriptures; and that he appeared to Peter, then to the twelve, then he appeared to above five hundred persons at once, of whom the greater part remain until now." That is, over two hundred and fifty people are still alive who saw Jesus after he had risen from the dead.

This throws light on the way in which those early witnesses were regarded. The Christian church in those days was small; it was surrounded on every side by foes. Every Christian was precious in the eyes of his brethren. A peculiar sanctity belonged to those who had seen Jesus before His Ascension. The death of any one of them was an event. Every decrease in that immortal company was noted. The church kept itself posted as to how many of these witnesses were still alive. Paul is able to say to the Christians in Corinth that over two hundred and fifty of the Palestinian witnesses are still living. "Then he appeared to James, then to all the apostles, and last of all he appeared to me also." The first facts he had taught the church in Corinth on the authority of Peter, but in addition to the testimony of Peter and the other apostles, he had his own personal experience. How absurd, therefore, for any member of the Corinthian church to deny the resurrection of the dead. "If there is no resurrection of the dead," he says, "neither has Christ been raised. And if Christ has not been raised, then is our preaching vain. Your faith also is vain. Yea, and we are found false witnesses of God; because we have testified of God, that he raised up Christ. If in this life only we have hope in Christ, we are of all men most pitiable."

That Paul believed that Jesus rose from the dead does not admit of question. And Paul was no dunce. He was so great an intellectual giant that he dominates a large part of Christian thought today. And what Paul believed, all the other disciples believed, also. You may say they might have been mistaken in their belief, but if they were deluded, it was a costly delusion. It is incredible that men should ever have acted as those men acted if they did not believe with all their mind and heart and soul what they preached. James would never have allowed his head to be cut off with a sword if he had not believed that Jesus rose from the dead. Nor would Stephen have allowed himself to be stoned if he had not believed Jesus was risen. All of the apostles, one after another, were killed except John. They all died in the same belief. Now these men either believed a truth or they believed a delusion. Which do you think is the more probable? If they believed a truth, then everything is turning out as it ought; but if they believed a delusion, then the whole Christian church is built upon that delusion, and we find that a delusion has perennial power to lift civilization Godward.

Delusions ordinarily are short-lived. As a general rule a delusion causes mischief, but here is a delusion which has proved to be the one greatest blessing of the ages. There are in the world today 550,000,000 Christians. Only nineteen centuries after Jesus's death the Christians outnumber the adherents of any other religion on the face of the earth. We are just in the beginning of Christian history. If only nineteen centuries after the Crucifixion over one-third of the race has given Jesus a name which is above every name, it is not hard to believe that the time is coming when the millions of Africa and of China, of India and Persia, and the islands of the sea will confess that He is Lord indeed.

Now this story of the Resurrection is inextricably embedded in a history that is full of miracles. If the miracles formed a sort of fringe to the story of Jesus's life, we could shear them off, or if the miracles were golden tassels hanging to the corners of the Gospel story, we could use our penknife. But the miraculous element is so interwoven with the other elements that it is impossible to get it out. Allusions to the miracles run into the narrative of Jesus's sayings in the most remarkable manner. Nicodemus goes to see Jesus by night, and among other things he says, "Rabbi, we know that thou art a teacher come from God: for no man can do these miracles that thou doest, except God be with him." Jesus passes condemnation on the cities of Galilee, saying, ". . . if the mighty works which have been done in thee had been done in Tyre and Sidon, they would have repented long ago in sackcloth and ashes." Peter on the day of Pentecost, addresses his countrymen thus: "Ye men of Israel, hear these words, Jesus of Nazareth, a man approved of God among you by miracles and wonders and signs, which God did by him in the midst of you, as ye yourselves also know . . ." The words of Jesus and the words of his apostles move on the assumption that Jesus is performing miracles. There is a thrill of wonder in the very atmosphere of the New Testament writings. If you cut out of the New Testament every account of a miracle and every reference or allusion to one, you have a book which is a mass of ruins.

But even if you destroy the New Testament, there are some things which cannot be destroyed. One of these is the Lord's Day. From the days of Moses down to Jesus the Hebrews had punctiliously observed the seventh day of the week as a day of rest. It was one of the most sacred of all their institutions. The Pharisees were sticklers for the letter of the law, and no Pharisee in his right mind would any more have thought of changing the day of rest from the seventh day to some other than he would have thought of shifting the foundations of the earth. But yet, for some reason, after the death of Jesus, the day of rest was changed from the seventh to the first. And it was changed by Jews. Paul, who was proud to say that he was a Hebrew of the Hebrews, uses this language in writing to the Corinthians: "Upon the first day of the week let every one of you lay by him in store, as God hath prospered him. . . ."

That is only one of many references. Why the first day? Certainly something has happened. There has been a revolution, and the revolution has been brought about by no ordinary occurrence. What has given a sanctity to the first day of the week which lifts it above the level of all other days? There is no explanation so simple and credible as the explanation which the New Testament itself gives: Jesus rose from the dead on the first day of the week. Through the Christian centuries the Lord's Day stands, a monument which storms and revolutions cannot overturn, testifying to the glorious fact that Jesus rose. And what is the meaning of our Easter Sunday? There is a line of Easters running straight back to the first century, and there the line stops. There was no Easter before Jesus died. Why should one Sunday of the year be singled out and given a glory which belongs to none other? Surely it must commemorate some extraordinary event in the experience of Christian people. There is no interpretation of Easter so reasonable as that which the New Testament supplies: it is the anniversary of the day on which the Prince of Glory rose. Here then, in addition to the New Testament, we have the Christian church, the Lord's Day, and Easter—all bearing witness to the fact of Jesus's Resurrection. If proofs such as these cannot establish the reality of an event, then nothing in this world can be established.

Having made certain of the Resurrection of Jesus, the greatest of the miracles, we need not tarry in our consideration of the others. Evidences equally strong cannot be brought in support of the other miracles. They become credible because they are associated with the miracle of the Resurrection. If Christ was indeed a person so unique and transcendently great as to be able to burst the bonds of death and to show himself alive to men, then it is not difficult to believe that He said to sick men, "Arise, and walk"; or that at His word a storm fell dead at His feet. The miracle of the Resurrection is so strong that it can carry all the other miracles on its back.

The miracles do not hold the place in apologetics which they held a hundred years ago. All through the eighteenth century it was customary for men, in proving the divine origin and authority of the Christian religion, to hold up prophecy and miracles as the strongest evidences which could be adduced. Christ did indeed come from heaven, men said, and what He said was divine authority because He worked these miracles and because He fulfilled the prophecies. That was the line of argument pursued in the days of Paley. But ever since the time of Coleridge, Christian scholarship has placed increasing emphasis on the contents of the Christian religion. Look at this character, men now say, listen to these words. Do you not know in your heart that a teacher such as this must have come from heaven?

Christianity itself, in its essence, bears witness to its truthfulness. And along with this we have an ever deepening and growing life in the Christian church. We cannot prove to the mind of our day and generation that Christianity is indeed divine because of anything that may have happened nineteen hundred years ago. The proof which carries weight today is a spiritual life in the souls of individual men strong enough to overcome evil and to reproduce the spiritual graces which are displayed before our eyes in the Gospels. There are indications in the New Testament that we are not to rely upon the miracles of Jesus forever as prime evidence of His divine mission. His miracles are most abundant in the earliest traditions. Matthew wrote down some of his recollections of Jesus. Mark, who was a special friend of Peter, wrote down many things which Peter remembered. Later on a Gentile physician, Luke by name, using the Gospel of Matthew and the Gospel of Mark, and also other documents, compiled the third of our synoptic Gospels. And in each of these three Gospels the miracles are abundant. But when we come to the Gospel of St. John, the miracles are only half as many as are to be found in the first three Gospels. John represents Jesus as speaking almost slightingly of his mighty deeds. To his disciples the Master is reported to have said, "Believe me that I am in the Father, and the Father in me: or else believe me for the very works' sake." In the letters of Paul there is but one miracle insisted upon, and that is made the foundation of everything—the Resurrection.

In the writings of the great preachers of the second century the miracles are not allowed to hold a foremost place. They seem to be steadily kept in the background. There were other arguments which the preachers of the second century felt would be far more convincing to the people of their day than the narration of miraculous stories. What was true in the second century is doubly true in our own. The preachers of today keep the eyes of the people on the central figure in the Gospel story, Jesus of Nazareth. They say to men: "Follow Him! Give yourself to Him! Take His yoke upon you and learn of Him." And it is through fellowship with Jesus himself that one comes to believe that the Gospel history is true.

Possibly a page of my own experience would be of interest to some young man here who may be perplexed in his efforts to find the truth. Nineteen years ago I found it exceedingly difficult to accept the stories of the miracles. I had been a teacher of chemistry, and later a student of law, and the result of my entire education had been to give my mind a bias against all miraculous stories of every sort. One day I had a talk with Phillips Brooks in his study. By and by the conversation came round to the miracles. I said to him in great earnestness, "Dr. Brooks, must I believe the miracles?" It was a vital matter to me at that time because I wanted to be a preacher, and felt I could not accept them.

His prompt reply to my question was, "I should not say that you *must* believe the miracles, I should say that you *may.*"

That little word "may" had magic in it. It changed the complexion of the problem entirely. I saw at once that I had been approaching the question in a wrong temper. I had felt that the church was trying to drive my mind, and against this compulsion I rebelled. I respected my intellect. I believed that it had rights which the church of God was bound to respect. I would not allow myself to be browbeaten, even by the apostles themselves. I had never heard any professor in a college say to his students on the threshold of a study, You must believe thus and thus: But when the great Boston preacher said, You may believe these things, there are reason for believing them, the pressure was removed, the mental irritation passed away. And with my mind acting freely, I plunged unto a study of Christian evidences with an alacrity which I had not been able to command before.

I imagine that many a young man is repelled from Christianity by a misapprehension of the temper of Jesus of Nazareth. I heard a lawyer one day give his opinion concerning the unreasonableness of Christianity. He did not often go to church, nor was he much acquainted with the New Testament. He knew, however, that in one of the Gospels some such sentence as this occurred: "Believe, and you will be saved. If you do not believe, you will be damned." That was sufficient for the lawyer. He wanted nothing to do with a religion so peremptory and dictatorial.

But if a man will read the New Testament carefully, he will find, as Matthew Arnold found, that the shining characteristic of the teaching of Jesus is its sweet reasonableness. Jesus was always reasonable. He always spoke to the reason. "Have you not read?" "What thinkest thou?" "You yourselves judge what is right." This is the manner in which He approached thoughtful men. He never shoved a man. He was full of truth, men were also sure that He was full of grace. When men, then, assert that Christianity says, "Believe, or be damned!" you can boldly say there is nothing of the sort in the New Testament. The word "damned" is not to be found in the New Testament, not the "damned" which you hear men speak on the street. It is a foul and vulgar word into which the venom of a thousand blasphemous lips has been poured. Jesus never used such a word, nor should we. The proper word is *condemned,* and in order to find out what the word "condemned" means, we must read the context. Jesus is giving his apostles their great commission. He says to them, "Go ye into all the world, and preach the gospel to every creature. He that believeth . . . shall be saved; and he that believeth not shall be condemned."

Believeth what? That Jesus stilled a storm, that Jesus opened blind eyes, that Jesus turned water into wine? No. He that believeth the good news, the great truth that God is our Father, and that man is his child, and that all men are brethren, and that a man's life lies in service—this is the gospel. And who doubts that if a man believes this and lives this, he shall be saved? And who would deny that a man is condemned who refuses to think of God as his Father, who refused to believe that he is God's child, and who persists in living like a brute instead of a man? Is it not clear that such a man is condemned—must be condemned in his own conscience and by his own heart, by the best men, and by God?

What shall we say in answer to the questions: Has any man outside the Christian church a right to join in until he can honestly say that he accepts all the miracles? And if a man is a member of the Christian church, has he any right to retain his membership if he comes to a point where he can no longer honestly say that he believes in the miraculous deeds of Jesus? These are important questions, and an answer for them, I believe, is to be found in the New Testament. According to Paul, the supreme miracle is the Resurrection. If a man denies that, he has gone as far as a man can go.

Now, fortunately for us, one of the apostles denied for a season the Resurrection. All the remaining ten believed; he alone doubted. What did the ten do with him? Did they disfellowship him? No. They allowed him to retain his place. He continued to pray with them and to live with them. By remaining in their company, the day at last arrived when he came to see as they did and to rejoice in their experiences. If a man is ever going to believe in the Resurrection of Jesus, he is far more likely to do it when he is in the presence of Christians than when he is away from their company.

Paul followed the example of the apostles in Jerusalem. Certain members of the Corinthian church, under the influence of pagan society, surrendered their belief in the Resurrection of Jesus. Paul was grieved, but he did not drive those people out of the church.

There was a man for whom Paul thought there was no room whatsoever in the Corinthian church. He was the man who openly violated one of the clear commandments of God, a man who was morally corrupt, and who was living a life which was an open scandal to all decent men. "Put him out," Paul cried with indignation; "don't you know that a little leaven will leaven the whole lump?" The Christian church cannot afford to carry along with it men who openly and defiantly transgress the laws of morality; but if men have doubts in regard to the interpretation of the New Testament, they are to be dealt with tenderly, instructed, persuaded. The error of their way of thinking is to be pointed out. They are to remain members of the Christian family, and grow as rapidly as they can and will to the full stature of instructed disciples in Christ.

Every man who is seeking first the Kingdom of God and his righteousness under the leadership of Jesus Christ has a right, I think, to come into the Christian church, and the right to stay there after he is once in, no matter what he thinks about any particular article of the creed. None of us is up to the standard. Each one of us falls short at some point or other. We are all moral delinquents. One man falls short in temper, another in disposition, another in the way he uses his time, another in the use of his money, another in his words, another in his home life, another in his business life, another in his treatment of his servants and inferiors. We are all sinners. We have all sinned and come short of the glory of God, but Christ is the friend of sinners. If our purpose is to do God's will, and our deep desire is to grow in grace, if our constant prayer is, "Create in me a clean heart, O God, and renew a right spirit within me," we certainly have a right to claim a place in the church. If moral delinquencies and shortcomings do not cause us to forfeit our place in the church, surely that place cannot be forfeited by our intellectual confusions and doctrinal aberrations.

We are all more or less ignorant, we are all more or less confused, we all see through a glass darkly. All that the strongest of us can say is: "I count not myself to have apprehended. I press toward the mark for the high price of God in Christ Jesus." And the prayer which we as a church need to offer continually is the prayer that Christ may more and more dwell in our hearts, till we all attain unto the unity of the faith and of the knowledge of the Son of God, unto a full-grown man, unto the measure of the stature of the fullness of Christ.

6

The Immortality of the Soul

"O death, where is thy sting? O grave, where is thy victory?"
I CORINTHIANS 15:55

It is a great day, and I bring you a great subject, the immortality of the soul. Nothing but a shout of triumph will answer for a text this morning. And I have found one in the most thrilling chapter which St. Paul ever wrote, the fifteenth chaper of the First Epistle to the Corinthians: "O death, where is thy sting? O grave, where is thy victory?"

"If a man die, shall he live again?" It is an old question, as old as the race. It has been settled a thousand times and then unsettled again, and it is just as live a question now as it was at the beginning. Men cannot let it alone. It has a fascination which draws and holds. One age decides it is a question which can never be answered, and therefore should be let alone. The future, they say, is a sphinx, and why should you torment a sphinx to give you answers? But the very next age comes back and throws itself down in front of the sphinx, and says: "O sphinx, tell us your secret. If a man die, shall he live again?" One generation immersed in business or in pleasure cares nothing for the question. It pushes it aside as a tedious piece of speculation. "One world at a time, this world is good enough for us"; so men shout as they hurry on to their business, and their pleasure. But the next generation picks up the discarded question and asks with even increased intensity of interest, "If a man die, shall he live again?" A man at one epoch in his life cares nothing for the question. It does not appeal to him. He cares nothing for any question which runs beyond the glowing horizon of this lovely world. But follow that man, and you will find him by and by sitting down with the old question. He, too, is now pondering the problem, "If a man die, shall he live again?" This, I think, is a remarkable phenomenon, that age after age, generation after generation, should ponder the same old question, and be unwilling to let it go.

The reason why men will not let this question alone is because death will not let us alone. If we could banish the death angel, we should banish the problem; but so long as death persists in coming and breaking the circle, in darkening the home, in crushing our castles, in putting out the light of the sun, just so long shall we be compelled to discuss the question, "If a man die, shall he live again?" For years we do not care to ask the question, it has no interest for us; and then death, like a conqueror, comes stalking through the palace of our life, leaving behind him an empty chair, and in the shadow which the chair casts the words flash out like the words on the wall of Belshazzar's banquet chamber, and we read them, "If a man die, shall he live again?"

It is surprising that this question should remain through so many ages an open question. Why has man not settled it long ago? Why has the world not been able to give a sharp, decisive "No"? Certainly appearances are against the probability of a man living after death. Why should a man live beyond the grave? Look at man! What a petty, insignificant creature he is, so frail that he must sleep almost one-third of his time, so fragile that a difference of a few degrees in temperature will wilt him down, so tiny that a fly can choke him, a pin scratch can kill him. Why should such a paltry creature dare to dream of immortality? Look at his mind! How sordid, how narrow are his sympathies, how petty his ambitions, how apparently fruitless his life! Upon what ground can such a creature dare to hope for a life as unending as the life of God?

If we are to be governed by appearances, then by all means let us say, if a man die, he shall not live again. The phenomena of our earthly life are suggestive of annihiliation. Watch a man grow old, see his body in the processes of dissolution, his eyes failing, his ears growing dull, his limbs becoming decrepit, his whole strength and substance gradually dissolving away. That a body is doomed to dissolution we know because the awful process goes on under our very eyes. But the mind itself seems to decay. Memory goes, judgment fails, imagination dies, reason at last totters and falls—the very soul seems to be in the process of dissolution, and if we are to be governed by appearances, then we must say that death ends all. But in spite of the disheartening phenomena of the death chamber, men persist in asking the question, "If a man die, shall he live again?"

Why do not men give the question up? In a scientific age like this, when demonstrative evidence is everywhere demanded, why should men persist in asking a question for which no demonstrative evidence is forthcoming? If the soul lives after death, nobody can demonstrate that fact; it can never be to us any more than a probability. No future event of any sort can be demonstrated scientifically. You cannot demonstrate that the sun will rise tomorrow morning, nor can it be demonstrated that you will reach your home at the close of this service, nor can you prove that your long-tried friend will be faithful to you five years from now. We build all our life on probabilities. We cannot demonstrate anything beyond the reach of our senses or the powers of the mind. Death passes beyond our reach. No eye has seen, no ear has heard, no instrument has grasped the soul of mortal man after his body has decayed. The immortality of the soul cannot be demonstrated, and yet this scientific century of which we are a part is asking the question with more earnestness than any age since men began to bury in the earth the bodies of their dead.

Since science is able to answer so many questions, why has not science answered this one? It has seemed more than once that science would close the question forever. Every now and then some bold scientist has shouted out with great assurance, "The question has been settled, there is no life beyond the grave." But when we have asked for evidence, we have received an answer which would not stand the test of thought.

The Christian world has received two great frights within the last fifty years. The first man to alarm us was the physiologist. He discovered that there is a closer connection between brain and soul than the ancients ever imagined. It was once counted proper to liken the soul to the tenant in a house, to a passenger on a ship; but the physiologist discovered that those illustrations are not valid. The soul is more than tenant, more than passenger. The soul is inextricably bound up in some mysterious manner with the very substance and fiber of the body. The physiologist discovered that we have different ideas in different portions of our brain. When we think one way, we use the frontal lobe; when we think another way, we use the occipital convolutions; when we think another way, we use the temporal lobes.

And if any lobe becomes injured or diseased, our thinking is impaired. The physiologist discovered that by injuring the brain at a certain point, it is possible to change, not only the color of a man's thought, but even his moral character, also. A man who has lived apparently a saintly life will, after an injury of a certain portion of the brain, manifest all the qualities of the brute or even the demon. After these things had been demonstrated, one man laid it down as an axiom, "No thought without phosphorus." Another man jumped to the bold conclusion that the brain secretes thought just as the liver secretes bile.

When these things were first asserted in the name of science, the Christian church stood affrighted, but the panic was only for a day. The psychologist came forward and told the physiologist that he was speaking beyond the limits of his knowledge. All the facts which the physiologist had discovered did not prove that the brain secretes thought as the liver secretes bile. The physiologist had proved that thought is a function of the brain; but there are different kinds of functions, and a function may be productive or it may be transmissive. Light, for instance, is a function of the electric circuit, it is produced by the circuit. Destroy the circuit, and you have no light. The function is productive. And if thought were a productive function of the brain, then the destruction of the brain would of course mean the annihilation of the soul.

But there is such a thing as a transmissive function. Music is the function of the organ, but the music is transmissive. Change the shape and size of the pipes, and you change the quality of the music; injure any one of the pipes, and you cause a deterioration in the tone. But the music, after all, is not produced by the organ, it is produced by the organist, and the music is in the organist and is transmitted to us through the organ pipes. Now the physiologist has never proved that the brain is an electric circuit. How does he know but that the brain is an organ upon whose delicately carved keys of gray the immortal spirit plays life's music? Change the condition of the brain's convolutions, and you indeed change the character of a man's thinking; but behind the organ stands the organist, and though the organ be destroyed, the organist lives on. The church is afraid of the physiologist no longer.

The second man who frightened us was the evolutionist. He discovered something that no preceding generation had ever seen so clearly. He found out that we are more intimately related to the animal creation than the ancients had believed. He pointed out the fact that we not only carry along with us many rudimentary organs, which are apparently an inheritance from the animal creation, but that in the mind itself, there is a vast inheritance of brute instinct and inclination. When this great truth first broke upon the world on the lips of the apostles of evolution, many men at once leaped to the conclusion that if a man is like an animal in his origin, he must be like an animal in his death. Men began to use the language of the Book of Ecclesiastes: ". . . that which befalleth the sons of men befalleth beasts; even one thing befalleth them: as the one dieth, so dieth the other; yea, they have all one breath; so that a man hath no preeminence above a beast: for all is vanity. All go unto one place; all are of the dust, and all turn to dust again."

The panic was a great one, but it lasted only for a week. Now that men have had time enough to think the doctrine of evolution through, it is discovered that probably no other hypothesis ever adopted by scientific men has so fortified the belief in immortality as this doctrine of evolution. For whatever may be said for or against the idea of evolution, it must be admitted that it has enlarged enormously the range of the imagination, it has broken down completely the little wall which we had built up behind us at the distance of six thousand years, and has persuaded us to think of immensities and eternities. It speaks naturally of myriads of ages, and will not allow us to think that either time or space is small. And along with this conception of vastness it has given us the idea of development. It tells us that there is a tremendous sweep upward. In the words of Emerson:

> A subtile change of countless rings,
>   The next unto the farthest brings;
> And striving to be man, the worm
>   Mounts through all the spires of form.

Evolutionists speak of transmitted tendency. They say that through the ages one increasing purpose runs. They note the fact that the whole creation travails and groans in pain, culminating at last in man. Now after evolution has convinced us that we have come so far, it is almost impossible to believe that we are not going any farther. If we have climbed so high, it is perfectly reasonable to believe that we shall climb higher. After all this tremendous outlay and cost, the mind will not believe that the creation bursts like a bubble at death. A creature who is the highest product of millions of years of development is not going to end at the tomb. The Christian church has no longer any fear of the evolutionist.

What has science, then, to say against the doctrine of immortality? Not one word. What evidence has science to bring against it? Not one shred or scrap. There is no evidence against it, said even John Stuart Mill, one of the keenest-eyed of all skeptics. We must make a distinction between science and scientists. There are scientists who say that there is no future life, just as there are other men who say the same; but they say it, not because of any scientific evidence in their possession, but because of a peculiar bias of the mind. When Haeckel says that the doctrine of evolution compels us to give up belief in the future life, John Fiske very properly points out the fact that he never deduced his belief from the doctrine of evolution, that he is simply echoing the opinion of a French atheist of the eighteenth century.

When we deal with the problem of immortality, we are in a region into which science can never go. We are in the world of probabilities. What has philosophy to say? It has many things to say in favor of the future life. It presents not one shred of evidence to prove that the soul is not immortal. Here we must distinguish between philosophy and philosophers. There are philosophers who say that death ends all; but as Fiske has pointed out, the assertion that the life of the soul ends with the life of the body is the most colossal and baseless assumption that is known to the history of philosophy.

Let us look this morning at twelve candles, all of which throw light upon the problem of the soul's immortality. Four of these have been lighted by history, four by philosophy, and four by science. They are the twelve-branched candlestick which stands at the center of our modern life. Or to change the figure, they are the twelve apostles which go out from the halls of reason to convince the world that if a man die, he shall live again.

Our candles are so many facts, and the first fact is that all tribes and peoples have pictured a life on the other side of death. The belief in another life has been so well-nigh universal, we need take no account of the isolated savage tribes which may have been too low down to enter into this idea, which is the natural possession of the race. Not only do all peoples now living upon the earth believe that there is something for them beyond the grave, but this has been true in every age of the history of the race. The paleontologist has dug up the bones of men who lived and struggled in the age of ice. Those prehistoric tribes of more than a hundred thousand years ago buried trinkets and utensils in the grave for the use of those whose spirits had left their bodies. That is a colossal fact: a race of beings through a hundred thousand years, holding to the belief that the soul does not die at death. It would seem that the human mind is so constructed that it bends in that direction.

The second fact is that this belief survives. Mrs. Browning has said that earth outgrows the mythic fancies sung beside her in her youth. But here is a belief that the earth has never yet outgrown. Fancies, dreams, and superstitions by the hundred have been outgrown and cast aside. Many of the conceptions of the early ages have been sloughed off as too narrow for our modern life; but here is a belief that has in it a vitality that shows no signs of waning. It has a stronger grip upon the thought of the world today than it had a thousand years ago. A belief that survives through a hundred thousand years, passing through the storms and revolutions of the changing seasons, a belief which no fire can burn up, or dagger kill, is surely a belief that has in it the vitality of God's undying truth.

The belief in immortality grows with the development of life. The higher a man is in the scale of being, the wider the sweep of his thoughts and the truer his affections, the more likely he is to believe that the soul is immortal. Men who are bestial and live close to the earth are not certain that they will live after death. It is the great-minded, great-hearted men of the race who have been the surest of the life everlasting. There were thousands of men in Greece, who lived little better than brutes, who did not know whether or not their souls would survive death. But when we come up to the great Greeks— Socrates, Plato, Euripides—we are in the presence of men who know that the soul is immortal. There was many a Roman who lived in the slime and had no convictions in regard to his soul's future; but when we come to a great Roman like Cicero, we hear him asserting in the senate chamber that death does not destroy a man. Many a superficial and godless Frenchman has known nothing about immortality, nor cared anything about it; but when we rise to such men as Montesquieu and Victor Hugo, we are in the presence of men who know they will not die. Millions of Englishmen have lived and passed away without any steadfast hope of life beyond the grave; but when we sit down and talk with the great Englishmen of the centuries—England's Shake-speares and Miltons and Gladstones—we are assured that the soul is immortal. This, too, is significant, then, that a belief which was born in a cave in the age of ice should be most vital and mighty in the hearts of the supreme men of our civilization.

Not only does this belief grow, but it conquers. It works mightily upon the thoughts and affections of men. It braces man for new con-tests, it nerves him for great struggles, it fires him for vast enterprises, it enlarges his sympathies, it purifies his affections. Under the sway of this belief man becomes both taller and stronger. The more firmly men grasp the world that is coming, the more heroically do they struggle to make this world what it ought to be. A man is able to do hard things which draw the blood, and to persist in doing them to the end of the day, if he knows that death is not the end. Men are stead-fast, immovable, always abounding in the work of the Lord, when fully convinced that their labor is not in vain in the Lord. History has lighted for us those four candles, and in their light it is safe to walk.

But philosophy has lighted candles also, and these burn no less brightly than those which we have just now considered. Not content with what lies upon the surface, the philosopher goes beneath appear-ances and studies out causes and relations. In his study of human nature he discovers certain facts, and from these facts he draws certain in-ferences. These facts, we may say, are candles.

Man has an instinctive yearning and longing for immortality. If he does not have this, it is because he is not a normal man. It is an instinct which cannot be strangled without lasting injury to the heart. If a man does not believe in immortality, he will believe in something else far less credible. If he will not believe in personal immortality, he will believe in corporate immortality. That is, he will believe that he will continue to exist in the complex life of humanity. George Eliot was a trustful, noble English Christian girl. At a critical period in her life she fell under the influence of a skeptical German professor who took away from her her Christian faith. She gave up her belief in immortality. But she could not go without belief altogether, and so she accepted the teaching of a Frenchman who was endeavoring to persuade his countrymen that the only immortality for which a man may hope is the hope of having one's life merged in the general life of the race. This became George Eliot's belief. She gave expression to it in her pathetic poem:

> O may I join the choir invisible
> Of those immortal dead who live again
> In minds made better by their presence.

Under the influence of this belief the heart of George Eliot grew sad. There are others who go further than she went, and who give up belief in immortality of every sort. In many cases these persons grow hopeless and bitter. The pessimism which has played such large part in the literature of modern Russia, Germany, and France has proceeded from hearts in which the belief in immortality has been crushed. What is pessimism but a great column of black smoke proceeding from a heart in which the hope of immortality has been burned to ashes? If a man remains normal, if he allows the current of his feeling to flow in the channel appointed for it, he believes in immortality. What are we to infer from this? Tennyson has expressed the inference:

> Thou wilt not leave us in the dust,
>   Thou madest man, he knows not why;
>   He thinks he was not made to die;
> And thou hast made him, thou art just.

Man has affections. They are an inextricable part of his life. They are as worthy of attention as are his thoughts. Love is as reliable as reason. The heart has reasons which the reason cannot understand. Now it is impossible for love at its strongest to believe that death ends all. From that horrid thought it shrinks back with a cry of pain. Poets are the prophets of the heart, and all the great poets teach immortality. After Tennyson had lost his dearest friend, he pondered for months the question, "If a man die, shall he live again?" He was familiar with the scientific and philosophic writings of his time, and all the doubts which had been suggested by the writers of England and the continent passed in long processions through his mind. Sometimes he could hear a voice telling him to believe no more. But no sooner had he heard this voice than—to use his own language—his "heart stood up and answered, I have fled." Tennyson came out with the conviction that Arthur Hallam was still alive—his heart convinced him of it. That is the revelation given to us by all the poets. John Greenleaf Whittier, in "Snow Bound," speaks thus:

Yet Love will dream, and Faith will trust,
(Since He who knows our need is just,)
That somehow, somewhere, meet we must.
Alas for him who never sees
The stars shine through his cypress-trees!
Who, hopeless, lays his dead away,
Nor looks to see the breaking day
Across the mournful marbles play!
Who hath not learned in hours of faith
The truth to flesh and sense unknown,
Life is ever lord of Death,
And Love can never lose its own.

Ralph Waldo Emerson was a great thinker. He sometimes threw beliefs out of the door of his mind which came in through the window of his heart. Standing beside the grave of his little boy, he ponders the old problem, "If a man die, shall he live again?" and there, with his boy's grave at his feet and God's sky above his head, he says:

What is excellent,
As God lives, is permanent;
Hearts are dust, hearts' loves remain;
Hearts' love will meet thee again.
Revere the Maker; fetch thine eye
Up to his style, and manners of the sky.

The heart is a great teacher of immortality. If God made the heart, will the heart perpetually deceive us?

A man has a mind, and his mind is too large for this world. There is no scope for the employment or satisfaction of all his powers. He is too great to be crowded within the narrow limits of seventy paltry years. We have in us latent powers for whose development we find here no opportunity. Our life at its best is fragmentary and unsatisfactory. As Emerson says, "God does not build magnificently for mice." Nor can we believe that God would build the human mind for the fleeting day of earthly life. The mind is never satisfied. It never knows enough. Those who know the most are hungriest for knowledge. Goethe had one of the greatest minds God ever intrusted to a mortal. He filled with industry a long life, and spent a great fortune upon the furnishing of his mind; but when he lay down to die, at the age of eighty-three, he died with these words upon his lips: "Light, light, more light!"

A man is never able to do in this world what he wants to do. We all lay down our work before it is half completed. Victor Hugo, on his seventieth birthday, said: "Winter is on my head, and eternal spring is in my heart. The nearer I approach the end, the plainer I hear around me the immortal symphonies of the worlds which invite me. It is marvelous, yet simple. It is a fairy tale, and it is a history. For half a century I have been writing my thoughts in prose, verse, history, philosophy, drama, romance, tradition, satire, ode, song—I have tried all. But I feel that I have not said the thousandth part of what is in me."

His language is the language of all great workers in the realm of character building. Who could have peace, if he felt that this life is all? If we are intended to grow into the image of God, we must have another life in which to do it; we can make only the beginnings here. Before we have chiseled out the statue, the chisel falls from our hand. The portrait which we paint is nothing but a charcoal sketch when the doctor tells us that we must die. The temple which we begin to build has not its foundations completed before the undertaker is at the door. We are made upon too great a scale for such a world as this, and there is down deep in us a quenchless desire for a fuller expression of our powers. " 'Tis life, of which our nerves are scant . . . More life, and fuller, that I want."

The world is incomplete. Everything is unfinished here. None of the processes is worked out. The world is inexplicable without another world. What inequalities! What wrongs! What abominations! What injustices! How many wicked men who are not punished! How many good men are not sufficiently rewarded! Right is on the scaffold, wrong is on the throne, and there is no explanation for this world unless within the shadow there is a world in which wrong shall be righted and justice be done. This world is unendurable unless there is another. The whole world is groaning and travailing in pain: what does it all mean? These tragedies—can we endure them? These enigmas—how shall we bear them? The world is filled with things that are dismal and dark; but pull aside the curtain, and when the light from another world falls on this one, all our pains and troubles flash like jewels in the sun. The conscience in man stands up and says: The Judge of all the world must do right. How can He do right with all His creatures unless He has more time?

Science has also lighted certain candles in whose light today many men are walking. One of the most stupendous discoveries of the nineteenth century is the discovery of the fact that matter cannot be destroyed. You can change its form, but not its weight. You may alter its shape, but not its substance. It cannot be washed away or burned up or blotted out. Nor is it possible, says science, to destroy energy. Force may be transformed, but not obliterated. Science has added to her creed the doctrine of the conservation of energy. If it be true, then, that force cannot be destroyed, we are allowed to hope that that peculiar form of force known as personality will survive the experience of death. If what we call the natural forces of the world cannot be annihilated, why should we not expect that affections and aspirations and the power of thinking should be equally indestructible?

Science has taught us that there is such a thing as the survival of the fittest. In her study of the processes by which the world has climbed to its present level, she has discovered that certain organisms find themselves unequal to the race of life and fall away, while other organisms persist and conquer. The weak and the unfit perish; the strong survive. Now of all the beliefs which have gone to make up man's spiritual possessions, not one has shown a greater degree of vitality and a greater power to resist the disintegrating influences of all changes in environment than belief in the soul's immortality. Many a fancy and many a notion has been sloughed off and cast as rubbish to the void, but the conviction that if a man die, he shall live again, has persisted in spite of all opposing forces; and the very fact that after so long a lapse of time it is still vigorous and buoyant suggests that this is a belief which is fit to live. Evidently it is one of the things which the Creator of the universe desires to grow. If the Creator of the universe is good, it is difficult to believe that belief in immortality is a delusion. The mind revolts from the idea that a lie is fit.

Science has also familiarized us with the fact that progress is only possible by the constant adaptation of faculty to environment. Without light, there would be no eye. Without sound vibrations, there would be no ear. Without water, there would be no fin. Without air, there would be no wing. Whenever we find a faculty, we discover in the environment something to which that faculty responds. There is always a correspondence between the internal life and the external reality. This is true throughout the entire animal creation up to man. In man we find things which do not exist in animals below his rank. There is in him the thought of immortality, and the craving for it, and the expanding conviction of it. The question now arises, Is there any external reality to which this internal hope corresponds? Among animals progress is conditioned on the adjustment of faculty to environment. How is it with progress among men? As man rises in the scale of being, his expectation of life eternal becomes increasingly strong. Does this internal condition correspond to any unseen reality? If not, then one-half the universe is made on one plan and the other half is made on a different plan: there is adaptation of faculty to environment among animals and no such adaptation among men.

Science has persuaded us all to believe in progress. It is her constant contention that through the ages there runs an unfolding purpose. She has pointed out the fact that everything passes from lower to higher, from less to more, from simple to more complex. And having gotten us into this forward-looking habit, it is well-nigh impossible for us to bound our vision with the tomb. With the apostle we cry out, "Now are we the sons of God, and it doth not yet appear what we shall be; but we know that when he shall appear, we shall be like him, for we shall see him as he is." Conservation of energy, the survival of the fittest, the adaptation of faculty to environment, the principle of progression—these are the four candles which science has lighted for the comfort and strengthening of men.

Thus far we have spoken of candles only. Let us now think of the sun. These candles would all be burning even though there were no Jesus Christ. But on Easter Sunday we can dispense with the candles and revel in the full light of the risen sun. Immortality has always been believed in and always hoped for; but it was Jesus of Nazareth who brought life and immortality to light. Jesus never argued with men concerning life beyond the grave, He took it for granted. God is not the God of the dead, but of the living—that to Him was axiomatic. In the presence of death He spoke with accents that never wavered. If you want to see the difference between philosophy and revelation, compare the Phaedo of Plato with the fourteenth chapter of the Gospel of St. John. Socrates, sitting on the side of the bed in his prison cell in Athens, indulges in long and abstruse arguments to prove to his disciples that the soul will not cease to live at death. Listen to Jesus saying, "In my Father's house are many mansions. . . . I go to prepare a place for you. And if I go and prepare a place for you, I will come again, and receive you unto myself; that where I am, there ye may be also." From first to last He always spoke in the tone which He used in the conversation with Nicodemus, "We speak that we do know, and testify that we have seen. . . ." But His words were no less wonderful than His deeds. He confirmed the truth of all which He had said by His rising from the grave. He told His disciples that on the third day He would rise, and so He did.

No event of history is more certain than that. For no event can stronger evidence be brought than can be brought for that. It has evidence of many kinds, and evidence which cannot be overturned. Paul, in writing to the Corinthians, sums it all up in a paragraph as compact as it is convincing. Paul assures the Corinthians that he has preached to them only that which he has received. He has had long talks with Peter and with John, and he knows just what has happened. He says that Christ appeared first of all to Peter, and later on He appeared to the Twelve, and still later to five hundred brethren at once, of whom over two hundred and fifty were living when the apostle wrote his letter. This was an immortal company; they had had an experience which had been given to no others. Furthermore, He appeared to James, the man who had not believed in Him, but who is now a believer and the head of the Jerusalem church. He appeared again to the Twelve, the official company which is the head of the church universal. "And last of all," says Paul, "he appeared to me." Thus far he has dealt with hearsay, he has been willing to stand upon the testimony of others; but now he enters the realm of personal experience. Nothing can shake him from his position; nothing can overturn the foundation on which he stands. The very idea that Christ has not risen is to his mind inconceivable, horrible, crushing. His language even yet burns after the winters of nineteen hundred years. ". . . if Christ be not risen, then is our preaching vain, and your faith is also vain. Yea, and we are found false witnesses of God, because we have testified of God that he raised up Christ. . . ." What terrible consequences follow the denial of the Resurrection: the apostles are liars, and all Christians are dupes, all preaching and all faith are vain. No wonder the apostle goes on to say, "If in this life only we have hope in Christ, we are of all men most pitiable." The supposition that Christ has not risen is picked up only to be hurled away.

But a page of one of St. Paul's letters is not the only foundation on which we build. We have something more substantial than one man's conviction for a foundation. How does it happen that the day of rest has been for centuries on the first day of the week? For centuries it had been on the last day. But suddenly the first day of the week has a glory which no other day possesses. When Saul of Tarsus, a Hebrew of the Hebrews, begins to instruct his converts in regard to what they are to do on the first day of the week, certainly something has happened to bring about so mighty a revolution. So great a change must have been wrought by some phenomenal event. And what does it mean that there is one Sunday of the year more glorious than all the others—a Sunday that walks like a jeweled queen in the midst of her sister Sundays? Something wonderful must have happened on an April Sunday in Palestine that at the distance of nineteen hundred years our Easter Sunday should still be glorious. The Resurrection of Jesus left its mark not only in the apostolic writings, but in the world's calendar. You may burn up the New Testament, but what will you do with the calendar?

Not only has the calendar been changed, but the institutional life of man has undergone a marvelous transformation. After the death of Jesus His disciples were discouraged and defeated. They were a company of nerveless, timid, cowering men. There was no song on their lips, nor any light in their faces, nor any fire in their voices; and yet after a few days these men, for some reason, became bold as lions, and fairly sprang upon the world. They were eloquent as archangels, entrancing men's hearts. They were mighty as Titans, and turned the world upside down. How are we going to account for a transformation so marvelous? These eleven men, filled with a burning conviction that Jesus had risen, began to organize men around themselves. In a short time the number was a thousand, and then it became ten thousand, and then ten hundred thousand, then ten millions, and then a hundred millions, and then two hundred millions, and then three hundred millions, then four hundred millions! The marvelous process has gone on steadily to the present hour, until it requires no great stretch of faith to believe that those eleven men will someday succeed in winding the entire race around themselves into one compact body of believing men, each one joining in the glad confession, "Now is Christ risen!" The Christian church is built upon the fact that Jesus rose from the grave. On Easter Sunday we stand upon that luminous and sovereign fact and call upon all men everywhere to join us in the exultant shout: "O death, where is thy sting? O grave, where is thy victory?"

7

Birds

Let me remind you at the start that I am not going to give you a lecture on ornithology. I have no ability as a lecturer, and I have no time to lecture. I am a preacher—a prophet. I am ordained to speak for God. My purpose is not to deliver a scientific dissertation on birds, for I know almost nothing of birds from the scientific standpoint. There are many men in this city who can speak to you learnedly about the nature and habits and value of birds. My aim is not to impart information. You can readily get that for yourselves. All the public libraries and all the bookstores have many volumes on birds, and special magazines and newspapers can tell you all you need to know. My sermon *is* a sermon—a spiritual discourse. My wish is that I may be able to open your eyes a little and your ears a little, and your mind a little to the wonder and beauty of the bird world, in order that you may cry out with a fresh rapture: "O Lord our Lord, how excellent is thy name in all the earth."

What a mystery a bird is! Tennyson, in one of his best known poems, has said that if he knew a little flower completely, in all its essences and relationships, he would know everything. But a bird is a greater mystery than a flower. It has higher potencies and wider possibilities. Little, timid, quivering, fluttering, scary thing, what is it but a ball of mystery wrapped up in feathers! How strange that a thing like that should come out of the earth! How remarkable that it should come out of protoplasm: that one pinch of protoplasm should be worked into a thing that swims, and another pinch, into a thing that crawls, and another pinch, into a thing that flies! How extraordinary that a bird should come out of the star-stuff! At first there was a great mass of stuff. Large pieces flew off and became stars; small pieces, tiny bits flew off and became birds. How amazing that a bird should come out of the fire-mist! In the huge ball of fire-mist the seeds of bird-life were hidden, and out of the mist there flew, in the fullness of time, a little creature with a spark of the primeval fire burning in its heart. Birds are the hottest of all creatures. They have a blood-temperature which would quickly burn us up.

But how could a bird come out of protoplasm, star-stuff, fire-mist? Only because it was, first, in the Mind of God. From eternity the bird idea was in the Divine Mind. One day God said, "Let us make birds," and they were made. He said that before He said, "Let us make man." Birds are older than man. We sometimes look upon them as interlopers, troublesome intruders, saucy upstarts, but they were here long before the first man made this planet his habitation. According to a Greek tradition, birds are the oldest of all created things. Before the sun and winds, before mankind, even before the gods, they were. And it was because they were supposed to possess primal powers and to reach back into ante-mundane times that soothsayers watched their flight and ministers of religion tried to find out from them the will of God.

Why did God create birds? A common answer is, He created them for man. That is pleasing to our vanity, but it is hardly a tenable explanation of their existence. If birds were made for man, then why did they exist millions of years before man was made? Why did they fly and sing, age after age, when there was no human eye to see them and no human ear to hear them? And why, even to the present hour, do many of the most beautiful birds in all the world make their homes in thickets and jungles and mighty forests, and on uninhabited islands where the foot of man has never trod? Why do they flash their gorgeous plumage in the sun, and pour their melodies on the air, where there is no human heart to enjoy them? It is true that God made birds for man, and it is also true that God made birds for Himself. He created them because He wanted them. He wanted them for Himself. He now shares them with man, but He wants them Himself. He likes them. He likes their plumage and He likes their song.

Abraham Lincoln used to say that God must like the common people because He makes so many of them. If that be a sound method of argument, then God must like birds because He makes so many of them. There are more kinds of birds than there are kinds of fish, and more than there are kinds of serpents, and more than there are kinds of animals. There are more species of birds than there are species of fish and serpents and animals combined. The largest of all the kingdoms of sentient life is the kingdom of the birds. I do not wonder that Jesus of Nazareth used to say, "Look at the birds!" God keeps His eye on them. Not one of them can fall without His noting its fall. Jesus felt that bird-life was a page in God's great Bible, and that by reading this page men would receive a message from their heavenly Father.

This leads us to another mystery: the majority of mankind is indifferent to birds. Men ignore them as unworthy of attention. Indeed, the human race may be said to be almost hostile to birds. Are there not societies organized for the express work of protecting them, and do not congresses and parliaments pass laws for the purpose of saving them from extermination? Mr. Hornaday, of our own city, set himself to raise a fund of $100,000 to save a particular kind of bird from extinction. In New York birds have decreased 46 per cent. But most men are not hostile to birds, they are simply indifferent to them. They do not care for them, never think about them, never read about them, simply pass them by as uninteresting and useless. To be sure, there are exceptions. There are bird-lovers in every community, men and women who take unceasing delight in birds, and the number of these bird-lovers is increasing every year. But, at present, the majority of people are not interested in birds.

This is a mystery. Birds are easily seen. Fishes are not. Fishes hide. In order that fishes may be seen, the city must catch them and put them in an aquarium and carefully adjust the lights. It does not seem that fishes were created to be looked at. Serpents also hide. They conceal themselves in the grass, behind rocks, in holes in the ground, and even if we could see them, we do not want to see them, for the sight of them causes a revulsion in our blood. But birds do not hide. They rise before us. They soar into the air. They wheel and circle above our heads, as if they would say, "Now you like to see men looping the loop, and performing other aerial stunts, just look at us! See how gracefully we can do these things, and how easily and without danger at all." Birds do everything they can to attract our attention, but most of us refuse to look.

Not only are they visible, but they are beautiful. They are beautiful in form, in movement, in color. The coloring of birds is one of the miracles of creation. In some of them the colors are splendid, in others they are gorgeous, in others they are positively dazzling. Oh, the delicacy and vividness of the patterns woven into the plumage of a bird! We think it wonderful when men can bring together bits of stone in such a way as to create those matchless mosaics in St. Peter's at

Rome. We count it marvelous that men can create such designs as one sees in the priceless tapestries of the Vatican; but all these masterpieces of human artistry are poor, cheap, faded things compared with the splendor of some of the most common of our birds. When you want to see delicate shadings, exquisite gradations of color, and artistic designs that cannot be matched in the studios and factories of men, go to the breast or the wing of a bird! There are more rich and vivid colors in the plumage of birds than you can find in the foliage of a landscape on a summer afternoon; more than you can see in the ocean when it breaks against the rocks and the sunlight is migled with the spray; more than you will find in the sky even when the day is breaking or when the sun is dying in the west. This color in the plumage of birds is the Lord's doing, and it ought to be marvelous in our eyes. Feathers do not come together to form exquisite patterns with every line unbroken and every matching of color perfect, without a superintending mind. But most of us do not care.

Birds, again, are vocal. It is difficult for birds to keep still. They are always chattering or twittering or chirping or calling or singing. They are so full of life, they cannot keep silent. By their singing they say, "Please listen to us!" But we turn a deaf ear. Most of us do not care for birds.

And yet they follow us. They like us. They come into the city. They take possession of all our parks. Central Park, New York, has nearly one hundred and fifty different kinds of birds within its bounds every year. But birds are not aristocratic. They do not confine themselves to stately parks. They will visit your back yard—anybody's back yard—no matter how poor or mean you are, provided you have a tree or even a bush there. A woman in Chicago counted fifty-seven kinds of birds which in one year visited her back yard. Is it not strange that we should ignore them when they are so beautiful, so musical, and so friendly?

How many birds do you know? How many kinds of birds live in our city? How many are here in the winter, how many in the summer, how many all through the year? How many transients do we entertain in the course of every twelve calendar months? Birds are coming and going all the time, just as people are coming and going. We are interested in city life—well, bird-life is a part of city life, and most of us ought to know more about it than we do.

One object of this sermon, then, is to persuade you to pay attention to birds, to look at them, to listen to them, to think about them, to come to like them. This is one of your religious privileges, this is one of the means of grace. God makes the birds. They are parts of His ways. He has something to say to you through them. If you ignore the birds, you lose a part of His message.

This sermon is specially for boys. Many boys do not think of birds. Because they do not think, they throw stones at them. A stone may break a bird's wing. A bird with one wing broken cannot use the other wing, and so it has no wings at all. A bird with no wings is helpless, ruined. It is in the same condition that a boy would be in if some one put out both of his eyes or cut off both of his legs. This sermon is specially for girls. Girls do not think about birds, and that is why some girls wear the dead bodies of birds on their hats. Some of the loveliest species of birds have become almost extinct because of the thoughtlessness and cruelty of girls and women.

This sermon is specially for grown-up people. None of us perhaps are as happy as we ought to be. We are not so happy as we might be if we were interested in a larger circle of things. Having eyes, we see not; having ears, we hear not; and having hearts, we feel not the things we might see and hear and feel. The result is that we get old early. Nobody gets old so long as he is interested in a large number of things. All of us know men and women in the upper eighties or early nineties who are yet young because they are interested in so many things. This sermon is to remind you that if you are not interested in birds, you will get old before your time. This sermon is specially for the old, for the men and women who realize they are old, who find the days somewhat tedious and who lament that must of the zest has gone out of life. Let me suggest that you enter the bird-world. Buy one of Charles M. Chapman's books and go to work. Begin this summer. Begin today. Introduce the bird-note into your life. You are going down the western side of the hill. Let the birds—God's choristers—sing for you all the way down until the shadow falls and you hear other voices sweeter still.

The bird-world is a fascinating field of study. One can devote his leisure hours to it for a lifetime and always have something new to learn. Every feature of bird-life is bewitching. The flying of birds—what a feat that is! Men have learned to fly in recent years; yet a sorry mess they often make of it. Look at the airplane! What a noisy thing it is! It makes a great ado, and every now and then it gets out of order and comes tumbling to the earth, killing the man who is learning how to fly. A bird is God's flying machine. In the machine there is a little engine—the bird's heart—not so large as the tip end of your little finger. How tiny, and yet how mighty! It can carry the bird a thousand miles, two thousand, three, four, five, six thousand miles. Some birds spend their summers in the Arctic Circle and their winters in Argentina. Twelve thousand miles a year they fly, just for the sake of being comfortable.

And how fast they fly: some birds, a mile a minute; others, two miles a minute. Experts declare that certain birds can fly three miles a minute. Against what obstacles they fly; right in the teeth of the wind, straight through the storm, on they go to their destination. What energy is locked up in those little engines! The albatross is a mighty bird. It measures, sometimes, seventeen feet between the tips of its out-stretched wings. It can fly day and night for three thousand miles, as fast as the fastest steamer can sail, sleeping on the wing, if it sleep at all, and at the end of the journey be apparently as fresh as it was when it started. And it flies without any observable movement of its wings. In the presence of such a bird the heart cries out, "O Lord, how manifold are thy works! in wisdom hast thou made them all!"

The migration of birds—you can study that for a lifetime. Many birds spend one season of the year in one country, and another season in a different country. The countries may lie thousands of miles apart. They lay out courses of travel and they follow these courses for thousands of years. They start south at the same time every year. They start north at a time that never varies. The experts can tell you almost to the day when certain birds will be here from the West Indies, when other birds will be here from Brazil, when still others will be here from Patagonia. They fly often at night. They fly in great armies. Sometimes they fly so low you can hear them shouting and calling to one another, at other times they fly high and can be seen only through the telescope, passing across the silver disk of the moon. The tides of the ocean are wonderful, so certain, regular, and mighty. But there are other tides, tides of feathered life, flowing north and south with the regularity of the trade winds and the precision of the movement of the stars; and these tides of bird life have ebbed and flowed every year through all the ages of human history, and through uncounted millenniums before history began.

O the depths of the riches both of the wisdom and knowledge of God! how unsearchable are his judgments, and his ways past finding out!

The economic uses of birds, the millions of dollars they save us by making war on the enemies of our orchards and crops—this is an interesting study, and a still more interesting study is the poetic uses of birds. What use did Homer make of them? Dante? Shakespeare? Wordsworth? Tennyson? Browning? our own American poets? Shakespeare, the world's greatest poet, apparently loved birds the best. Six hundred times in his dramas he brings them in, and sometimes with magic effect. In the love scene in *Romeo and Juliet,* in the moment of intensest passion, a bird is heard and the maiden cries:

> "It was the nightingale . . .
> Believe me, love, it was the nightingale."

But Romeo better understands the notes of birds, and his reply comes sadly:

> "It was the lark, the herald of the morn,
> No nightingale. . . ."

How did the Hebrew poets deal with birds? They saw in them a partial revelation of God. They noticed how birds will break up their nests and train their young ones to fly. So does God break up men's resting places. He wants men to soar aloft. The tenderness and solicitude and faithfulness of the mother bird made a profound impression on the Hebrew heart. The downy softness, the warm tenderness, and the all-surrounding security of the protecting wings were hints, the poet thought, of qualities existing in the heart of the Eternal. There was an old poet of Israel who did not hesitate to think of God under the image of a bird: "He shall cover thee with his feathers, and under his wings shalt thou trust. . . ."

Birds are man's companions in every quarter of the globe, and yet they are removed from him by a gulf both deep and wide. They do not come so close to him as a horse, or a dog, or a cat. They do not like to be held in the hand. They resent a caress. They cannot talk to us as a dog can. It is impossible for them to express in any way which we can understand what they think or feel or wish. They cannot look us in the eye, nor can we look into their eye. They look at us, but they do not look into us. Matthew Arnold had a dog, Rover, and when Rover died, Arnold wrote no poem. He had a cat named Atossa, and when Atossa died, he wrote no elegy. He had a bird named Matthias, and when Matthias died, Arnold wrote a poem expressive of his remorse and sorrow. His heart was pierced because he had not known the bird was going to die. He had not suspected even that the bird was sick. He had offered him sugar and cake and seed, and had spoken jocosely to the bird even when he was under the shadow of death, and it was this sense of ignorance and inability to understand a bird that wrung from Arnold's heart one of the most beautiful poems he ever penned.

But though we cannot understand them, birds are company for us. They relieve our loneliness. They are comrades along the perilous road. They never forsake us. They are faithful to the end. One of the darkest features of the tragedy of human life is its increasing loneliness as the years multiply. One by one, our friends, our acquaintances, our companions in pleasure and work, leave us. The boys and girls we played with when we were children, our schoolmates, our friends of the early years, drop out, one by one, and we find ourselves attended by an ever diminishing company of those who care whether we are alive or not. Charles Lamb was not an old man when he wrote:

> I have had playmates, I have had companions,
> In my days of childhood, in my joyful school-days.
> All, all are gone, the old familiar faces.

Tom Moore was not aged when he wrote:

> I feel like one,
> Who treads alone
> Some banquet-hall deserted,
> Whose lights are fled,
> Whose garlands dead,
> And all but he departed.

But he who makes friends with the birds will have them with him to the end. Birds never change. So far as you are concerned they never die. You probably never saw one die. You never saw its body after it was dead. There are just as many pewees and juncos, sparrows and swallows, orioles and robins, as there ever were. And they do not change either their form or their color or their voice. The robin will sing to you this summer just as he sang when you first heard him sing, and the whippoorwill will speak to you out of the dusk with the same accent which he used long years ago. No matter how old you live to be, when it comes time to die—if you die in the season of the singing of birds, if the window is open—you will hear the birds singing the same songs which they sang to you when you were a child. There are two things which never forsake us—the stars and the birds.

And although they cannot look into our eyes, they can sing their way into our hearts. Martin Luther, in an hour of terrible depression, was lifted up and strengthened by the spectacle of a little bird swinging on a twig and sending forth a song of perfect trust. Thomas Carlyle walked one day to Edinburgh on a disagreeable errand, and on his way home his heart was heavy with care. But the larks rising and singing around him made him think of his father's house, and he was comforted. Dan Crawford, years ago, went as a missionary to Central Africa. He sat one day on a cliff overhanging a lovely lake, feeling as desolate as Robinson Crusoe felt before he found his man Friday. While he was pondering the fact that Scotland was four thousand miles from where he sat, suddenly there came the tapping of a woodpecker on a tree immediately behind him. "What a warmhearted tap that is!" he said, and, at once, it seemed that Scotland was just round the next bend of the lake.

In one of the finest of his poems, Wordsworth tells the experience of a poor woman who went every morning to her humble work in a crowded part of London. On her way she passed a corner at which hung a thrush in a cage. When the thrush sang there came before her eyes the cottage in which she was born. She saw the path through the meadows along which she had tripped with her milk pail when a girl, she saw the woods, the mountain, and the river. The whole scene of her childhood rose before her, as by enchantment, at the singing of this bird.

Charles Silvester Horne was one of the radiant and anointed spirits of our time. For many years he was Pastor of Whitefield's Tabernacle in Tottenham Court Road, London. He was elected to the British House of Commons, and wherever he was, he was a champion of noble causes, the loyal servant of mankind. Horne's death came when he was but fifty, and when he died, a darkness fell upon the hearts of those who knew and loved him. It was a sad-hearted company which gathered round his open grave. They had lined it with moss and wild flowers, but they could not cover up the wound in their hearts. Mrs. Horne was there with her seven children; Horne's two brothers and his sisters were there; and a large company of men of distinction who had been his comrades in many a hard-fought campaign. When the minister began to read the committal service, and every heart was at the point of breaking, a thrush in the oak tree poured forth a jubilant song. The human heart was not able just then to say: "O grave, where is thy victory? O death, where is thy sting?" and so God said it through a bird.

The most original poem ever written by an American bears the name of a bird, "The Raven." It is by Edgar Allan Poe. The weirdest poem ever written by an Englishman telling the story of how a curse fell on a man for the killing of a bird is *The Rime of the Ancient Mariner,* written by Samuel Taylor Coleridge. For days the hero's life was a long-drawn agony. Because of the softening of the man's heart the curse was finally lifted, and the poem closes with the noble thought:

> He prayeth best, who loveth best
>   All things both great and small;
> For the dear God, who loveth us,
>   He made and loveth all.

8

The Impossible Commandment

"Love your enemies. . . ." MATTHEW 5:44

This is a commandment of our Lord. It expresses the climax of Christian duty. It places before us the distinguishing characteristic of Christian morality. It has been called "The Impossible Commandment."

Love your enemies! It falls upon us with a shock. It is not a shock of surprise, for the words have been familiar to us from the days of childhood, but the commandment comes to us even now with a shock of bewilderment and almost consternation. Our first impulse is to say, What does He mean? What does He mean by that word "love"? Love is a word of many meanings. With what significance does He use the word in this commandment? Enemies! What is an enemy? Who are one's enemies? Which enemies are we to forgive? Our first inclination is to quibble about the meaning of Jesus's words. He knew that we would do that, and so He defines the meaning of this commandment with greater care than He ever defined the meaning of any other sentence that He ever spoke. He says, "Love your enemies! By that I mean, bless those that curse you"; but here again we are likely to stop and ask for further definition. What is it to *bless?* What does He mean by *curse?* Our enemies do not curse us. For the most part they are not cursing people. What does He mean by *bless* and *curse?* and the answer comes immediately, "I mean this: do good to them that hate you."

Ah, now we have come down to the fundamental forms of speech. There is room now for no further quibbling. *Do good*—we know what that means. *Hate*—we know what that is. We have gotten into the heart of that bad word. We have hated, and we have been hated. And when He tells us to love our enemies, or, in other words, to do good to them that hate us, we have no further opportunity to say we do not understand the meaning of His words. But suppose our enemies will not let us do them good; suppose they keep out of our way and we cannot come near them, then certainly this commandment will let us go free. He anticipated all that, for He never closed His sentence until He said, ". . . pray for them which despitefully use you, and persecute you."

Oh this severe, and pitiless, and relentless, and unescapable Jesus of Nazareth! When He once gets on our track, there is no getting away from him. He cuts off every avenue of escape. He pursues us to the end of the road. When He has gotten us with our back to the wall, there is nothing to do but look into His face and listen to what He says. If He had only given me a chance, I could have explained that commandment to my entire satisfaction. I have dictionaries and encyclopedias and all sorts of learned books, and I could have seized that word "love" and toned it down and given it a meaning which would have made the commandment easy for me to keep. I could have taken that word "enemies" and bent it in such a way as to give my natural disposition a chance to act. But He knows the trickiness of my nature, and so He locks every door and will not let me out. He tells me that love is not a sentimental thing to be buried deep in the recesses of the heart; it is a disposition which must express itself in language. My good will must pour itself into speech. When my enemies throw at me words which blast and cut, I must throw at them words which caress and heal.

And even this is not enough: I must not only speak my good will, but I must also live it. My kindly disposition must be poured into forms of conduct. I must not only bless, but also do good. But even this is not enough. If He had given me the opportunity, I could have evaded the law even here: I could have spoken sugared words and poured honey upon the sentences so that it would drop from every syllable. I could have done all sorts of gracious deeds, and at the same time carried the dagger in my heart. But He says that there must be no shamming, that my speech must be genuine, and my conduct must be honest. I must love my neighbor in the deepest recesses of my soul, and carry him to the throne of grace, and ask from the great good God the same blessings upon him which I would ask for myself. And in order to make His meaning clear beyond all question, He says, ". . . if ye forgive not men their trespasses, neither will your Father forgive your trespasses." He shuts the door of heaven and writes above the door, "No soul shall enter here who has an unforgiving disposition." If this is the law of the Kingdom of God, who can be saved?

This is a familiar question, we have heard it before. It is a question that always leaps to the lips of men whenever the gospel of Jesus is squarely preached. When Jesus talked to men in Jerusalem and in Capernaum, men listened to him dumfounded and amazed. "Are there many that be saved?" they cried out as He made the conditions high and hard; "Who, then, can be saved?" "This is a hard saying, who can hear it?" "How can these things be?" "Lord, increase our faith!" These were the ejaculations that sprang spontaneously to the lips of the men who drank in His severe and lofty words. But never did He apologize for anything He ever said, and never did He go to men with any suggestions of a compromise. He pushed up His standards higher and higher, and left them shining there. He took His position on certain principles, and all the learned men of His day could not budge Him from the spot on which He stood. He laid down the law of love and never modified it in a single syllable.

He had a strange way of repeating his hardest sayings. In that He imitated nature. Nature often seems unreasonable and cruel. We cry out against her. "Do not do that, nature!" And nature goes right on and does the unreasonable thing again. We ask nature to give us a reason for her conduct. We say, "Tell us why, O nature, why you persist in doing that," and the only answer that comes back is, "Verily, I say unto you, I am going to do it again." So it was with Jesus. He said to Nicodemus, "You must be born again." When Nicodemus asked for the reason, His answer was, "You must be born again." To the men in Capernaum He said, "You must eat my flesh and drink my blood"; and when they asked for an explanation, His answer was, "You must eat my flesh and drink my blood." There were certain facts which He would never allow His hearers to get away from. He never would allow them to escape from the fact that to enter the kingdom of God, they must be changed. The change must extend to the roots of their being. They must be built up anew from the very foundation. This change could be wrought by God, and God only.

Because God is almighty, and human nature can be changed, the Christian religion does not hesitate to put at the very forefront of all her teaching this impossible commandment, "Love your enemies." That high doctrine was not spoken in a corner and is not hidden away in some footnote in the New Testament; it is written large on the very forehead of our faith. All the enemies of Christianity have known that it is the command of Jesus that His followers shall love their enemies. This has been in every age a stumbling block and a rock of offense. Men have derided Christianity because of his high teaching. They have said it teaches a groveling and cowardly disposition, it commands a man to abdicate his manhood. It takes out of him a virile and noble spirit. So men have always said, and so they are saying still. Others have found in the law of love something beautiful to think about, but impossible to live. They have said Christianity is a lovely dream, but it is absolutely unworkable in a world like this.

But no enemy of Christianity has ever ventured to suggest that the Carpenter of Nazareth does not teach the doctrine of love to enemies. We know it is the teaching of our religion, and we measure Christians always by this law of love. Whenever we find a man or woman who is spiteful and revengeful, ugly and unforgiving, we say he is not much of a Christian. Instinctively we condemn him if he does not live up to this law of love. We measure ourselves by the same high standard. Whenever we allow hateful feelings to take possession of our hearts, whenever we breathe revenge or keep alive the fire of hatred, we feel so out of sorts, so wretched, and so unworthy that we know we have parted company with the Lord, and there is no peace for us again until we have allowed Him to take all the bitterness away.

We may say sometimes that our religion is unpractical, but we are not honest when we speak so. It is not true that Christianity cannot be lived upon this earth. It has been lived here once, and it can be lived here by every man who is willing to give himself to God. Did not Jesus live the doctrine which He preached? What other man in all human history has ever been so misrepresented and maligned, so hooted and hated and hounded? What man ever had greater exasperations and more numerous provocations to retaliate and strike back, and yet it is impossible for us to conceive of Jesus of Nazareth entertaining a malicious feeling. On one occasion two of His disciples, disgusted by the boorish action of some Samaritan peasants, wanted to burn them up. They rushed to Jesus for the permission to do this. His only reply was, "You do not know my spirit. I am not come to destroy men's lives, but to save them. No matter what they do to me, it is my mission to do good to them." What an illustration of self-control we have in His treatment of Judas! The despicable wretch steps out in the moonlight and imprints a kiss on Jesus's cheek. Certainly any man with any spirit in him will hurl the traitor off as he would spurn a viper. No, His only rebuke is, "Judas, betrayest thou the Son of man with a kiss?" He would not strike him with a sword; He struck him only with a glance of His loving eyes. "Father, forgive them; for they know not what they do. . . ." So he kept repeating as the Roman soldiers drove the nails through his quivering hands. Never allow any man to tell you that Christianity is not practicable, that it cannot be lived upon this earth. That assertion is a lie. Christianity has been lived here, else our New Testament does not speak the truth.

But someone says, Jesus was unique, He was different from all the men who have ever been or ever shall be. There was that in Him which has never been in any other man, and therefore conduct which to Him was possible is beyond the reach of ordinary men.

It is true that Jesus was different from all the other members of our race, but it is not true that ordinary men cannot follow Him in obeying this law of love. The New Testament tells us that other men besides our Lord were able to love their enemies. Within a short time after Jesus's death one of His followers was stoned. As the stones came crashing into his flesh, he fell upon his knees and prayed, ". . . lay not this sin to their charge." What Jesus did upon the Cross, Stephen did upon the ground.

Nor is Stephen the only man who did that. St. Paul was able to forgive his enemies as Jesus forgave the men that hated him. Wherever Paul went, he was misrepresented and misunderstood. He was made the offscouring of the world; but harsh treatment never soured him, and injustice never made him vindictive. In one of his letters he sets forth the manner of his living, ". . . being reviled, we bless; being persecuted, we suffer it. . . ." Not only did he suffer all sorts of abuse at the hands of the pagan world, but he suffered still greater insults at the hands of his Christian converts. Never did a minister have a more cantankerous and unreasonable and ungrateful church than St. Paul had in the church of Corinth. But he treasured up no malice against these quarrelsome people in the Grecian city. After they had done their worst, he says, "I will very gladly spend and be spent for you; though the more abundantly I love you, the less I be loved." The apostles were all able to live up to this golden law of love.

But someone says, That was nineteen hundred years ago, that

was in the age of the apostles, after the descent of the Holy Spirit; but you cannot expect such dispositions in these later and colder times.

Do not say that. Do you mean to say that forgiveness is such a delicate plant that it blossomed once upon our earth, to blossom no more forever! Has there been only one tropical age when this plant could put forth its bloom, and have the petals been scattered on the icy winds of this chill world? No, forgiveness is a plant that grows and blossoms in every time where human hearts are willing to give access to God's eternal spirit. There are men and women living now, and they are numbered by the thousands, who obey this law of love. You have known some of them, and so have I. I think of one just now, Dr. John G. Paton. Who that has ever known that man would hesitate to say that there is at least one man upon this earth who cannot think a malicious thought or nourish a resentful feeling. His heart is as sweet and tender as the heart of the beloved disciple. We have had in this country at least one president who was near and dear to the heart of Christ. We have had others; but I am sure of this one, for in his life there was a marvelous manifestation of the spirit of the Gospel. It was our President who said, "With malice toward none; with charity for all. . . ." Abraham Lincoln was great in many ways, but the crowning proof of his transcendent greatness was his Christ-like freedom from resentment.

But while the law is practicable, there are various questions which are certain to arise in every thoughtful mind. Is there a limit to this forgiveness? Can we set boundaries to love? How many times may a person do me a wrong and still have a claim upon me for forgiveness? It is a living question in our day; it was a living question in the time of Christ. For hundreds of years the rabbis had been arguing about that question in their various schools, and in the time of Jesus they had reached the conclusion that after a man has forgiven his enemy three times, forbearance ceases to be a virtue. One day when Jesus was talking about offenses, he spoke in such a tone as to arouse the curiosity of His disciples. Peter restrained himself for a little while, and then broke out, "Master, how many times must my brother offend against me, and I forgive him? until seven times?"

That question of Peter's is full of meaning. It gives us a revelation, not only of Jesus, but also of the man who asked it. The rabbis had decided that three forgivenesses were sufficient; Peter knows that three will never satisfy the heart of Jesus, and so he suggests the figure seven.

He knows that Jesus is unlike all the other religious teachers of the land; His mercy outruns their mercy, their forgiveness is no match for His. And so Peter runs far beyond the rabbinical law—goes more than twice as far as any rabbi has ever gone, and sets the stake down at what seems to him the farthest limit of the demand of God—and then says to Jesus, Shall I forgive a man seven times? The question of the disciple shows what a profound impression the Master had made upon the men that were nearest to Him. The question also gives a revelation of the heart of Peter. Peter knew that vengeance is sweet, and he did not like the idea of having every possibility of retaliation taken from him. His natural disposition was like a tiger. He was willing to hold it in once, twice, thrice, even seven times, but he could not allow himself to think that the natural disposition must be held in forever. Master, he said, shall I hold the tiger in seven times, and then let him spring?

Jesus's reply was, "Forgive thy brother seventy times seven." O Peter, you do not know what Spirit you are of, you have not yet gotten out of the sphere of law into the sphere of love. Love never counts, you must quit your counting. So long as you count, you are not in the world of affection. Forgive your brother seventy times seven. This, interpreted into our modern speech, means, Forgive your brother a million times. When we say we have done a thing a million times, we do not mean we have done it 999,999 times, plus one. Nobody ever counted up to a million; that expression is simply a figure of speech. It means "always." When we say we have done a thing a million times, we mean to say we have always done it, it is our habit to do it, we would not think of doing anything else. And so when Jesus says forgive your brother seventy times seven, He says you must always forgive him. There must never be in your heart any malice or vengeance. You must always and everywhere maintain the spirit of love.

Are we, then, to say that we must take no notice of any wrong whatsoever? Are we to submit to injustice without rebuke? May people injure us with no remonstrance from our lips? Are we to be blind and deaf to every unkind word and every unjust deed? Are we to allow people to walk over us as though we were a worm? Certainly not. We are to do our enemy good. In order to do him good, it may be necessary to rebuke him. Jesus gives His disciples instruction on this point. Read what He says in the seventeenth chapter according to St. Luke: "If your brother offend you, rebuke him, but do it in a brotherly way;

do not make a fuss about it in public, but go and have a quiet talk with him in private. Tell him that he has done you a wrong. Try to show him the sin which he has committed. By being brotherly, you may bring about a reconciliation. But if he will not listen to you alone, then take a friend along. Possibly two or three of you together may accomplish what one cannot do alone. If he will not listen to you and your intimate friends, then make the matter public, bring it to the attention of the Christian brotherhood. If the man is still unrepentant and goes on in his evil way, then have no more to do with him; separate yourself from him. Let all the world know that the man has been guilty of unchristian conduct, and that your disapprobation rests upon him."

All this, of course, must be done, not for vengeance, but in love. We must treat our enemies in such a way as to do them good and bring them, if possible, to repentance. And so there are occasions when it is necessary and Christian to hand evildoers over into the custody of the civil law. It is not right for any man to allow himself or his family to be abused with impunity. If a man breaks my window or cuts down my trees or insults my wife or beats my children, it is my duty to bring him to punishment. He is not only my enemy, but he is the enemy of society, and I owe it to society to bring that man, if it is possible, to a better frame of mind. I must do everything in my power to do him good. I must call upon the state to help me in my efforts to do him good. To arrest him may be to him a means of grace. A few months in jail may bring him to repentance. Love does not always caress. Love may sometimes strike. Blows may be necessary to redeem. God loves us, but He rebukes us. He rebukes us because He loves us. He chastens us because He has compassion on us. He hands us over to the tortures of our conscience because He is not willing that any should be lost, but wishes that all men should come to repentance. Love may seize upon painful measures in order to bring the transgressor to himself again. Jesus was not teaching unmanly conduct when He told men to love their enemies. We always do Him wrong when we interpret His language in such a way as to take out of human life the elements essential for its preservation. No flimsy, sickly sentimentalist was He, but the manliest, bravest, sanest man that ever lived.

Another question is, Can we forgive an injury? We sometimes hear people say, I will forgive, but I cannot forget. It is often said in a very significant tone. When people say that, it is pretty certain there is no forgiveness in their hearts. When a man has really forgiven, he never makes any such speech as that. Forgiveness puts on no qualifying phrases, does not add an appendix in which to state that the wrong will never be forgotten. In a superficial sense it is true that nothing that ever happens to us can be forgotten. The intellect holds on to it and will recall it as long as the soul endures, but in a deeper and truer sense, we do forget. The Bible everywhere assures us that God Almighty forgets. "As far as the east is from the west, so far does he remove our transgressions from us." He casts our sins behind His back so that He cannot see them. He casts them into the depths of the sea, covers them so that they are hidden forever. He blots them out. He remembers our iniquities no more. When He forgives, the old estrangement is done away with and the reconciliation is complete. He not only forgives, but He forgets.

The heart has mysteries which the head knows nothing at all about. This forgetfulness is not a trick of the brain, but an art of the heart. A mother knows what it is to forget. Her boy some evening speaks to her an insolent or contemptuous remark. It hurts her, and for a day or two her heart bleeds, and then it is all forgotten. She forgets it, but the boy does not. He remembers it. He does not think of it much at the time, but by and by it comes back to him—ten, fifteen, twenty years later he begins to realize what a sin he has committed. Finally he determines to speak about it. He says, "Mother, do you remember the evening when I said that hateful thing to you?" She replies, "Why, I had forgotten all about it." Mothers know how both to forgive and to forget—so does everybody who knows the meaning of love.

Can we feel the same toward our enemies and friends? Certainly not. But that is not essential. God does not expect this. No two kinds of love are alike. One cannot feel the same toward his parents as he feels toward his wife, or toward his wife as he feels toward his children, or toward his children as he feels toward his brother, or toward his brother as he feels toward his friend. Those are five different types of love, and one love differs from another love in glory. They are all genuine and they are all sweet, but no two of them are alike. So is it with the love toward our enemies and the love toward our friends. They are different, but they are both genuine. Anyone who has lived close enough to God to be able to forgive his enemies, and who has taken his enemy to the throne of grace again and again, and prayed for his soul as he has prayed for his own, knows that there is no love any finer or higher or sweeter than the love which the soul can feel for its enemies. Jesus did not use the wrong word in this commandment. He used the word "love," and love it must always remain.

Let us consider the motives which Jesus puts behind this great act of the soul. He never urges us to great duties without laying mighty motives before us.

He tells us to love our enemies because this is the condition of God's forgiveness. One day He gave His disciples a sketch of what true prayer ought to be. He told them the manner of it and the spirit of it, suggested the direction in which the petitions ought to move. Right in the middle of the prayer He put this strange petition, "Forgive us our debts as we forgive our debtors." As soon as He had completed the prayer, He went back to give a word of explanation on that strange petition. He said, "I have put that in because unless you forgive those who trespass against you, your Heavenly Father will not forgive you your trespasses." The gates of the Kingdom of Heaven are closed to the unforgiving heart.

We ought to love our enemies as a recognition of God's forgiveness of us. No man has done us as large a wrong as we have done God. No man owes us so much as we owe God. If He is willing to forgive us our trespasses, we ought out of sheer gratitude to forgive the transgressions of our enemies. In order to make this plain, Jesus one day told the parable of the unforgiving servant. A certain king came to make a reckoning with his servant. One man owed him $10,000,000. He could not pay his debt. The king ordered him and his wife and his children to be sold. And the poor debtor in great distress throws himself on the ground and says, "Have patience with me and I will pay you all." The king's heart is moved with compassion, and the man is forgiven. But no sooner is he loosed than he goes out and finds a man who owes him $25. He takes him by the throat and says, "Pay me what you owe me." And although the man begs to be released and promises to pay all, his petition is spurned, and the man is cast into prison. The word is immediately carried to the king, who orders his debtor to be handed over to the tormentors, to be kept by them until he has paid the entire debt. Jesus ends the parable with these awful words, "Even so shall my heavenly Father do unto you, if ye from your heats forgive not every one his brother their trespasses."

Love your enemies, says Jesus, in order that you may be children of God. This is the aim of the Christian religion—to make men God-like. It will stop at nothing short of that. We must reproduce His disposition and temper. We must be like Him in order to be with Him where He is, and behold His glory.

Is not this a gospel for us all? How hard it is to live in a world like this without offending and without being offended. We have such different temperaments and dispositions, and we live so close together that there is friction somewhere all the time. If God should strip us naked this morning and lay open the secret recesses of the heart, I wonder how many alienations and estrangements, how many enmities and hatreds, how many grudges and un-made-up quarrels are hidden in this single congregation!—how many unforgiving spirits have come up to worship in the temple of our God! Let me bring to you the command of Jesus, "Forgive your enemies." Some of you are brooding over wrongs that have been done to you; quit it! Quit it immediately! You are never so completely in the Devil's power as when you are thinking of the things your enemies have done. Some of you are nursing your resentments—do not do it! Resentment is a fire that burns up the very tissues of the soul. If you have misunderstandings, make them up! If you have quarrels, get rid of them! Do it all before Easter. Do not say that you will go half the way—go all the way. Be like God. Christ did not come halfway to earth, He came all the way. He did not descend half the way into the depths of humiliation. He descended even to the death on the Cross. Unless you die with Him, how can you ever expect to reign with Him?

Let me give you six reasons why you ought to forgive your enemies. In the first place, the offenses are trivial. The sins which men commit against us are not great sins. They do not burn down our houses, or kidnap our children, or slap us in the face. All the offenses are only penny debts. Somebody insults us or snubs or misrepresents us on some insignificant matter, or somebody does not agree with us in art or music or politics or religion, and we are mortally offended. Or somebody lies about us because he does not know us. If he only knew us, he would quit his lying. But because he has lied about us, we are burning with the fire of vengeance. What are these but penny debts? Little boys and girls occasionally keep banks in which they drop their pennies from day to day, and now and then they shake the bank to see how the pennies are increasing. Grown men and women sometimes act like children: they keep a bank in which they drop from day to day the slights and insults and misunderstandings and disagreements and cruel words and unkind deeds, and every now an then they shake the bank to remind themselves how fearfully the old world is abusing them. The next time you go to your little bank, remember God's great bank; when you count up your penny debts, calculate your great debt to God. If you expect His forgiveness, how mean it is in you not to forgive your offending brother!

Love your enemy! Forgive him now, for he may die. He may die before Easter. In Ian Maclaren's recent story the hero, on approaching Communion Sunday, thinks of a misunderstanding he had had with a college friend years before. That misunderstanding lies like lead upon his heart. One night he does not go to bed, and after midnight he walks a long distance to the telegraph station and sends a message to the man to whom he has not spoken for many years. It so chances the man is on his deathbed, but before he dies, he regains consciousness long enough to send a message in reply.

That is the way it happened in the story, but that is not the way it generally happens in the world. Usually we wait too long. We wait until our enemy is dead, and then we say, "If he were only back, I would not be so proud. I would put out my hand. I would take the first step forward. I would work to bring about a reconciliation."

Love your enemy! Forgive him, and do it now, for you may die before Easter. What would you say if you should go into the presence of God and admit that the preacher had made it all plain; that he had read to you the parable of the unmerciful servant with its great words of warning at the close? Would it not be an awful confession to make, "I had my attention called to it . . . I wanted to do it . . . I was half inclined to do it . . . but I would not do it. I did not do it, and here, O God, I am!"

Love your enemy, because you may live. God may give you many years yet upon the earth, but no matter how long you stay here, you will never know what life is so long as you hate a single human being. Life is not life when there is hatred in the heart. Those of you who have ever had a misunderstanding or a quarrel and has made it up, know that after your pride had been crucified, and you had done the disagreeable and long-postponed duty, a flood of joy came into the heart that could not be expressed in words. It is after such experiences as that that one comes to know the meaning of the phrase, "The peace that passeth understanding."

Love your enemy! Forgive him because God has forgiven you. Do not be ungrateful. Do not be mean. If God will wipe out a debt of $10,000,000, shame on you if you will not wipe out a debt of $25.

Love your enemy, and by so doing become a child of God. He causes the sun to rise on the evil and on the good. He sends His rain on the just and on the unjust. Be like Him. Reproduce His disposition, and by and by you will behold Him in His beauty.

It sometimes happens that men who have been harsh and hard all their lives become strangely sweet and mellow on their deathbeds. A man who was not known the meaning of forgiveness will sometimes, in the closing hours, manifest the sweetest graces of the spirit. "Wife, bring to me the writing pad, there is a man out west—we had a misunderstanding years ago—I have been proud and so has he, and neither one of us has ever been willing to take the first step toward an explanation, but I am going to write to him. I am going to ask him that it all may be forgotten and forgiven. And there is a man downtown to whom I have not spoken for a dozen years. He did a mean thing to me. I felt very hateful at the time. I wonder if he would come to see me if I should write to him. I think after we have shaken hands it will not be so hard to die."

Why do men so often act thus? Undoubtedly it is due to the work of the Holy Spirit. When the world begins to recede, its noises grow distant and faint, its hubbub and thunder die out of the air; and in the awful silence that precedes the hour of dissolution, the soul can hear, as it could not hear in the noisier days, the voice of Jesus, saying, "Verily, I say unto you, love your enemies."

9

The Silent Years

"And Jesus advanced in wisdom and stature, and in favour with God and man." LUKE 2:52

I want to think with you about the silent years of Jesus. By "silent years" is usually meant the period between the day on which Jesus was found in the temple and the day on which He appeared at the river Jordan to be baptized by the Prophet John. Through all this stretch of eighteen years we do not catch a glimpse of Jesus or hear a syllable from His lips. We listen, but there is not the suggestion of a rustle. We shout our questions, but the silence sends back no echo. This period is a sort of Sahara Desert, with not one oasis in it at which the weary Bible student can pause and quench his thirst. From the age of twelve to the age of thirty the years of Jesus are silent.

And the same may be said of the years between His birth and His appearance in the temple. These twelve years may be added to the following eighteen, so that we have thirty years of silence. How little is told us of the birth and infancy of Jesus. We know He was born in Bethlehem, that wise men visited Him there, that He was brought when a few weeks old into the temple of Jerusalem, that He was carried for safety into Egypt and thence to Nazareth in Galilee; and that is all. The years come and go, and not a voice breaks the silence until the Boy is twelve years old. Then the curtain is lifted, but only for an instant. We catch a glimpse of a boyish face, we hear the music of a boy's voice asking a question, and then the curtain drops, not to rise again until the man Jesus meets the prophet from the desert at the river Jordan.

It is surprising that since that curtain fell, no one has yet been found strong enough to raise it. It is one of the wonders of the life of Jesus that thirty years are silent. When you count the miracles of the New Testament, do not forget this miracle of silence. When you marvel at the things which are said, do not fail to marvel at the things which are not said. How surprising it is that almost nothing of those thirty years has yet been discovered. Why did not the apostles go back to Nazareth and gather up information in regard to what Jesus said and did as a boy and write it down for the instruction of countless generations which would have treasured every word? Or why did not one of the more than six hundred converts whom Jesus left behind Him on the day of His Ascension question the men and women of Nazareth about their townsman and find out at least some of the things which He did as a boy, a youth, a man?

It is amazing that of all the Christians who lived in the last half of the first century, not one was able to put down on paper a single item of information concerning these thirty long and wonderful years which has reached a modern eye, although thousands of keen-eyed men have searched diligently for just such a priceless treasure. Here is a thing which the wisest men of our time are not able to do—they are not able to find out what Jesus did or said through these thirty years of silence. They can do almost anything else. They can soar into the dark stellar spaces, and measure the stars and weigh them; they can delve into the earth and read the secrets of the rocks; they can dive into the ocean and make a map of its wonderful floor; they have been for many years ransacking the mounds and tombs and ruins of buried cities, bringing forth all sorts of treasures; but not one scrap of authentic information concerning those thirty years of silence has as yet been brought to light. A mangled sentence here and there has been discovered which may possibly have come from His lips, but uncertainty hangs round all such sayings, and not one of them adds anything of value to the information already given in the four Gospels.

Why these long years of silence? The mystery becomes greater when we bear in mind who Jesus was. He was the greatest man who has ever lived, the holiest of the mighty and the mightiest of the holy. He was the Prince of Glory, the Prince of Peace. He was the Messiah, the Saviour of the world, God's only-begotton Son, God's well-loved Son whom all men are to love and honor, the Lamb who takes away the sins of the world, the Teacher who said, "Heaven and earth shall pass away, but my words shall not pass away." And yet nine-tenths of the life of this Man of men, this King of the nations, is a total blank.

The curtain is down, and no one can lift it. The curtain is thick, and no one can see through it.

If you ask why this silence, my answer can be but a guess, but the guess is this: It pleased God to give Jesus many silent years in order that in all points He might be as we are. In living in obscurity, He entered into the lot of mortals. Had all His life been open, recorded, trumpeted, He would not have been so near us as He is. The world never thinks it worth its while to chronicle the cooings and the prattlings of a baby. What does the world care for the plays, the games, the sorrows, and the joys of a boy? What do the bookmakers care for what goes on in a carpenter's shop, or in any shop where things are made and sold? The routine drudgery of the world goes on from day to day and from year to year without being heralded or written. The wise men did not write down the things which you and I did when we were children, nor have they written the things which we older folks have done as men.

Life is too ordinary, prosaic, common, to tempt the pen of genius, and the average man has, as Jesus had, a life of silent years. If we were asked to write the story of our own life, the story would not be long. It is shorter still when the writing of it is left to others. Only a fraction of Jesus's life was ever put on paper—just enough, as an apostle puts it, to persuade the world that Jesus is the Son of God.

But while in one sense the years are not recorded, there is a sense in which every year is written in ink which cannot fade. We may not write our life on paper, but we write it on the Book of Life. There were in a deep sense no silent years in the life of Jesus, no years which did not record themselves in the big book of human life. Jesus wrote Himself on Mary's heart and on Joseph's heart and on the hearts of all the members of the Nazareth home. He left a record of Himself on the mind of every boy with whom He played in the street or with whom He roamed over the Galilean fields. He impressed himself on every man He knew in Nazareth, or with whom He did business, or by whose side He sat in the synagogue; He was recording Himself all the time.

And that is what we do. We begin the writing of our life in our cradle. At least one man and one woman were different after we came. We have influenced, more or less, every one with whom we ever played and with whom we ever worked. We have written ourself on the hearts of all our teachers. All our friends bear in themselves the evidence of our living. And so there are no unrecorded years. In the silent years Jesus wrote Himself deep in the life of Palestine. In those thirty years He influenced the thought, the feeling, and the choices of every one with whom He had to do, and that is what we all are doing all the time. Whether we are conscious of it or not, we are writing ourselves down in the great volume of the world's life.

And because this is true, we must not be surprised to learn that the so-called silent years all sooner or later break into voice, and the hidden years, so called, all burst upon the sight. No writer has told us on paper what Jesus did up to the age of thirty, and yet we know without being told. We have the record of three flowering years, and from this record we can tell just what Jesus said and did in the so-called years of silence. Let us look at some of these things for a moment.

He learned to love nature before He was thirty. Nazareth stood in one of the loveliest spots in all Palestine. Looking north, He could see the snowy top of Hermon; and looking eastward, the rounded dome of Tabor. Looking southward, His eyes swept the lovely plain of Esdraelon; and in the west He saw Carmel and the shimmering surface of the blue Mediterranean. Every spring the fields around Nazareth sparkled and blazed like the robe of a king, and the great night sky with its constellations kept right on declaring the glory of God and showing forth His handiwork. While a boy, He bathed himself in the loveliness of nature, became drenched with its perfumes and glories; and so, when as a man He opens His mouth to speak, one catches the scent of the fields in His sentences and feels the beauty of spring in His sermons. How naturally He brings in the birds and the flowers, the grass and the rain, the trees and the clouds, seeing in all of them intimations and self-disclosures of God. No man begins to love nature at thirty. That is a grace which must be developed in the days of one's youth.

He learned to read men as well as nature. Human nature is a difficult book, but He could read it. He loved to study men. He watched the children playing in the streets, overheard their laughter and their quarreling; He watched farmers at their work and women at their housekeeping. He knew life in the street and in the fields and in the home. A little town is the best of schools in which to study human nature. In the quiet ongoing of the untroubled and unhurried days, men have ample opportunity to show themselves; and in the close contacts of the little world, men come to know what human nature is.

For thirty years Jesus lived in a narrow country town, and at the end of that time He was master of the secrets of the heart. He knew men's weaknesses and biases, their prejudices and passions, their whims and inconsistencies; as one of the Evangelists boldly puts it: ". . . he knew all men, and needed not that any should testify of man: for he knew what was in man."

Another book which He learned to read was the Scriptures. From a boy He had been familiar with them, and as soon as He comes before us, we hear Him quoting the Bible. He does it in a way which shows how well He knows it. It takes a deal of study to learn the Bible so thoroughly that one can use it in the critical moments of life. Jesus always used the Scripture in beating back His foes. When the Devil tempted Him, He discomfited him by hurling Scripture at him. When His enemies attacked Him in the streets, He overwhelmed them by quotations from the writings of holy men of old. When they tried to trip Him up by quoting only a part of a sentence, He could go on and complete it and show them they had grasped only a fragment of the truth. In His dying hour He comforted Himself by repeating sentences from the Psalms. He could use Scripture as a sword, a staff, or a pillow. All those years of silence must have been filled with Bible study, for no man begins at thirty to use the Scriptures as Jesus used them if he has never studied them before.

In these thirty years He formed the habit of praying. All through His public life He is a man of prayer. He prays naturally and always. He prays before He enters on his work, after He has won his victory, and in the stress and strain of crowded and fatiguing days. He prays early in the morning, He prays far into the night. So often does He pray that men who know Him best ask Him to teach them how to do it, too. For Him to pray was easy and satisfying and joyful, because from a boy He had poured out His heart to God in the shop and in the fields in adoration and thanksgiving. Men who do not learn early how to pray are handicapped in their later years, and often find it difficult to pray. Those pray with greatest freedom, faith, and rapture who formed the habit of often speaking to God in the simple, trustful days of childhood.

He also formed the habit of going to church, or as the people in Palestine expressed it, of going to synagogue. After thirty we see Him always in His place in the church on the Sabbath day. One of the Evangelists tells us it was His "custom" to be there. The custom was formed in the thirty years of silence. From the earliest years He had been taken to the synagogue, and to be absent from a Sabbath service would have created a scandal among all good people in Nazareth. The modern foolishness had not yet taken possession of parents' hearts, that in religion and in religion only we must let children do what they please. To the end of His life Jesus was a churchgoer because He had established that habit in the days of His youth.

He had also formed the habit of thinking. As a boy He had asked questions and meditated, and as a carpenter He had thought as He had worked. It is a mistake to suppose that men who work with their hands do not think. Some of the sanest and finest thinking in the world has been done by men who all the time kept working with their hands. Mind and hands can work at the same time. How long and carefully Jesus had thought can be seen by the daring way in which He speaks when He comes out of His obscurity at the age of thirty.

He has a message, and He speaks it without a quaver or a hesitation. It is a message which is so strong and radical that it stirs the nation to the core. Even that great thinker John the Baptist fades away in the glory of this fresh thinker from the little shop in Nazareth. His sentences are as clear as crystal. Only men who have done much thinking are able to express themselves with clearness. The reason there is mud in much that is said today is because men who write and speak are too hurried to think themselves out into clearness. His paragraphs are as beautiful as they are clear. His parables are gems. Not a writer in nineteen centuries has been able to write parables equal to His. These parables were not made on the spur of the moment: some of them, I doubt not, took their shape in the carpenter shop in Nazareth. His words carry with them a certain atmosphere which the sensitive soul can feel, and this atmosphere is the creation of a mind which is much given to meditation. There is a calmness and a restfulness in the words of Jesus, given to them by a mind which has thought the problem through.

In those silent years He had formed certain convictions which went with Him to the end. The difference between an idea and a conviction is that we hold the first, while the second holds us. A conviction is an idea which has gotten such a grip upon us that it molds and directs our life. In the silent years certain convictions took shape in Jesus—conceptions of God and man, of right and duty, of this world and the next—which determined the character of His conduct and His teaching. And these convictions were not surrendered or even modified by the fierce opposition of the world. A pitiless storm beat upon His head all the way from Nazareth to Golgotha, but not one conviction melted down under the fury of the awful blast. The rain descended and the floods came, and the winds blew and beat upon that house; and it fell not, for it was founded upon a rock. Through the years of silence the deep foundations had been laid with fidelity and care, and nothing could overturn the structure built upon them.

He had built up a disposition which was also incapable of destruction. The two tempers which strike us in the man Jesus are, first, His abhorrence of evil and, secondly, His love for human beings. How He hated insincerity! Snobbery and foppery, pretense and putting-on, all shams and humbugs were odious to Him. He struck them whenever He got a chance. And if more grown people nowadays had a deeper hatred for show and sham, there would be less humbugging than there is! And then He despised cruelty. Unkindness to a human being, especially if the man or woman was sick and forlorn or despised or poor, stirred His soul to blazing indignation. As a boy He had learned to hate hypocrisy, and to look upon every kind of cruelty with fiery detestation.

Boys, if you do not hate evil when you are young, you are not likely to hate it when you are men. You will compromise with it and raise plausible excuses for it. His hatred of evil was matched by His burning love for everything that was beautiful and good. He loved men. He pitied them. He sympathized with them. He loved them with a love which even the meanest of men could not break down. No matter what men said about Him or did against Him, they could not turn Him sour. He was sweet to the very center of His heart. When the soldiers drove the nails through His hands, He said, "Father, forgive them; for they know not what they do. . . ."

To put it all in a sentence, Jesus had in the silent years built up a character that is the wonder and admiration of the world. Inside that garden, surrounded by the hedge of silence, there had grown and blossomed in these hidden years a flower of paradise whose fragrance has filled all the world. In the dingy shop in little Nazareth there had been crystallized a character which to the end of time shall be the model and ideal of our race. And so, even though the New Testament does not tell us in so many words what Jesus thought and said and did in the thirty years which preceded His baptism in the river

Jordan, we know substantially everything of value which took place, for the three years of recorded life are but the unfolding and interpretation of the years which were hidden.

And what is the lesson for today? Boys and girls, don't overlook yourselves. In the New Testament the big folks overlook the little folks. That is bad, but it is still worse for little folks to overlook themselves. Do not think for a moment that you are only getting ready to live; you are living now. Do not imagine you are getting ready to do some big thing later on. What is a big thing, the biggest thing which one can do in this world? Is it keeping a store, or making a lot of money, or arguing a case before a jury, or preaching a sermon, or publishing a paper, or making a book, or healing sick people? No, no, no; the biggest thing which any one can do in this world is to build up his soul, and that is what you are doing now.

You are forming habits. Be careful not to form any which you will have to fight in your later years. Jesus never formed a habit which caused Him trouble after thirty. Would to God we older people could all say that of ourselves. Many a man is harassed and tormented all his afterlife by habits formed before he was thirty. An evil habit is like a tiger lying at the door. Every now and then it springs, and the man must fight with it, losing time and strength and blood!

Now is the time to let the convictions form which shall hold you through the storms of the sea. Thousands of men are like so much seaweed, rising and falling with the tide, drifting with the current because they are without convictions. What is seaweed worth in the making of a world?

In these silent years certain dispositions are taking shape which will color all the years which are to come. Many a man and woman here this morning is unhappy, losing out of life the best things which life has to give, all because in the silent years dispositions were allowed to grow which were contrary to Jesus.

These are the years in which you are to decide what you are going to do. Now is the time to frame your plan. Jesus had His plan completed at the age of thirty. From the hour of His baptism onward, he never wavered, hesitated, or doubled back upon His track. Men tried their best to hasten Him, retard Him, or turn Him aside, but every time He pushed steadily forward saying, "I must!" He accomplished much because He lost no time in retracing His steps. The men who have no plan are the men who march bravely up a hill and then march down again. They go forward for a mile, and retrace their course because their purpose is uncertain. They go in a roundabout way, losing strength and time, when they could have cut across lots, had they carried in their eye a goal.

If you want to quadruple the length of your life, decide early what you are going to do. A plan is the greatest of timesavers. The public life of Jesus was only three years long, but so much was accomplished that we forget how short it was. When we hear the name of Methuselah, we think how long he lived; there is nothing else to think about. But when we hear the name of Jesus, we do not think of the number of His years, but of the mighty work which He accomplished. Every stroke counted, every word told, every effort deepened the impression and widened the influence, so that at the end of his brief life He could say, "I have finished the work which thou gavest me to do."

In the silent years the roots of the soul established themselves in the soil. Some men are always surprising us; they do better than we thought they would, because they were better rooted than we knew. Other men are always disappointing us. They never come up to expectations, because in the silent years the growth of the roots was interfered with and stunted. The little oak is scarcely noticed standing among the beeches and birches and poplars and pines. Through ten and twenty years it goes on growing, but its progress is silent and its glory is hidden. But slowly through the century, while its neighbors fall and perish, it rises and spreads until every traveler who passes that way stops and exclaims, "What a magnificent tree!"

Boys and girls, I urge you to remember this: The so-called unrecorded years are every one recorded; the silent years will someday surely speak, and everything which is hidden will sometime—if not here, then yonder—burst upon the eyes of men and of God!

IO

The Individual Is the Key
of the World Problem

To the thoughtful mind the world is a problem. By *world* I mean the world of men and women, the world of human society, a wonderfully intricate and complicated organism, shot through with inflammable stuff and explosive forces, and pregnant with a thousand possible catastrophies. The problem is how to keep society from degenerating, disintegrating, rotting. Jesus of Nazareth, the Man who understood the world better than any other man who has ever lived in it, said that the world needs two things, light and salt—light to keep it from tumbling into a ditch, and salt to save it from putrefaction.

The rise and fall of empires has long been a subject for the contemplation of historians. A tragic theme it is. The dissolution of nations, the disappearance of races, this is a pathetic and doleful tale. Lord Byron read history, and at the end of his reading, this is what he wrote:

> First Freedom and then Glory—when that fails,
> Wealth, vice, corruption—barbarism at last.
> And History, with all her volumes vast,
> Hath but one page.

Will our civilization go down? We do not know. We know that other civilizations have vanished. The civilization of Assurbanipal, of Nebuchadnezzar, of Ramses II, of Cyrus the Great, of Pericles, of the Antonines, of the Goths and the Saracens and the Aztecs—all these arose, flourished, and dissolved. Will ours also go down? We only know it cannot go on as it is. It is too dishonest. Society is honeycombed with hypocrisies and shams and lies. It cannot go on indefinitely. It is too unbrotherly. The men at the top are too indifferent to the way in which the men at the bottom are obliged to live. Races are too snobbish in their attitude to one another, and classes are too cruel in their treatment of one another. It cannot go on. It is too stupid. Great Britain and France and the United States are spending hundreds of millions of dollars on armies and navies, notwithstanding they have just come out of a war loaded down with debt. Here is stupidity in its densest and deadliest form. It cannot go on. Unless our civilization is improved, it is doomed.

What can be done? One reply is that nothing can be done but to pull it down, rip it up, blow it to atoms, and make room for something different. That is what the Bolshevists say, and the Communists and the syndicalists and the anarchists—groups of alert and determined men who are working in every country to disseminate the philosophy of destruction.

The majority of men, however, are not concerned with the problem at all. They do not want to be bothered with it. They go on eating and drinking, marrying and giving in marriage, making money and spending it, willing that civilization should drift on, God only knows whither.

But there are groups of noble-minded men in every country who believe that humanity can be reformed, the world can be reshaped, if only resolute men once get their hands on it. But there men are not agreed in regard to what must be done. The reformation cannot come, so it seems, through the state or the church or the school or the press. All these agencies seem to be impotent, and labor spent on them is apparently futile. We have no instrument at hand with which we can reform the world. Where shall we seek for a solution for the world problem? Where shall we find the key which will unlock the closed door? Let us consult the Prophet Jeremiah and see what suggestion he has to offer.

Do you ever use a concordance? You can learn things from a concordance which you can learn from no other book. You can learn, for instance, in a moment that the word "heart"occurs more frequently in the Book of Jeremiah than in any other book in the Bible except Proverbs and the Psalter. It occurs so frequently in the Psalter because the Psalms were largely written by poets who were powerfully influenced by Jeremiah. The word occurs several scores of times in the

Book of Jeremiah, because religion in him has for the first time become intimate and personal, inward and individualistic.

In the earlier stages of Hebrew development religion was tribal. There were several Semitic tribes inhabiting Western Asia, and each tribe had its own God. There was a God of the Ammonites and a God of the Canaanites and a God of the Edomites and a God of the Midianites and a God of the Moabites and a God of the Philistines, and also a God of the Jews. This last God was named "Jehovah." He looked after his people. He rewarded them when they did well, he punished them when they did wrong. He gave the tribe prosperity in peace and victory in war. By and by the twelve tribes of the Jews were amalgamated into a nation, and their religion became a national religion. Church and state were united. The individual had no religious or political existence apart from the nation. No Jew had any rights or responsibilities as a human being. His rights and responsibilities belonged to him solely as a member of the Hebrew nation. The nation was the religious unit, and throughout the Old Testament, the nation is spoken of as though it were an individual. Sometimes it is called God's "wife." He is the husband. The nation and God have been married. Lack of loyalty to God is adultery. Sometimes the nation is God's "son." Such it was to Hosea when he wrote, "Out of Egypt have I called my Son." Sometimes it is called God's "servant." Such it was to Isaiah. Through hundreds of years the religious thinking of the Jews was done in nationalistic terms. God is the God of Jacob. Jacob was the name of the nation. God is the God of Israel. That was another name for the nation.

But in the eighth century a terrible thing happened. Ten of the twelve tribes of the nation were carried off into captivity by the monarch of Assyria, and they never came back again. In the sixth century something still more terrible occurred—the other two tribes were carried off into captivity by the monarch of Babylon. This time Jerusalem was destroyed, the Temple was burned, the nation was blotted out. A crisis had come in the history of the human race.

In this dark hour there appeared a man—Jeremiah was his name—who caught an idea which has left its mark on all subsequent generations. This man got his eyes on the individual. In the destruction of Jewish institutions, there was one object which remained, the individual man. Society was dissolved into its primordial elements, and out of the chaos there emerged a new hero—the one man. All the political and ecclesiastical machinery went up in smoke, and through the black clouds of rolling vapor, Jeremiah caught glimpses of the glory of the individual soul. For the first time he came to realize the dimensions of human personality. He was driven in on himself. He came into a fuller knowledge of himself. All the bonds by which he was bound to other men were broken. The ties of fellowship between him and the king and between him and the princes and the prophets and the priests and the people, all were dissolved. He had no wife or children. He dwelt in isolation. He lived in an awful solitude. And in this solitude he came to know as no man before him had even known, the depth of the heart, the reach of the mind, the strength of the spirit, the worth and dignity of the soul. He saw for the first time that the only power which can break the force of inherited tradition is the power of a man linked with God. The only influence which can overcome a false public opinion is the influence of a man who is true to God. The only way to check the lurch of the world toward the abyss is to throw against it the inflexible determination of a consecrated man.

And thus did a new conception of the power of the one man come into the world. A new sense of personal responsibility was born. A fresh sacredness came into the word "duty." From this time onward religion is going to revolve round the dignity and immeasurable worth of the individual soul. Henceforth men are to be taught that the individual is the key of the world problem.

Let us note how this idea is expressed in the Book of Jeremiah. It comes and goes like a ghost, it flits to and fro, it appears and disappears; sometimes it is so subtle, it will escape you unless your eyes are keen. You catch a foreshadowing of it in the fifth chapter. The prophet says that God told him to go through the streets of Jerusalem and try to find an honest man. God says that if he can find one honest man, the city shall be pardoned. There was an old tradition among the Jews that God long ago had declared that he would save a certain city if ten righteous men could be found in it. But Jeremiah makes a great advance on the earlier idea. He sees that even ten men are not essential. There is hope for a city if in that city there lives one man willing to stand up for the truth!

In the seventeenth chapter you come to the same idea expressed in a picturesque form. "Blessed is the man that trusteth in the Lord, and whose hope the Lord is. For he shall be as a tree planted by the waters, and that spreadeth out her roots by the river, and shall not fear when heat cometh, but her leaf shall be green; and shall not be careful in the year of drought, neither shall cease from yielding fruit." That strikes a new note in the history of religion. Long afterward a poet, whose name we do not know, seized upon this idea of Jeremiah's and worked it out into the exquisite literary gem which is known to us as the First Psalm. It is an interesting fact that when a group of Jewish editors got together to pick out of Hebrew literature 150 of the best poems, they said to one another, "Let us place on the front page of our volume the picture of a good man imaged by Jeremiah under the likeness of a tree."

In the thirty-first chapter we find the same idea expressed in relation to sin. "In those days they shall say no more, The fathers have eaten a sour grape, and the children's teeth are set on edge." The Jews had become fatalists. They had come to feel the tremendous force of heredity so keenly that they had lost the sense of personal responsibility. The generation preceding them had sinned, and they were forced to pay the penalty for their ancestors' transgression. There was no escape. They were all in the same boat. No matter what they did or did not do, they were doomed.

It became an adage among them that the fathers had eaten sour grapes, with the result that the children's teeth were set on edge. Jeremiah picks up the adage and repudiates it. He says, "That is not so! Men are not punished for the sins of others. Every one shall die for his own iniquity; every man that eateth the sour grapes, his teeth shall be set on edge." In that declaration you behold a mighty stride forward in the progress of religious thought. Here is a man who has come to see that no one can be punished for any sin but his own. Under the government of God no man is ever punished for another man's misdoings. Every man is punished for his own sin and for his own sin only. Evil consequences, of course, flow down over the innocent. We often suffer from the sins of others, but our suffering is not punishment. If I happen to be passing through the street where two men are fighting with revolvers, I may be struck by a flying bullet, but that would not be punishment. I would suffer for the sin of another, but I should not be punished. Every man stands on his feet before the judgment seat of God and answers for the sins committed in his own body. Jeremiah is right. ". . . every one shall die for his own iniquity: every man that eateth the sour grape, his teeth shall be set on edge." The individual is responsible for his own sin.

In the third chapter we are taught that repentance cannot be national, it too must be individual. Every man must do his own repenting. This is the way the idea finds expression. "Return, O backsliding children, saith the Lord; . . . and I will take you one of a city, and two of a family, and I will bring you to Zion. . . ." The repentant sinners shall be received one by one. Possibly there will be only one person out of an entire city, possibly only two persons from a whole clan, but every one who repents will find his way back to Zion. The redeemed will not come in crowds. They will come one by one.

The teaching reaches its climax in the thirty-third and thirty-fourth verses of the thirty-first chapter. ". . . I will put my law in their inward parts, and in their heart will I write it. . . . And they shall teach no more every man his neighbour, and every man his brother, saying, Know the Lord: for they shall all know me, from the least of them unto the greatest of them, saith the Lord."

This is an amazing declaration. It is an emancipation proclamation for the human mind. The prophet asserts that no man is to be dependent for his knowledge of God on other men, or on groups of men or on institutions. Every man is to do his own thinking, his own repenting. Every man is to form his own convictions. No one else can form them for him. They are to be formed by his own meditations and choices. Every man must cleanse his own heart, enrich his own mind, strengthen his own will. Every man must shoulder his own responsibilities and do his own duty. Religion is not to be a matter of tradition or hearsay, but a matter of personal vision and conviction. Every man is to know God in his own heart. This is the highest peak in the thinking of Jeremiah.

What is the matter with our modern world? Is not one of the secrets of our tribulations the fact that we have lost sight so largely of the individual? He has been slowly disappearing. In some quarters his image has completely faded out. This is due in part to the growth of our cities. The rural population has been for years pouring into our cities, giving us great aggregations of strangers in which the individual is lost in the crowd. We speak familiarly about the "masses," showing by our language that we have lost the outline of the individual man. The man of sixty or seventy who has spent his entire lifetime in a village is an interesting character because of his strong individuality. He thinks for himself, has his own ways of expressing himself.

He is original and racy. In the city we are standardized. We think and talk and dress alike. The edges of individuality are blurred. Moreover, we are living in an age of organized activity. We do everything through societies, groups of men organized to accomplish specific ends.

The result is that the businessman has disappeared. He has vanished in the corporation. As soon as he enters the room of the board of directors, we see him no more. He is lost from the public eye. Whatever is done, is done by the corporation. And so it has become an adage that a corporation has no soul. Why? Because so many soulless things have been done by corporations within the last fifty years. When wrong things are done, no one man is blamed. It is all the fault of the "system." The individual is excused.

The wage earner has also vanished. He has hidden himself in the "Union." He is no longer accountable for anything he does. It is the "Union" which acts. All the diabolical things which are now done in the realm of industry are not done by the individual man. They are done by the "Union."

The editor has disappeared. We once had an editor in New York who was known by the whole country. His name was Horace Greeley. We have no editor now—none that we can see. We have newspaper owners, and they hire editors, and these editors never sign their names to anything they write. When you read an editorial, as you sometimes do, packed full of sophistry and half-truths, you do not know who wrote it. It is the paper which does the thinking and the talking. Or to use a term more dignified and impressive, it is the "Press" which does the talking and the thinking. Those big cylinders turned by electricity running the white paper over the black inked types, it is these which influence public opinion and tell us what we ought to think and do.

The politician has also disappeared. We once had a politician whom everybody could see. His name was Daniel Webster, but he vanished long ago. We are now ruled by political parties. It is the "Party" which writes the platform. No particular man writes it. It is the "Party" which conducts the campaign. Individual men have little to do with it. It is the "Party" which raises the money, and the "Party" which spends it. Only now and then does the public get interested enough in political matters to tear away all the external coverings and get down to the individual men who are raising and spending the money and making the "Party" what it is.

The Christian is in danger of disappearing. He has a tendency to vanish in the church. In many churches the individual has become invisible. We have been asking, "What is the church doing?" That is a stupid question. You get nowhere by asking a question like that. The important question is: What is Mr. A. doing? He is a prominent man in the church. What is he doing? What is Mr. B. doing? He holds a high position in the church, but what is he doing? What is Mr. C. doing? He has belonged to the church for twenty years. What is he doing? That is the kind of question in which God is interested. That is the kind of question which is all important and should be answered. It is the conduct of Mr. A. and Mr. B. and Mr. C. which is the key of the church problem.

You hear men talking about the amount of money which the church has raised. How much did the church raise last year? It is a bootless question. The question of importance is, How much did Mr. D. give? and how much, Mr. E.? and how much, Mr. F.? What is the ratio between what these men spend on themselves and what they contribute toward the work of making this a better world? That is the question with which God is concerned, and it is not till that question takes the uppermost place in our own mind that we shall have the key of the problem of church finance.

It is often said that the church of today is cold. What makes it cold? The common answer is, "It is the 'Age' which makes the church cold. It is a worldly minded age, you know." How shallow! Why make the "Age" a scapeboat? Why not ask, How much ice is there in the heart of Mr. G., and of Mr. H., and of Mr. I.? They are church members, and what is the temperature of their hearts? Is there any fire burning? Is there any spiritual passion in them? It is not the atmosphere of the "Age" which makes the church cold. It is the iciness of the hearts of Mr. G., and Mr. H., and Mr. I.

One often hears the lamentation, The church in our day is impotent. It performs no miracles. It does no mighty works. Why is it impotent? The popular answer is that the world is not interested in religion. Men are giving their thought to other things. How unsatisfactory! Why not ask a question about Mr. J., and Mr. K., and Mr. L? They are church members, and the power of the church depends on them. How much moral energy is there in Mr. J.? How much spiritual force is there in Mr. K.? How much strength is there in Mr. L. when it comes to carrying a cross? We have a fatal fashion of ignoring the deep questions and playing with abstractions.

And so the sense of personal responsibility is growing feeble. Nobody is responsible any more for anything he does. The criminals are not to be blamed. Poor men, they are victims and not culprits. They are not responsible for their actions. It is "Society" which is to blame. They are the product of "Society," and therefore if "Society" punishes them, they are martyrs. They are to be praised and not condemned.

If we do not blame the murderers and thieves, we shall not be likely to blame ourselves. A prominent man said a few years ago that no sensible person worries today about his sins. Of course not. Why should he worry? We are not responsible for our sins. They are the result of our heredity. What is heredity? A crowd of ancestors. A convenient crowd to hide behind. Our conduct is the result of our environment. What is environment? A crowd of circumstances in which we can hide ourselves. By the use of big words we slip down into the slough of sloppy thinking.

It is because we lose sight of the individual that we content ourselves with generalizations. We talk about the rich as though all rich people were alike, and we talk about the poor as though all poor people were alike, and we talk about the youth of today as though all young men and all young women were thinking alike and acting alike. There are as many kinds of young people as there are kinds of old people, and it is absurd to sweep them all into one class and speak of them as though they were a unit. Whenever we think of human beings in masses, we think both foolishly and falsely.

We need Jeremiah. Where did he get this idea of the place and power of the individual man? He got it from God. We can be sure of that because Jesus of Nazareth adopted it and made it His own. Did you ever notice that nearly all of the parables of Jesus are organized around a "certain man"? It is a "certain king," a "certain householder," a "certain rich man." He does not tell parables about races or nations or classes. He focuses the eyes on the one man. In the parable of the Prodigal Son, we are not told about fathers or fatherhood, but about one father who had two sons, each son being different from his brother, and the father dealing with the boys in two different ways. Every individual stands out sharp-cut and unforgettable. In that parable you have the gist of the wisdom which all fathers and sons need to know. In the parable of the Good Samaritan, it is "a certain man" who goes from Jerusalem to Jericho—one man and not a caravan. It is one priest who passes by, not a deputation of priests; it is one singer who looks on, and not the whole choir; it is one Samaritan who appears, and not a committee. Four characters, each one distinct in his own individual traits; and in that parable you have the essence of all the wisdom ever needed in the realm of philanthropy.

Jesus had the individualizing eye. He always saw the one man. He instinctively picked the individual out of the crowd. He one day met a deaf man, and Mark tells us that He took the man aside from the multitude privately, and dealt with him there. He was always doing that. He picked up the blind beggar and the paralytic at the pool and the widow who cast in the two mites and the invalid woman who was lost in the crowd. Peter saw only the crowd; Jesus saw the one woman who needed Him. He picked up his disciples one by one. He did not take His place in front of the crowd and say, "Come on men, let us go to work and reform the world." He picked His men. He said: "Come Simon," "Come Andrew," "Come James," "Come John," "Come Nathaniel."

Nathaniel was amazed that Jesus knew him. "Where did you see me?"

"I saw you under the tree when you were praying, and I made up my mind that you were the kind of man who could help me."

I can hear Matthew saying to him, "When did you see me?"

I can imagine Jesus replying, "I saw the expression on your face one day when I was preaching in Capernaum, and when I saw the look in your eyes, I said to myself, "That man has in him the stuff out of which heroes are made. I will make him one of my helpers." Jesus dealt with each disciple privately. It pierced His heart to be compelled to say, "One of you is going to betray me." He longed for the personal loyalty of each individual heart. When we see Him and Peter face to face for the last time, this is the question: "Simon, do you love me?"

Jesus in His mind's eye saw the destruction of Jerusalem and the burning of the Temple and the blotting out of His nation, but He believed that the world could be saved by one man, one man who belonged wholly to God. It is the message of the Christian religion that the world problem can be solved by one man. The solution is not an isolated event, but a process, a solution worked out by one man wholly committed to God, who is followed by a long succession of men, each one of them ready to die for the truth.

I I

The Social Vision of Isaiah

"The vision of Isaiah the son of Amoz, which he saw concerning Judah and Jerusalem . . ." in other words, which he saw concerning his nation and his city. He saw things concerning them because he thought much about them. He carried them in his mind. It is the things which we carry in our mind which gather around them all sorts of ideas and wishes and dreams. He saw things concerning his country and his city because he bore them on his heart. He loved them, believed in them, and it was his love for them that gave new lenses to his eyes. It is love which enables us to see. A mother carries her boy upon her heart, and that is why she sees so many things concerning him—his welfare, his education, his future.

Isaiah has been thinking recently about Judah and Jerusalem more than usual. The King, the Great King Uzziah, is dead. Death is always solemnizing, more solemnizing perhaps to a man in the early twenties than it is on any other period of his life. As we grow older, we grow more accustomed to death. Almost every day we hear of the death of someone whom we have known. By and by we talk in this tone: "Your father lost a father. That father lost his, and therefore you must not grieve too much."

King Uzziah was the greatest Hebrew king since Solomon. He had been on the throne for more than fifty years. We Americans do not know what that means. We have had twelve Presidents within the last fifty years, and we kept no one of them long enough to become attached to him in the way in which the citizens of monarchies become attached to a good king who has reigned through two generations. Those of you who visited England within the last ten years of Queen Victoria's reign found something there the like of which we have never had in this country, and never can have. There was a reverence for her, a devotion to her, and an affectionate worship of her which cannot be created in a republic which changes its ruler every four years.

Isaiah, like many another Jew, was devoted to King Uzziah, and now that Uzziah is dead, it seems as though the very heavens have fallen. The young man does not know what is going to become of his country. A wind is blowing, and there is no telling what it may blow to tatters. He hears the rumblings of subterranean fires, and he cannot tell at what moment there may be an eruption of hot lava which will scorch Jerusalem to cinders. It is growing dark in Jerusalem, and in the darkness Isaiah sees things which he had never seen in the light.

It is a singular thing that we can see some things better when it is dark than when the sun is shining. For some things, light is indispensable; for instance, the threading of a needle, or the finding of a coin which has rolled out of sight. The woman in the parable, as soon as she lost a piece of silver, lighted a candle and got her broom and began to sweep diligently in search of the treasure that was lost; and when at last the light fell upon the piece of silver coin, the coin laughed aloud, saying, "Here I am!" It was the light which brought the woman and the coin together. The astronomer works upon a different principle. He loves the dark, and when now and then the sun becomes dark in daytime, the astronomer rushes for his broom and sweeps diligently in search of the secrets that have escaped him in the light. We all know from our own experiences that we can see things in the dark.

> Who never ate his bread in sorrow,
>   Who never spent the darksome hours
> Weeping, and watching for the morrow,—
>   He knows you not, ye heavenly Powers.

In the darkness Isaiah saw something he had never seen so clearly before: he saw God, and he saw his country and his city in the light which fell on them from God's face.

This heading of the first chapter of the Book of Isaiah strikes the keynote of the whole book. If you will turn to the second chapter of the book, you will find the heading substantially the same as that of the first chapter: "The word that Isaiah the son of Amoz saw concerning Judah and Jerusalem." After the second chapter this heading disappears, but the content of all the chapters from the beginning until chapter thirteen is concerning Judah and Jerusalem. Those are Isaiah's two great themes. He never can get away from them. He thinks habitually of religion in civic and national terms. When you come to the thirteenth chapter, you observe that his vision widens; he now begins to see things concerning nations round about him. He has revelations concerning Babylon and Egypt and Ethiopia and Arabia and Moab and Damascus and Tyre. He sees things concerning all the nations around Judah and all the foreign capitals within sight of Jerusalem. This man is an internationalist. He believes God is a God of cities as well as a God of individuals. He believes that God plans cities, builds cities, watches cities, sympathizes with cities, makes use of them in carrying out his eternal plans. Isaiah believes that God is interested in nations, that He plans them, waters them, trains them —desiring that they may bring forth blossoms which shall exhale the fragrance of heaven. It his His purpose that nations shall produce fruit which shall feed and refresh the human heart.

"Every man's life is a plan of God"; so said Horace Bushnell over fifty years ago. Every city's life is a plan of God, and every nation's life is a plan of God; so thought Isaiah twenty-six hundred years ago. My subject is "The Social Vision of Isaiah."

This is a profitable subject for study, because we have been brought up in a different school of religious thinking. We are individualists, more thoroughly individualistic in all our thinking than we realize. We talk, when we talk religiously, about men's souls. It is not easy for most of us to talk about either cities or nations in the church. When we talk of those, we feel that we are getting out of the religious realm into the political. If one wants to know how individualistic we are in our thinking and feeling, all one has to do is to compare our hymn-book with the hymnbook of the Jewish church. It is in the hymnbook of a church that you find the heart of the church. The things which we sing about are the things which we carry in our hearts.

And what is it that the Hebrews are always singing about? Open the Psalm Book almost anywhere and you will hear the choir singing about Jerusalem. Here is an illustration from Psalm 48: "Beautiful for situation, the joy of the whole earth, is Mount Zion, on the sides of the north, the city of the great King. . . . Walk about Zion, and go round about her: tell the towers thereof. Mark ye well her bul-warks, consider her palaces; that ye may tell it to the generation fol-lowing." In other words, count the towers and see how many there are. Take notice of the bulwarks and see how strong Jerusalem is. Let your mind dwell upon her palaces, that you may take in her magnificence and tell the story to your children. Do not allow this beautiful memory to die out, but hand it on as a glorious tradition from one generation to another. In that psalm you get an expression of what was deep in the Hebrew heart.

Or take this from Psalm 122: "Pray for the peace of Jerusalem: they shall prosper that love thee. Peace be within thy walls, and prosperity within thy palaces. For my brethren and companions' sakes, I will now say, Peace be within thee."

Or take this from Psalm 137: "If I forget thee, O Jerusalem, let my right hand forget her cunning. If I do not remember thee, let my tongue cleave to the roof of my mouth. . . ."

That is the way the Hebrew sang both in the temple and in the synagogue. That is not the way we Americans sing. We do not sing about our cities. We never sing of Washington City, beautiful though it is. We never sing about New York City. It is beautiful for situation, the greatest city in the New World, but we never sing about it. We never sing about the city in which we live, no matter what our city is. In our hymnbook there is no hymn about a city. We scold about our cities, growl about them. We cudgel them, blast them, sometimes stamp upon them in anger or in scorn. Possibly that is the reason why they are no better than they are. If we should stop kicking and cuffing them and begin to sing about them, perhaps they might grow in grace and in the knowledge of Jesus Christ, our Saviour. We accept Cowper's line as truth: "God made the country, and man made the town." And some of us believe that after God made the town, He turned it over to the Devil, who has owned it ever since; and so we never bring our towns and cities within the circle of public worship. We leave them out in the outer darkness. We do not sing about them, because we do not have the social vision.

There are no hymns about cities in our hymnbooks, and only a few hymns about our nation. When you open the Jewish Psalm Book, you hear the choir always singing about the nation. The Jews had two names for their nation: one was "Jacob" and the other was "Israel." Glance up and down the pages of the Psalter, and see how many dozens of times those two words occur. There was nothing in which a Jew so exulted as in the opportunity to sing about his nation. Take Psalms 105 and 106—both of them great national hymns, both of them between fourteen and sixteen stanzas long when measured in the terms of our hymns. Our national hymns are short and very few in number. It is amazing how few we have. Our best loved national hymn is "My Country 'Tis of Thee." But we waited fifty-six years before we had that hymn, and then we had to wait seventy-two years more before Katherine Lee Bates wrote "America the Beautiful." We have three or four other hymns that are sung now and then, but one of them which we often call a national hymn is not national at all—Leonard Bacon's hymn "O God, beneath Thy guiding hand." That is a hymn for the Puritans of New England. The hymn, "God of our fathers, known of old," is sometimes sung in our churches, but it was not written by an American. We are so poor in national hymns, we have to go to Great Britain to borrow one for our worship. We do not sing often of our nation because we do not have the social vision.

Turn the pages of your hymn book and notice how individualistic nearly all our hymns are. The hymns that we like the best and that we sing with greatest fervor are nearly all individualistic. Here is a specimen from the eighteenth century, written by Philip Doddridge:

> O, happy day, that fixed my choice
>   On Thee, My Saviour, and my God!
> Well may this glowing heart rejoice,
>   And tell its raptures all abroad.
>
> Happy day, happy day,
> When Jesus washed my sins away!
> He taught me how to watch and pray,
> And live rejoicing every day;
> Happy day, happy day,
> When Jesus washed my sins away!"

It is a beautiful hymn. We ought to sing it. It has a right to a place in the hymnbook, but you will observe that there is in it no reference to Judah, no thought of Jerusalem. The whole hymn circles around my own heart and its relation to Jesus Christ.

And now pick out a representative hymn of the nineteenth century. There is probably no hymn more characteristic of nineteenth-century Christianity than the hymn of John Henry Newman, "Lead, kindly Light, amid the encircling gloom." You will observe that it is just as individualistic as the hymn of Doddridge. "Lead, kindly Light, amid the encircling gloom, lead Thou *me* on." Notice the first personal pronoun always. "The night is dark, and *I* am far from home;

lead thou *me* on. Keep thou *my* feet; *I* do not ask to see the distant scene—one step enough for *me*." That is the tone of the hymn all the way through, until at last you come to the vision of "Those angel faces smile, Which I have loved long since, and lost awhile." I do not criticize the hymn. It is a good hymn to sing, but you will observe that there is no thought of Judah, no glance in the direction of Jerusalem.

These are only samples of a great collection of hymns, some of which already come into your mind; for instance, "Jesus Lover of my soul," and "Just as I am without one plea," and "Nearer, my God, to Thee, nearer to Thee," and "When I can read my title clear." There are only a few of the great host of hymns that our heart loves. Here are some others: "My Jesus I love Thee," "I am trusting Thee, Lord Jesus," "I lay my sins on Jesus," "I need Thee every hour," "I've found a Friend; O such a Friend." In not one of these is there any reference to Judah, any allusion to Jerusalem. As Christians, we do not have the social vision.

I am calling attention to this interesting fact for the reason that it throws light on certain phenomena which have undoubtedly puzzled us. One of the outstanding phenomena of our day is the criticism of the Christian church. It is constant, and it is widespread. The criticism does not come from the foul mouths of godless blasphemers, but from many of the best people in the community—men and women of education and culture—of high intelligence and noble purpose. One often hears people saying that the church is asleep. That is a mild and gentle thing to say. If a critic has a gracious tongue, that is what he always says, "The church is asleep." But if a critic is somewhat rougher in his criticism, he says that the church is narrow and bigoted, or the church is wrapped up in its little creed, or the church is engaged in denominational bickerings and controversies. There are critics who go further than this. They say the church is filled with hypocrites —people who say one thing and do another thing.

Now, most of us would never agree that these criticisms are accurate or just. We are acquainted with thousands of Christians, and certainly they are not sleepy. They are just as wide-awake as any set of people in the world. We cannot agree that Christians are narrow and bigoted. There are a few bigots here and there, but a bigot always attracts attention because he is a rare bird. There are not many

Christian bigots yet alive. And as for Christians being hypocrites, that is malicious slander. It is absurd to think that the church of Christ is made up of conscious rogues and liars, men and women who are playing a sham, saying one thing and believing another. Why then, are all these hard things said about the church? Why do men and women, ordinarily fair-minded in passing judgment on other matters, indulge in such wholesale condemnation when they come to deal with the Christian church? I think it is because the world is in such a deplorable plight. Everybody concedes that the world is in a lamentable condition, and it is difficult to account for this when one remembers how many Christians there are upon this planet.

The statisticians tell us that there are now 556,000,000 Christians in the world, and with all these hundreds of millions consecrated to the Son of God, how did the world ever get into such a mess as it is in, and why does it not get out of it? We have a Christian nation. There are scores of millions of church members in our country. Our churches are large and rich and influential, and yet what a plight the United States is in. The experts have been placarding the record which we made in the year 1924. What a dismal and heartbreaking record it is. In that one year $100,000,000 was stolen in forgeries; $2,500,000,000 was stolen in holdups; $6,000,000,000 was stolen in swindling stock operations. This is a part of the story on the financial side, but think of the thousands and thousands and thousands of murders; of the thousands and thousands and thousands of divorces; of the thousands and thousands and thousands of culprits who stood in our juvenile courts. Certainly this is a record to make the heart sick. Dr. Russell H. Conwell, who has been all his life an optimist, always persisting in looking on the bright side of things, said on his eighty-second birthday, "I believe that American morals are worse than they have ever been to my knowledge." Now, when we have all these millions of Christians and find the country full of vice and crime, it is not surprising that some people say the church must be asleep, or the church must be attending to something else, or the church must be a sham and a fake.

I shall never forget an experience I had a few years ago when I was visiting a ministerial friend in a western city. At the dinner table he told me how prosperous Christianity was in that city, and how large and successful the churches all were, what good congregations they had, and what great contributions they made to missions and philanthropic causes. I was delighted to listen to so cheering a story. Later on in the evening we began to talk about the city in general, and my friend at once began to paint a picture black as night. Everything in the city seemed to be wrong. The mayor was an incompetent and low-grade politician. The board of aldermen was made up of men totally unfit for the office. The courts were in a demoralized condition, and society was honeycombed with immorality and every kind of corruption. I was greatly impressed by the contrast between the prosperity of the churches and the wickedness of the city. Wickedness and worship seemed to thrive side by side. There seemed to be no point of contact between the life of the church and the life of the city. I could easily understand why critics in that city might say that the church is asleep, or the church is attending to other matters, or the church is a fraud.

Not long ago there appeared in one of the highest magazines of our country an article entitled, "Can Christianity Survive?" I was struck at once by the radicalness of the title. We are accustomed to read articles on, "Can the Pulpit Survive?" To many people the answer is easy. It is almost axiomatic in many quarters that the pulpit cannot survive—it is already decadent and on the way to extinction. Sometimes the question is put thus: "Can the Church Survive?" and many persons are swift to answer "No." They believe that the church is obsolescent, and that it is destined for the scrap heap. Humanity is going to leave it behind. It is not often, however, that you find a writer discussing the question, "Can Christianity Survive?" I was all the more surprised to see such a title because I had only recently been reading the church statistics of the last ten years. Many persons do not realize what rapid advances the church in this country is making. Whenever you hear people talking as though the church is losing members and also ceasing to function in the life of the people, you may rest assured you are listening to persons who need information. The church membership is growing all the time, and the benevolent and missionary enterprises are increasing year by year, and the activity of the churches has never been so intense as it is now. When you compare the church of our day with the church twenty or thirty years ago, you must be astonished at the enormous strides forward which the church has been making. I have just been reading how many millions of Methodists there are, and millions of Baptists, and millions of Lutherans, and millions of Presbyterians, and millions of Roman Catholics.

I have read that there are over a million members of the Church of
the Disciples, and over a million Episcopalians, and hundreds of thousands of a dozen other denominations.

Coming fresh from these statistics, I was somewhat startled to find
in one of our highest magazines a sober discussion of the question,
"Can Christianity Survive?" The writer began by confessing that
he is not so radical as some. For instance, Mr. Bertrand Russell believes
that religion cannot survive. This writer is sure that religion can
survive, but he wants to discuss the question, "Whether Christianity
Can Survive." One of his first assertions was that Christianity is not
at present a vital factor in our civilization, and that Christianity is
no longer reckoned with in the more complex problems and the
wider social relationships in which the destiny of our civilization is
being determined. I found the writer to be a man of intelligence
and learning, a keen observer of the life of our generation, a man
who had at his command a great array of facts; and I asked myself,
How can this be? How can a man of intelligence and information
discuss a question like this while at the same time churches are making
amazing advances in every department of church life and work?

The only answer I could think of was one which I have already
given. It is the impotency of the church in the presence of modern-
day problems that drives men to ask, "Can Christianity Survive?"
The question was coming to the front before the war, but the war
pushed it upon the vision of wider circles of thinkers. The Great
War demonstrated that something was wrong. The Christian church
did not prevent that war. The question is, "Why did it not?" That
war started in Europe, the oldest of all the Christian continents.
The church is mighty in Europe. There are 375,000,000 Christians
on that continent, and 90,000,000 of those are Protestants. There are
three great hierarchies of ministers and priests—the Roman Catholic
hierarchy, the Greek Catholic hierarchy, and the Protestant hierarchy
—thousands and tens of thousands of ministers and priests, all of
them educated, all of them consecrated to the Prince of Peace, and
under these hierarchies hundreds of millions of professing Christians
consecrated to brotherliness and service, and yet in the presence of
this mighty host dedicated to love, a whole continent slips down into
hell!

There is something wrong somewhere, and no Christian should
allow himself to get away from the problem which that war has

presented. Not only did the church fail to prevent the war, but it did nothing to alleviate the horrors of the war. The war would not have been more horrible than it was if there had been no church at all. Men did their utmost in the way of cruelty and atrocity. They whipped the horses of science into a faster trot, that they might carry mankind on to new exploits of horror. It was one of the beastliest and ghastliest wars ever waged, so fierce and so inhuman that the non-Christian peoples of Asia looked on with amazement, and even the barbarians of Central Africa listened to the tale of atrocities, and wondered. There is something wrong somewhere. No thoughtful Christian should allow his eyes to wander from the problem which the war has presented. The Christian church did not shorten the war by so much as a day. It would not have been longer if there had been no church at all. The carnage was not shortened because of anything which the church did or said. The war was brought to an end solely through the physical exhaustion of Germany. All the nations in the fall of 1918 still had the will to fight. The spirit was willing, but the flesh was weak, and because the body of Germany crumpled, the war came to an end.

Here, then, we had a demonstration in the sight of the whole world of the impotency of the Church of Jesus Christ. The problem becomes all the more vivid and baffling because during the fifty years before the war began, Christianity in Europe had been prosperous. Millions of Roman Catholics had gone right on from year to year, making the sign of the cross, sprinkling themselves with holy water, saying their Ave Marias and their Pater Nosters, and thousands of priests had celebrated millions of masses, offering up a daily sacrifice to God through Christ; and millions of Protestants had said their prayers, and had sung hymns no different from the hymns which we often sing:

> Peace, perfect peace, in this dark world of sin,
> The blood of Jesus whispers peace within.

And yet, notwithstanding all this worship, the whole continent of Europe slid down into an abyss of blood and tears. There is something wrong somewhere. It is high time we were finding out where it is. "Can Christianity Survive?" It seems to me the answer is easy. It cannot survive in its present form. Christianity of the present type has not saved the world, is not saving it, and never can save it. The present type of Christians must unfold into a type that is more Christian. We must get out of our individualism and gain the social vision. Without the social vision, we never can have a social conscience. Without a social conscience, we can never save the world.

We make a vast distinction between public sins and private sins. We judge men by the standard of individualist ethics. We condemn a man if he is addicted to vices that mar individual life. A man feels he is a good man if he does not drink or swear or gamble or commit adultery or refuse to pay his debts. His wife stands by his side, saying, "He is indeed a good man, for he does none of the things which bad men do." His neighbors say to one another, "He is a good man, for he reads the Bible, and he goes to church nearly every Sunday."

But he does not think of Jerusalem! He has no interest in Judah! His neighbors do not measure him by the standards of social ethics, nor does he measure himself by such standards, and the result is that public sins abound.

Let me remind you of two of them. Ellis Island has for generations been a public sin. It is the front door of America. Through that door nearly all the men, women, and children intending to become citizens of our country come in. We have provided a vestibule there in which it is necessary for them to stand for a little while before we permit them to enter. It goes without saying that that vestibule ought to be beautiful and spacious and clean. It is important that we should make a favorable and wholesome impression upon all our future citizens. We are a rich nation. We have more than half of all the gold in the world. Our wealth has reached fabulous proportions, and therefore we ought to have provided buildings on Ellis Island ample for their purposes. The buildings should have been the best that our architects could devise or that our builders could build. They should have been provided with every convenience, if not with every comfort. All the officers and attendants on Ellis Island ought to have been men and women of fine breeding, high ideals, courteous manners and soft voices.

But, alas, what has Ellis Island been in all these years but a scandal and a disgrace—a stench in the nostrils of the whole world. In America we have scores of millions of followers of Jesus who are consecrated to the service of "the first true gentleman who ever lived," and yet all these millions of Christians have allowed that scandal to go on year after year and decade after decade, until by and by the situation became intolerable, and it was necessary for Great Britain to offer a protest. The move was carried out in a most diplomatic manner. She made use of one of the most gracious and winsome of all her public servants. He visited Ellis Island, used his eyes and ears and nose, and sent in his report to Downing Street. His report was written with great restraint and was delicately worded, a constant effort being made not to irritate or offend more than was absolutely necessary. Congress took the hint and provided a small sum of money in order that Ellis Island might be cleaned up and new accommodations provided. Oh, the pity of it! The shame of it—that our republic should wait until nudged by a Christian neighbor across the ocean to be decent in our treatment of immigrants! What is the explanation of this? There is no explanation except that we have little social vision. We are individualists in religion, and we do not carry our religion into the affairs of Judah and Jerusalem.

One other illustration: We are having great difficulty in enforcing the Volstead Act. Tens of thousands of Americans break the law, and not a few of these are members of Christian churches. It is not simply foreigners in our great cities who are trampling upon the law, it is men and women in our highest American homes—men and women of culture and great social influence who openly deride and trample on the law of their country. How can you account for that? There is no explanation but this: These people have been brought up in the individualist school of ethics. They argue in this manner: "Alcohol does not hurt me, and therefore I propose to drink whenever I please." They do not think of Judah. They have no thought of Jerusalem. "Alcohol does not hurt me. I think of myself first. I think of myself last. I think of myself all the time. I do not think of anybody else but myself!" Oh, the pity of it—that we have members of the Christian church who have no social vision, and therefore no social conscience, and who therefore begin and end with themselves.

There is no hope for us unless we come up and accept the religion of Jesus. People sometimes talk of the "Old Gospel." That is the very gospel I am speaking about. The "Old Gospel" is the "Social Gospel." Sometimes they speak admiringly of the Simple Gospel. That is indeed the gospel that we all want. The Simple Gospel is the Social Gospel. This individualist gospel is no gospel at all. Dip down into the teaching of Jesus anywhere you please, and you will find him preaching the Social Gospel. "If you are bringing your gift to the altar, and remember that your brother has anything against you, leave your gift before the altar, go and be reconciled to your brother, and then come and offer your gift"; that is, social relationships come before worship. You cannot truly worship God until your social relationships are right. Your worship of God is meaningless and offensive until you are in right relations with your neighbors. That is the Simple Gospel. That is the Old Gospel. We must come up to it in order to be saved.

Or, take this: "Go and learn what this means: 'I desire mercy, and not sacrifice.'" The religious people of Palestine criticized Jesus because he ate with publicans and sinners. They thought it was not nice. His action filled them with disgust. They were good people measured by the standards of their circle. They pretended to revere the Scriptures. They read them often. He told them to go and read them again and find out the meaning of a simple sentence like this—something that had been written in the eight century—something that Hosea had said—something that Hosea had put into the mouth of God: "I desire mercy. I desire humane social relationships rather than worship." That is the Simple Gospel—that is the Old Gospel, and we must come up to it or we are lost.

Or take this: When a man asked Jesus to name the great commandment, Jesus replied, "Thou shalt love the Lord thy God with all thy heart, and with all thy soul, and with all thy mind, and with all thy strength. . . . The second is . . . this, Thou shalt love thy neighbour as thyself." The man to whom he was speaking wore on his forehead a little leather box, in which he carried the First Commandment, "Love God." He carried a similar leather box on his left arm. In that box also he carried the First Commandment. Jesus said to him, "You must put into your little box, 'Love thy neighbor as thyself.'" Those two commandments go together. You cannot separate one from the other. Upon these two everything worth while hangs. That is the Simple Gospel. That is the Old Gospel. We must come up to it, or we are lost.

On the last night of his life, in the upper chamber, Jesus said, "A new commandment I give unto you, That ye love one another, as I have loved you. . . . By this shall all men know that ye are my disciples, if ye have love one to another." Here again the emphasis is on social relationships. Men are to know that Christians belong to

Christ, not by the form of their worship, or by the phrases of their creed, or by the form of their church government: they are to prove their Christian discipleship by their relations to men. That is the Simple Gospel. That is the Old Gospel, and without that gospel we cannot be saved.

II

LECTURES

12

The Shepherd's Temptations

They are many. Let us look at but two. These two are singled out because they are the two against which our Lord and two of his apostles uttered special and repeated warnings, and because the experience of nineteen hundred years has demonstrated that these two are most insidious, most constant, and most fatal. They are the love of gain and the love of power: covetousness and ambition, inordinate desire to possess for personal gratification, and an unlawful love of advancement, prominence, authority. Christian history makes it clear that these are the cardinal sins which ever lie like crouching beasts at the shepherd's door.

Covetousness is often associated in our mind with money, and it seems absurd to say that one of the two besetting sins of the minister is an inordinate love of money. The world is always ready to accuse the minister of this, probably because the average man is himself so susceptible to the alluring power of gold. One of the traditional taunts hurled at the minister is, "the bigger the salary, the louder the call." A layman, no matter how great a saint, may exchange one position for another if by so doing he increases his income without the sacrifice of important interests; but this in a minister is by many people counted reprehensible, even positively disgraceful. There is in many quarters a jealous solicitude lest ministers get more money than they ought to have, and think more highly of their salary than they ought to think.

But this accusation is not justified. Ministers, as a rule, are not abnormally fond of money. No other set of men in all the world think so little about it, or care so little for it. That a man is in the ministry is presumptive evidence that he does not worship the golden calf. What a dunce a man would be to go into the ministry for the sake of making money. Is not the average minister's salary pitifully small, and are not thousands of salaries a disgrace to the church? Every man who goes into the ministry takes, in reality, the vow of poverty. He turns his back on all the avenues which lead to wealth. He surrenders all hope of ever becoming a rich man. No man in this country has ever become rich in money by his services as a minister. Occasionally a minister comes into possession of wealth, but it is not through his salary as a pastor of a church. There is only the smallest fraction of ministers whose salaries are large, and these few are large to meet the extravagant expensiveness of living in great cities. When, therefore, the critics accuse ministers of having an itching palm, they deal in calumny. That in this money-loving, money-seeking, money-crazy country a multitude of young men are every year turning their backs on the glittering financial inducements held out by other callings and dedicating themselves to a profession which dooms them to be poor is one of the sublimest phenomena of our century, and an indisputable proof that the Spirit of God is still among us.

But covetousness does not necessarily mean love of money. It is an excessive desire for anything which gratifies one's own cravings. It is the disposition of having and for getting. Money is not the only thing which can be had or gotten, and the very fact that money is shut out from the possible acquisitions of the minister possibly makes him more covetous for those things which do lie within his reach. Covetousness is a part of our unregenerate human nature, and if it cannot exert itself in one direction, it endeavors to make conquests in another.

When one speaks of the salary of the minister, he should not stop with the sum of money which the minister annually receives. Money is only one element in the minister's stipend. He is paid money, and also gratitude, and praise, and applause, and admiration. He is given not only dollars, but social privileges and positions which are worth more to a man of culture than bank notes. He has opportunities for study and self-cultivation, for meditation, and for those quiet pursuits in which the studios nature takes delight. Compensations come to him which are more valuable than rubies, satisfactions subtle and sweet are his which the man of the world knows nothing about. While in one sense the minister is the poorest-paid man in the community, in another sense no man is so generously rewarded. The minister who is really called of God to lead men in the way of life has a remuneration which cannot be computed in the terms of our earthly arithmetic, and which he would not exchange for the income of the highest-salaried man in the town.

It is right here, then, that the pastor meets one of his two most dangerous temptations. He is tempted to make himself the center of the parish, and like a medieval baron, exact illicit tribute from the people. A Puritan preacher once declared that "a covetous person lives as if the world were made altogether for him, and not he for the world." Are there no ministers who, according to this definition, are covetous? Do they not often think and act as though the parish were made for them? Men sometimes come out of the seminary with no conception of Christian servantship, no idea that the church is to be first always, no notion that the church does not exist for the pastor but that the pastor exists for the church. There is nothing more dismaying than the tone of the talk in which some ministers indulge. They confess quite blandly that they are looking for a church that will pay them a living salary while they carry out a cherished plan. The church they are looking for must be in a certain locality, must pay a certain salary, must have a certain kind of parsonage, and must be made up of a certain type of people. Sometimes ministers speak of their personal schemes, unabashed and without a blush, and go into their first parish with no other thought uppermost in their mind but that of their own personal advantage.

When such a man gets a church, the tragedy begins. He lays out a line of study according to his own taste. He delves in fields to which his intellectual proclivities carry him. He finishes certain investigations, perhaps, which were begun in the school. He gives himself to sundry branches of philosophy or science for which he has a liking. As for the people, who are they? They ought to be satisfied with anything. Every sermon has something in it, and it is the business of laymen to find what that something is. Sunday after Sunday the hungry sheep look up and are not fed. The minister is working, perhaps, for a postgraduate degree; he is, possibly, laying up material for a coming book. He is a greedy, selfish man, and his people droop and die. The physician has come. The patients are before him, but he does not study their diseases. He is experimenting in the laboratory with some new serums and cultures. The sheep are waiting to be guided and fed, but he fleeces them simply to clothe himself. If his conscience is thoroughly dead, he uses the church solely as a base of supplies. He goes into the lecture business, or some other form of remunerative occupation, allowing his people to pay him for the work which he does not do. While he is building up his fame and fortune, souls whom God has entrusted to his guidance are left to the mercy of the wolves, and noble causes which might by his leadership be carried to their coronation are permitted to languish and fail. A church going to pieces through sheer neglect while its appointed leader is dabbling in outside ventures is a spectacle which brings pain to the heart of every true lover of God, and must cause anguish among the angels in heaven.

Sometimes the church is used simply as a steppingstone to something better. A minister goes into a parish with no desire to extend Christ's Kingdom there, but solely for the purpose of stepping at the earliest opportunity from that parish into one more nearly level with his deserts. Such men are, as a rule, egregiously conceited. Covetousness is a soil in which all sorts of briers and brambles grow. If the poison of covetousness flows in a man's blood, there is no limit to the foolish things he will think and do. By brooding on himself, he generates an abnormal estimate of his worth. Nothing is too good for him. He thinks the highest pulpit in the land hardly worthy of him. He is always aspiring to churches forever beyond him. He thinks he is going to be called by committees who have never once thought of him, and never will. His dreams are pitiable and also disgusting. This is one of the elements in the awful retribution which God inflicts on those who profess to follow in the steps of Jesus, and who are really living solely for themselves. Throughout the country there are, here and there, sour and disgruntled ministers, their hearts in constant ferment, all because they have been denied that recognition which in their opinion their shining merits indisputably deserve. They speak with scorn of "favored brethren" who, without half their intellectual resources and with only a fraction of their merit, have by means of influential friends or chance, or possibly the Devil, succeeded in outstripping them. "Put to death covetousness," says the Apostle Paul, "it is idolatry." The idolatry of self always leads to hell, and never so swiftly as when the sinner is a minister.

Covetousness leads to conceit, and also to vanity. Every human being has in his heart a peacock, and the peacock is ever hungering after crumbs. The covetous man feeds the peacock in him all the time. People praise his sermons, and this praise makes him voracious for more praise. They compliment his voice, or his memory, or his beautiful diction, and this wakens an appetite which, growing by what it feeds on, is never satisfied. This abnormal love of praise is in reality a form of covetousness. It is a sort of avarice which is as fatal as the greed for money. Praiseful words are coins, and some men itch and burn for them as other men do for silver and gold. Sometimes this disease makes such progress that the poor man becomes an object of ridicule in the parish. He seeks habitually for compliments, and every man whose heart is sound secretly despises him. The last man of all men upon the earth who ought to hunger after the sugar of popular commendation is the minister of Jesus of Nazareth. If the applause-seeking brother were not spiritually dead, he would hear a voice saying, "How can you believe who receive honor from men, and seek not the honor which comes from God only?"

Covetousness has still another sprout, carelessness. A man who thinks too much about himself has not sufficient time to give thought to others. Self is a big subject, and when one goes into it, there is no getting through with it. The covetous man is sure to become neglectful of those forms of work which are distinctively pastoral. Ministering in the homes of the sick and the poor, work that involves quiet and obscure labor which no one but God sees, it is here that the covetous minister shows what manner of man he is. There are many duties which a minister cannot escape. No matter how covetous he may be, he will attend to these, for these make for his advantage. He cannot stay away from a wedding, or absent himself from a funeral, or remain at home from a prayer meeting, or go off on a visit over Sunday. Public duties hold him as in a vise. The worst of men will do things which are for their profit, but it is in the doing or not doing of private duties that a minister's true self is disclosed. If he be selfish, he need not go today to call on the woman who is ill, he can go tomorrow. The world will not know. If she dies tonight, she will never tell that he did not come. He need not go out of his way to comfort a man who lost his only son last month. An omission of that sort never gets into the papers. The outsider living without hope and without God in the world has an open claim on him, and the claim of the last magazine is imperious, and therefore he can give time to the magazine to the neglect of the outsider. Looking up a member of his church who has grown negligent is not so congenial a task as many another. The wandering sheep does not want to be looked after. Why pester him with pastoral attention? The town will go on just the same with one sheep less in the fold. A bad boy who is breaking his mother's heart needs a bit of admonition, but if he does not get it, he will not divulge the pastor's neglect. A hundred little things ought to be attended to, but every little thing eats up energy and time, and even though these little things are really important things in the lives of human beings, they are matters that can be omitted without the minister being called to account.

It makes a vast difference in the tone and trend of parish life whether the minister is faithful in that which is little, or whether he devotes himself solely to the things which are conspicuous and big. A considerable part of pastoral work can be slighted without the lightning falling. Many of the finest and most critical things can be neglected without bringing the minister to open shame; but when a pastor allows things to run at loose ends in his parish, and is careless in his response to obscure but vital needs, he may win golden opinions from many sorts of people, but he rests under the condemnation of the Good Shepherd.

Covetousness also manifests itself often in cowardice. A covetous man, as a rule, runs at the sight of a wolf. A man careful of himself has no fondness for danger. He will save himself, whosoever else may be lost. A crisis arises in the parish, and he hands in his resignation. Enemies of the flock have appeared, and in the hour when the people most need guidance, the leader abdicates his position. A great moral question is at issue, but he is afraid to come out boldly for the truth and the right. When skies were blue, he seemed brave enough; but when the storm burst, he was the first to seek cover. In days of peace he blew a furious blast, calling the cohorts to battle; but when the enemy appeared, he slunk ignominiously from the field. This was because he was a covetous man. He was abnormally fond of his own skin. Covetousness is one of the most subtle and deceitful of all sins. One does not know how covetous he is until tested. The finest test of covetousness is the open mouth of the wolf. In the flash of the fire of a wolf's eyes a man's soul is startlingly revealed. The man with a covetous heart is everywhere and always a coward. When he sees the wolf coming, he flees.

It would be impossible to paint with colors too black the enormity of the sin of covetousness in the envoys of the Son of God. Nothing is so destructive of the Christian faith as a selfish minister. There are laymen whose faith has been destroyed forever by the unworthiness of their pastor. They once had confidence high and glad in Christian ministers, and were foremost workers in the church; and then, alas, one day there came a minister who, preaching with his lips the gospel of unselfishness, hid behind his preaching the rank corruption of an avaricious spirit. Little by little it became revealed that the minister was working for himself, that the welfare of the parish was not in all his thoughts. And when the crisis came, he sacrificed the parish to secure his own advancement. When laymen have at their head a covetous leader, they oftentimes say nothing—they sicken spiritually and die. They lose their faith in their minister, and then their faith in all ministers. They lose their interest in their church, and finally, in all churches.

Woe to the minister who by his selfish heart not only loses heaven himself, but closes the door so that others cannot enter—he is the worst man in the parish, he is worse than a robber. A robber may wrong his victim and still retain a certain sense of honor. Robbery may be his business, and with open face he may acknowledge his unwillingness to be an honest man. But a minister who lives for self is not only a robber but a sneak. He pretends to live for others, and if under his pretense he lives solely for himself, he is the most despicable of all extant rascals. He is the steward of heavenly treasures, and if he looks out mainly for himself, he is recreant to the highest trust which God commits to men. He is a leading citizen of the heavenly Jerusalem, and if at the expense of others he works for his personal aggrandizement, he is a traitor to the Kingdom of God.

He is also a blasphemer. He blasphemes himself, and he causes others to blaspheme. He becomes the things which the Son of God abhorred with all the intensity of his infinitely pure and honest heart, a hypocrite—a wolf in sheep's clothing.

Jesus has a name for the covetous preacher. He calls him a hireling. "A hireling," he says, "is not a shepherd at all." He lacks the shepherd's heart, and he cannot do the shepherd's work. A hireling is a man who works exclusively for pay; his eyes are ever on his wages, his deepest motive is gain. He is always counting up his profits. His god is self. It is amazing how the breath of Jesus has glorified certain words forever. *Servant,* for instance, has never been the same since Jesus spoke it, nor has *love.* He gave some words a luster which will outlast the stars. Other words, however, he tarnished, and left them to make their way down the centuries, disgraced and branded. One such word is *hypocrite,* another is *hireling.* One cannot speak the word "hireling" free from the accent which Jesus gave it. We cannot make it a sweet and adorning word. We cannot lift it to the seats of the respectable. It is a degraded word, and when we wish to condemn a man, we call him a hireling. He is a man whose heart is not in his work. He does it solely for what he expects to get out of it. Jesus sketches the robber and the hireling side by side in his shepherd allegory. But there is no doubt for which of the two men he had the deeper abhorrence. One can almost catch the scorching hiss of moral detestation in this sentence: "The hireling fleeth, because he is an hireling, and careth not for the sheep."

It is noteworthy that Peter in his instructions to shepherds should warn them against the sin of covetousness. "Tend the flock of God . . . not for filthy lucre, but with a ready mind." The exhortation must have been called for by something which the apostle saw in the lives of church officials. Already that sly serpent covetousness had crawled into the garden of the Lord, and was working havoc in the hearts of the Lord's anointed. It is equally striking that Paul in his pastoral address to the elders of Ephesus should say this: "I have coveted no man's silver, or gold, or apparel. Yea, ye yourselves well know, that these hands have ministered unto my necessities, and to them that were with me. In all things I gave an example, that so labouring ye ought to help the weak, and to remember the words of the Lord Jesus, how he himself said, 'It is more blessed to give than to receive.'"

In his first letter to Timothy, Paul lays it down as one of the essential qualifications of a bishop, or shepherd, that he shall be no lover of money. By money we are to understand every earthly thing which men count a treasure. There were in apostolic days no comfortable parsonages, no delightful studies, no richly filled bookshelves, no ministerial discounts, no famous pulpits, no eulogizing organizations, no fawning society, no applauding world. Ministers were reviled, persecuted, defamed, made as the filth of the world, the offscouring of all things. There was only one earthly blessing which it was possible for them to covet, and that was money. Do not set your heart on it, pleaded Peter and Paul. And if they were speaking to ministers today they would say, "Do not set your heart on the earthly advantages which are offered by the ministerial office—time for study, quiet for meditation, opportunity for self-culture, compliments of women, gratitude of men, applause of the world; do not make these the burden of your heart's desire."

And the Master would add, "Beware of covetousness. A man's life consists not in the abundance of the things which he possesses."

But the love of things is not more deep-seated or destructive than is the love of power. The love of power is innate in the soul of man. The man is maimed who does not have it. All virile and vigorous men are ambitious. It would be strange if ministers of the gospel had no ambition. The love of prominence, the craving for distinction, the desire for exalted rank, these are deep-seated instincts in our human nature, and a course of study in theology does not eliminate them. Like all the native appetites of the soul, they may become abnormal, bringing to their victims suffering and death. No other sin has wrought such havoc among the ministers of Christ as the inordinate love of place and power. What is the story of a thousand years of church history but the tragic narrative of how the ministers of Christ, little by little, compacted themselves into a hierarchy which became at last the most blighting and intolerable despotism that the world has ever known? The tyranny of the medieval Church was the tyranny of clergymen. Laymen were crowded out of the place appointed them by the Church's founder. Reduced to mere spectators, they had no voice whatever in the government of the Church, all authority being gathered up into the hands of ecclesiastics who, rising rank above rank, formed a compact organization culminating in one supreme head who claimed authority transcending that of the mightiest of the Caesars, and whose agents, distributed throughout the world, lorded it over the consciences of men, gathering into their clutches all the kingdoms of life.

It is the supreme tragedy of Christian history that this ecclesiastical passion for power in the medieval Church brought a disgrace upon the cause of Christ from which it will not recover for another thousand years. The whole world suffers today because of what medieval clergymen did. The cause of Christ is hampered everywhere because of the prejudice planted in the human heart by the imperious and high-handed policy of the ambitious leaders of the

Church of Rome. The stories of that tyranny are the property of all mankind. Wherever the name of Jesus is preached, the enemies of Jesus unroll the record of the ambition and cruelty and despotism of the ordained ministers of Jesus, and thereby close the hearts of many. With the history of the church open before him, every young man preparing for the ministry has a warning which he should heed as coming straight from heaven. Those clergymen of bygone days were men of like passions with ourselves. They did not start out intending to disgrace and ruin the church of God. They were not conscienceless enemies of Christ. They had good reasons for formulating their plausible policies, and they were able by specious reasoning to justify all they did. They were not wholly depraved and reprobate. In their hearts was many a noble aspiration, and in their generation they did many noble deeds. But, alas, ambition—the sin by which the angels fell—gradually darkened the mind of the clergy and led it into courses which well-nigh wrecked the world.

We are Protestants and have broken away from the despotism of Rome. We rejoice and call ourselves free men in Christ, we believe in the priesthood of believers, in the brotherhood of the Lord's disciples. We recognize the danger of church heirarchies, we are on guard against every increase of ecclesiastical authority, we know that the minister of Christ, if dominated by theories of priestcraft, is the most dangerous enemy which humanity has to face. And yet while thus open-eyed to historic facts and teachings, we may be blind to the evil forces working in our own hearts. Self-assertion, lordly pretension, and autocratic temper are not confined to any one branch of the Christian church. Protestantism has not escaped entirely the despotism and the ways of Rome. The old virus still runs in human blood, and today, as always, the old injunction is timely: "If any man thinks he stands, let him take heed." We cannot play the monarch in the splendid and dashing way of the medieval bishop, but it is possible for a Protestant minister to be as insolent as the lordliest of Cardinals, and as despotic as the most tyrannical of Popes. If one were to go up and down our Protestant world, noting carefully the sins of clergymen, would he not write down in his list such as these: autocratic manner, imperious temper, consequential air, dictatorial disposition, self-assertion, hankering after distinction, ambition for higher place, arrogant presumption, refined but earthly lordliness?

Every man has in him the elements out of which Rome built a despotism which enslaved the world.

It is worth noting how many things conspire to develop in the minister a proud and imperious disposition. His relation to Christ the Son of God, the consciousness that he is the ambassador of the King of kings, tends to give him a sense of dignity which may easily pass into a vice. The fact that he is entrusted with the oracles of God, and is ordained to minister in holy things, separates him from men engaged in secular occupations; and this, if dwelt on, has a tendency to beget the feeling, "I am holier than thou." One wonders, sometimes, how much the shepherd metaphor may be to blame for the exaggerated notions of ministerial prerogative. A metaphor, like every other good thing, is always dangerous. It may be carried too far. The shepherd idea, if rightly used, is illuminating; but if abused, it is false and dangerous. It can be construed in such a way as to imply that laymen are weak and silly creatures, while clergymen are wonderful beings endowed with supernatural powers, enjoying unique and exclusive favors from heaven. Never did Jesus use the word "sheep" in a depreciatory or disparaging sense. He called little children "lambs" because *lamb* is a love name for a child. He called grown people "sheep" because the word was dear to Hebrew ears, and his countrymen had been singing for centuries: "We are his people, and the sheep of his pasture."

Literally speaking, men are not sheep at all. They do not belong to an order of creation lower than that to which the shepherd belongs. The life of pastor and people is on the same level. There is no gulf between the minister and his flock. Pastor and people are members of the same family. They have the same natures and the same privileges. All alike have free access to the throne of grace, all alike are redeemed by the Son of God, all alike are heirs of immortality. It is possible, however, for ministers so to use the shepherd metaphor as to exalt themselves at the expense of the laity, and to set up pretensions which are expressly ruled out by the Good Shepherd.

Whatever the influence of the shepherd metaphor may have been, there is no doubt the nature of the preacher's work has a tendency to feed his love of rulership and to quicken his appetite for absolute dominion. What liberty a minister enjoys in the disposition of his time! No other man but the retired millionaire is such a monarch of his day as in the minister. He can read on Monday morning, or write, or walk, or mingle all three, just as he deems best. On Tuesday morning he can attend to his correspondence, or catalogue his library, or eat the heart out of some new book, or meet a company of friends, just as he decides. The order of his going out and coming in is largely at his own discretion. Within wide limits he is the monarch of all the hours he surveys. Such liberty is dangerous, it has spoiled its thousands.

His dominion over his sermons is still more wonderful. He is free to say what the text shall be, the topic, the illustrations, the arguments, the conclusion, and no one can interfere. He can adopt any style of preaching that he likes, he can follow whatever line of thought he chooses. A merchant has to give his customers what they ask for, a hotelkeeper must supply what his guests desire; but a preacher can give what he thinks his hearers ought to want and ought to have, no matter what their needs and wishes really are. For half an hour or more every Sunday morning, everything is silent while he speaks. This unparalleled immunity from the noises and interruptions and contradictions which other men are subject to begets in certain types of men a tone of mind which says, "I am Sir Oracle, and when I ope my lips, let no dog bark."

In social life a minister is ever at the front. He is the observed of all observers. Wherever he sits is the head of the table. He has his critics and detractors, but they are not visible at social functions. In social life, especially in small towns, there is a deference paid to ministers which no other man receives. This burning of incense before the minister has a tendency, in many cases, to turn his head, and to lead him to think more highly of himself than he ought to think. Is there a celebration in the town? The minister must attend it. Is the fitting word to be spoken on a state occasion? The minister must speak it. Here is a true description of ministers not a few: "They love the chief places at feasts and the chief seats in the synagogue, and the salutations in the market-places, and to be called of men, Rabbi." They love these things because they are human and because they are accustomed to them, and because they think they have a right to them. Constant deference and obedience have a tendency to beget in men of a certain grade a haughty and unlovely disposition.

But mightiest of all the forces working for the undoing of the minister's heart is the liberty he has in devising and shaping the policy of the church. Laymen, as a rule, are too busy to take continued interest in church affairs. The result is that in many parishes almost everything is rolled upon the pastor's shoulders. Is a change to be made? He must make it. Is a new work to be undertaken? He must start it. Is there a fresh responsibility to be assumed? The pastor must shoulder it. In a multitude of parishes the minister must not only preach and conduct the prayer meeting, and make all the pastoral calls, but he must also superintend the Sunday school, manage the finances, map out the work of every organization, and possibly act even as leader of the singing. No wonder that ministers come to feel sometimes that they are of considerable importance. It was in this way that church government blossomed into Romanism. The laity in the early Christian centuries were largely ignorant, incompetent, and indifferent, and the whole shaping and managing of the church fell inevitably into the hands of its clerical officials. Laymen in our day are not ignorant or incompetent, but many of them are indifferent because they are so busy. They have no time to bother with church affairs. Church administration is left, therefore, largely in the hands of the pastor. This is bad for him, and it is bad also for the church. It makes it easier for the minister to build up in himself a dictatorial disposition and to nourish in his heart the love of autocratic power.

Note some of the ways in which this lordliness of temper shows itself. It is manifested sometimes in the tone of the sermon. Many preachers preach with an overbearing, dictatorial air. They assume that their congregation is a stiff-necked, rebellious generation, and they proceed to ram the truth down the people's throats. They talk too loud. There is too much push in their voices. I do not mean that a minister is never to speak loud. If he has a great voice, he has a right to let it out in thunder when the thought flashes and his emotions rise in tempest. But bellowing simply for the sake of making a noise is always bad. There is often an excess of the magisterial, and not enough of the friendly. There is too much omniscience, and not enough of the humility which Jesus loves. Truth, to go in, need not be driven in. Sledgehammers are not essential for the introduction of ideas. Keats once said, "Poetry should be great but unobtrusive." So ought a sermon. It ought to be great, but it ought not to obtrude itself. If men go away saying, "That was a great sermon," it falls short of the ideal. When men listened to Demosthenes, they did not go off saying, "That was a great oration." They said, "Let us march against Philip."

There are preachers who by the expression of their face, the poise of their body, and the character of their gestures say quite plainly, "This is God's truth! Do not dare to deny it! Take it! Take the whole of it! Take it immediately!! By the Eternal, I will make you take it!!!"

It is not necessary to put grass into the sheep's mouth. Cram the grass down the sheep's throat, and the animal is so flustered he will not eat at all. Put the grass within reach of the sheep, and he will eat it himself. So it is with truth. Hold it up so that people can plainly see it; bring it within comfortable reach of them; give them time to get at it; and they will eat it. Charles Lamb used to say that "the truth of a poem ought to slide into the mind of the reader while the reader is imagining no such thing." The truth of the sermon ought to glide into the mind of the hearer without the hearer really knowing what is going on. It is not an encouraging sign when men go away saying, "What a tremendous fellow that is! What a mighty effort that was!" It is better when they think nothing of the preacher, but go away with a heart disquieted by the memory of things they have done amiss, and teased by the haunting image of a bright ideal; a heavenly perfume hanging round their spirit as sweet as that which filled the room in which Mary broke the alabaster cruse upon the Master's head. Dictators are out of place in the pulpit. Dictatorship is a form of carnal striving after power.

This ecclesiastical lordliness shows itself sometimes in the tone of condescension with which opponents are dealt with, and the haughty insolence with which skeptics are brushed aside. The supercilious and scornful ease with which unbelieving philosophers and materialistic scientists are attacked and overwhelmed by young men, and old men too, in the pulpit, is a sad exhibition of an unchristian spirit. The fact that these opponents of the Christian faith cannot be present to make reply lays upon the minister an extra responsibility to be scrupulously fair in all his quotations and beautifully just in all his judgments. To rush furiously upon the ideas of a famous and learned man who is hundreds of miles away and hold these ideas up to coarse and flippant ridicule when the man can neither explain nor defend himself is not the action of a gentleman.

It is the same spirit which exhibits itself in the vociferous defense of orthodoxy. Every minister is of course under bonds to proclaim and defend what he conceives to be the truth, but he is also under bonds to proclaim the truth in love. If he struts like a rooster and exalts himself like a braggart, he may deceive the ignorant into thinking that he is a defender of the faith; but all who have discerning eyes know that he has surrendered it. No man is doing anything for the advancement of the religion of Jesus whose heart is vindictive and bitter and who attacks alleged error by misrepresenting men who differ from him. Every generation brings forth a company of stalwart champions who assume that they alone are the true custodians of the truth, and who by a blustering manner and a swaggering rhetoric induce the undiscerning to accept them as special agents of heaven. These high and mighty ones to whom the slaughtering of the heretics has been entrusted are not really prophets, speakers for God, they speak for themselves. It was when Elijah had a swollen head over his victory at Carmel that he conceived the idea that he alone in Israel had not bowed the knee to Baal.

In the realm of parish administration a puffed-up shepherd exhibits symptoms which have been often deplored. He resents all divergence from his opinions. Men who do not agree with him are set down as his foes. He treats them as traitors to the cause of truth. All who will not carry out his wishes have the mark of the beast. He is irritated by the least opposition. He is mortified by the failure of a single plan. Any independence of thought he considers a personal affront. If a household refuses to receive him, he calls down fire from heaven upon it. Strong in a clear conscience, he proceeds to break down opposition by the force of his ingenuity. He schemes to get ahead of the insurgents by adroit management. He succeeds—but success can be bought at too heavy a price. The price is always too heavy when success is bought at the expense of the highest Christian spirit in the heart of the shepherd. Many a minister has in the church meeting made a great triumph, only to discover the next day that he was overthrown. A majority of votes was secured for his project, but that amounted to nothing because of the number of hearts which were estranged. A minister may carry his measure, and at the same time lose his cause. What cannot be secured by sweet persuasion had better be gone without. It is only a bully who tries to tyrannize or club people into advocating his projects, and the minister who attempts it is a man whose heart has been eaten out by the overweening love of power. It is a good thing for a minister to be defeated now and then in order to find out that he is not invincible, and that there are other people in the world besides himself. Victory is often only by way of the cross. A good shepherd ought not to shrink from an occasional crucifixion.

A little Protestant despot, a petty parochial Pope, is a sorry caricature of a minister of Jesus Christ. A minister who boasts under his breath that he proposes to run things and who chuckles at his adeptness in manipulating people, and who says by his manner that he is the boss of the parish, is a man who is a stumbling block in the way of Christian progress. If to the minister the people are only silly sheep, fit for nothing but to be shorn now and then, he is certain to put on airs and bring the Christian ministry into disrepute. He will scold in the prayer meeting, play the part of a dictator on Sunday, move with a patronizing air among the poor and a supercilious smirk among the rich, give orders in a loud voice to all the officials in the town, while wise men blush for his folly and the church mourns the loss of a leader who, because he has not the spirit of Christ, no longer belongs to the Master he ostentatiously professes to serve.

The pastor is possessor of a power that is extraordinary and hence he must be evermore on his guard against the temptation to play the lord. Peter in writing to the pastors in his day said: "Tend the flock of God, not as lording it over the charge allotted to you, but making yourselves examples to the flock." In other words, your power is not denied, no man can take it from you. It is given you by God himself. Be careful how you use it. Do not strut. Do not clothe yourself in pomp. Do not play the tyrant in your sacred robes. Exert your power in the ways that the Lord has appointed. Exercise dominion after the Lord's own fashion. Be a pattern man after which men can shape their lives. Be a model toward which the people can ever look. Be an example through which the power of Christ can reach and transform the hearts of men. This is the charge given by the leader of the Twelve, and He got His instructions from the Chief Shepherd.

In the training of the apostles there was no virtue so often extolled and insisted on as humility. The Twelve were intensely human, and under the influence of Jesus's personality and ideas, new ambitions awakened in them, and they began to dream of lofty places which they were going to fill in their coming kingdom. It is one of the mysteries of sin that men can have their minds filled with thoughts of self-abnegation and unselfishness and at the same time be dreaming of pre-eminence and power. The men who were with Jesus at Caesarea Philippi and heard His words about the coming tragedy of the Cross began immediately to discuss the old fascinating and tormenting question, which one of them was to be the greatest. They were not sinners above all others, we are men of like nature with them. We, too, can listen to the words of Jesus about humility and self-renunciation, and repeat them to our people, and at the same time nurse in our hearts ambitions to climb and shine and dominate.

There are certain passages in the Gospels especially appropriate for ministers, paragraphs which ought to be read again and again in the inner chamber when the door is shut. One of them is the eighteenth chapter of Matthew's Gospel, with its story of Jesus summoning the Twelve and taking a little child and setting him in their midst, and saying, "Except ye be converted and become as little children, ye shall not enter into the kingdom of heaven. Whosoever therefore shall humble himself as this little child, the same is greatest in the kingdom of heaven." The simplicity and unpretentiousness of an unspoiled child is a revelation of what Christ expects in his ministers.

A second classic passage is Matthew, the twenty-third chapter. . . . "be not ye called Rabbi: for one is your teacher . . . and all ye are brethren. And call no man your father upon the earth: for one is your Father, which is in heaven. Neither be ye called masters: for one is your Master, even Christ. But he that is greatest among you shall be your servant. And whosoever shall exalt himself shall be humbled; and he that humble himself shall be exalted." There is danger lurking in titles. The word which Rome selected for her priests has had much to do with perpetuating her error and riveting her power. It is not good for ministers to be called by their people "Father." It is not good for the ministers themselves. It assumes a dignity and prerogative in the minister which do not exist, and an immaturity and dependence in the people which are not normal or wholesome. Ministers are not teachers in the sense in which Christ is a Teacher. They are not masters in the way in which Christ is a Master. They are His representatives, but they do not take His place, nor possess His power. There is but one Lord, Jesus Christ, God's Son.

A third chapter for pastors is the thirteenth chapter of the Gospel of St. John. The tragedy in the upper chamber is one of the darkest in human history. The twelve men who have spent years in the close companionship of the most unselfish Man Who ever lived, enjoying the illumination of His teaching and the cleansing power of His prayers, are still so petty and so selfish at the very end of their Master's life that they cannot sit down to partake of a farewell dinner without childish squabbling over the order of their places at the table. It was when their hearts were feverish and resentful that Jesus took the basin and the towel and proceeded to wash the disciples' feet. After the work was completed, He said: "Ye call me Teacher and Lord: and ye say well; for so I am. I have given you an example, that ye should do as I have done to you. . . . If ye know these things, blessed are ye if ye do them."

From the upper room Jesus went to the garden of Gethsemane, and from Gethsemane, to the Cross. It made men laugh to see a king crucified. They had never seen a king without a plume and without a crown. He was crucified, but King He was, and is, and shall be forever. From His Cross He rules the world.

In His hands He holds all souls. His claim upon no one of them has ever been relinquished. He is the Shepherd, and all the sheep are His. The minister speaks of his church, his people, his parish— and this is proper if he understands the meaning of his words. As distinguished from one another, one parish belongs to one man and another parish belongs to another man, but in the deep sense, all parishes alike belong to Christ. The human shepherds come and go in a continuous procession. A minister arrives in town, unpacks his books, does his work, and then sleeps with his fathers. "He cometh up and is cut down like a flower; he fleeth as it were a shadow, and never continueth in one stay." But Jesus Christ is the same yesterday, today, and forever. He is with His people even unto the end of the world.

When Jesus handed over to Simon Peter the charge of the Christian church, he was careful to use the possessive pronoun "my."

"Feed my lambs! Tend my sheep! Feed my sheep!" It is the mightiest pronoun in the New Testament for the saving of the minister from lordliness. "Simon, son of Jonas, feed my lambs. They are not yours, they are mine, but I wish you to look after them for a little while. Tend my sheep. They are not yours. I do not give them to you. They belong to me. Mine they always shall remain, but I ask you to tend them for a season for me. Feed my sheep. They are not yours. Not one of them shall ever pass from my possession, but I am going away for a few days, and I leave them with you. Guard them, feed them, guide them, be good to them for my sake. Follow me. Remember my gentleness, my watchfulness, my considerateness, my patience, my compassion, my readiness to help, my swiftness to heal, my gladness to sacrifice. Be the kind of shepherd to my lambs and my sheep that I have been to you. Follow me!"

13

The Dimensions of the Work

A minister of the gospel is expected to do a wider variety of things than any other man in the community. The division of labor has been carried further in every other profession than in the ministry. His work is multiform, and it is impossible in five brief lectures to cover more than a small fraction of it.

The minister is an administrator. His church is an organization, and like all organizations, it must have an executive head. The minister is that head. It is in one sense a machine, and like all machines, must be run. Friction must be reduced, the wheels must be lubricated, repairs must be made, every part of the mechanism must be subjected to constant scrutiny and supervision, in order that the machine may do the work for which it has been created. The work of administration is of great importance, but into that kingdom we cannot enter now.

The minister is a pastor, a shepherd of the flock. He must tend and feed the sheep. He must know them all by name, and he must know also their dispositions, needs, and habits, and knowing these, he must be acquainted with the pastures where the grass is greenest and most abundant, and he must know where the most refreshing waters flow, and he must know the character and the methods of the enemies by which the flock is most likely to be attacked. The work of shepherding is of vast concern, but into this province we cannot go.

The minister is a priest; he officiates at the altar of worship. He is the spokesman of the people as they offer up their sacrifice of praise and prayer. He leads the congregation to the throne of grace. Upon his lips the desires and thoughts of many hearts become vocal. He reads the Scriptures, interpreting by emphasis and intonation the revelation which has come through holy men of old. While he does not lead the singing, it is for him to decide what shall be the character and amount of the music in which the church shall express its adoration and thanksgiving. He is the ordained ministrant in the service in which the Lord's people bear public testimony to their faith, and to him is intrusted the entire conduct of worship in the house of prayer. It is a critical and difficult work, but into this wide region we cannot make our way.

The minister is a moral and religious leader. As a guide he has relations not only to his own congregation, but to the entire denomination of which he is a representative, and to the church universal of which he is a member. And not only does he have relations to organized Christianity, but he is related to the great philanthropic and reformatory movements of his age, and belongs in a special sense to the entire community in the midst of which he does his work. All these relations bring with them unescapable obligations and multitudinous duties. The work of minister as patriot and citizen is one of far-reaching influence and significance, but from all this territory we are for the time shut out.

The minister is a prophet of the Lord. By prophet is meant a man who speaks for God. He is pre-eminently a speaker. His business is to speak for another. He is a truth-teller, and, therefore, first of all a truth-seeker. He must dig for it as for hidden treasures, and having found it, he must coin it and put it into circulation among the people. Like a Moses, he must go up into the mountain and talk with God face to face, coming down and giving his brethren his latest revelation. He is a missionary intrusted with the good news, and he must speak his message without diminution or any blurring of its contents. He is an ambassador sent from the court of heaven to the court of earth, and his life is one long and passionate appeal to men to become reconciled to God.

This work of speaking for God is only a part of the modern minister's duty, but it is a realm of such wide dimensions that we shall be justified in confining our attention exclusively to it. But in passing over all the other departments of ministerial activity and shutting ourselves up with preaching alone, I would not have any one of you think that these other forms of work hold in my mind a place of comparative unimportance, or that in my judgment a minister can shirk all his duties but that of preaching and still accomplish the work which God has given him to do. If time allowed, I could speak for five evenings on each branch of work to which reference has been made, and still be unable to say all that can reasonably be said about their importance to a minister who wishes to be a workman that needeth not to be ashamed.

My ground for directing your attention especially to preaching is not because I underestimate the other forms of ministerial duty, or because I would have you ignore them in your own thought and work; but because there are just now several special reasons why a minister of the gospel should give himself with renewed zeal to the great work of preaching. The considerations which have led me thus to limit the scope of these lectures are:

1. The work of preaching is the most difficult of all the things which a minister is called to do. Indeed, it is the most difficult task to which any mortal can set himself. It is at once the most strenuous and the most exacting of all forms of labor. It requires a fuller combination of faculties and a finer balance of powers than are required in any other department of human effort. It is a difficult thing to paint a portrait. To gain the skill required to place the features of the human face on the canvas in such a way as that they shall breathe and speak requires the unflagging toil of years, but how much more difficult it is with human words to paint the face of Christ so that he shall woo and win the hearts of men.

It is a difficult thing to master the mysteries of the world of tone, and create harmonies and melodies which will set the nerves a-tingling, but much more difficult it is to catch the music of the world eternal and translate it into human speech so that human hearts on which it falls shall give back the same celestial vibrations.

It is a great thing to chisel the marble into forms which seem alive, but immeasurably more difficult it is to chisel character by means of words into forms which will please the King.

It is a difficult thing to act upon the stage, to interpret adequately the lines of the masters of the drama. One of the greatest living actors, now over seventy years of age, says that he began to study the art of acting when a boy of three, and that he is studying it still. But how much more study and practice is required for the right rendering to human hearts of the thoughts and purposes of God.

The lawyer has a difficult work. It is hard to apply human law to all the tangled and complicated affairs of men, but to apply the law is not half so difficult as it is to apply the Gospel.

The work of the physician is arduous, and without skill and knowledge he is nothing; but to minister to a mind sin-sick, to soothe a conscience crying out in pain, "to pluck from the memory a rooted sorrow" and "raze out the written troubles of the brain" and "cleanse the stuff'd bosom of that perilous stuff which weighs upon the heart"—this requires a skill and knowledge and wisdom and power greater than any which the doctors know. Because the work of preaching is so difficult it is my first reason for speaking to you about nothing else.

2. But notwithstanding the work is above all others difficult, ministers are just now in danger of receiving less help in mastering the art of preaching than in learning any other form of work. Fresh emphasis is being placed on the work of administration. With the increasing complexity of human life, the church as a machine is becoming more and more intricate. Social and industrial problems are at the front, and expert hands seem to be more needed than instructive tongues. The minister's study has fallen into the background, and the minister's office is the place in which he is expected to do his work. In a commercial age it is assumed that a clergyman must have the knack of doing things, and the business aspect of religion is the one which is uppermost in the public mind.

Along with this new emphasis on administration there is fresh interest in ceremonialism. Our forms of worship are discovered to be altogether too colorless and too bare to suit a generation which has developed all the nerves of taste, and so men are discussing everywhere the advisability of enriching the forms of service. There is a widespread feeling that the forms must be more stately, dignified, and elaborate, and that the advantages of a liturgy without its dangers are within the reach of every church. But with this increased emphasis on the value and place of liturgy there is a slackening sense in many a student, for the ministry is today more concerned about the ordering of worship than about the creation of effective sermons.

Even in our seminaries, which are in theory schools in which men are trained to preach, the multiplication of new and fascinating studies has had a tendency to throw homiletics into the shade. Archaeology, historical criticism, and sociology have but recently come to their best estate, and the worlds which they bring to our attention are so vast and stimulating and important that it is not to be wondered at that many a student is far more interested in the latest results of criticism and research than in the art of presenting New Testament ideas in such a way as to open the springs of the heart and turn the streams of conduct into new channels.

Moreover, there is a widespread feeling that preaching as an institution is more or less obsolescent. Sermons, men say, have had their day. Just as our national Congress has ceased to be the arena for interesting and instructive debate, so the Christian pulpit has ceased to be a center to which men look for either instruction or for uplift. And so the preacher is in disrepute. Coleridge once said that in "older times writers were looked up to as an intermediate beings between angels and men; afterwards they were regarded as venerable and perhaps inspired teachers; subsequently they descended to the level of learned and instructive friends; but in modern days they are deemed culprits more than benefactors."

A similar process has been going on in the public mind concerning preachers. Once they were more than human, then supremely human, later on, interesting and useful; but more recently they are regarded in many sections of society as impertinences and bores. The opinion of the world cannot fail to influence the thought and feeling of ministers themselves. It is not uncommon to hear ministers speak in disparaging and apologetic tones about their sermons. And even though they say nothing slightingly with their lips, the place which they give the sermon in their thought and preparation reveals only too clearly that they have lost their faith in its importance and their ambition to make it what a sermon ought to be. Rome was near her fall when the priests who ministered at her altars joked about the Mass. It is a sign of skepticism and decadence in the Protestant pulpit that so many ministers can joke about their sermons and listen to attacks upon the work of preaching without indignant protest or swift rebuke.

3. The greatest danger confronting the church of Christ in America today is a possible decadence of the pulpit. Let the pulpit decay, and the cause of Christ is lost. Nothing can take the place of preaching. There is no power under heaven equal to the power of a God-inspired pulpit. Anthems and hymns, responsive readings and creed recitations, prayers written and prayers extempore, all have

their place, and when rightly used are means of grace; but all of them put together cannot take the place of the exposition of God's word by a man whose lips have been touched by a coal from off God's altar. An ignorant pulpit is the worst of all scourges. An ineffective pulpit is the most lamentable of all scandals. The cause of Christ is hopelessly handicapped and blocked when Christian preachers forget how to preach. We must guard the pulpit with all diligence, for out of it are the issues of life. Any signs of decay in it must fill all well-wishers of the church with regret and alarm.

And history will not allow us to escape the fact that it is easy for the pulpit to decay. The prophet has always had a tendency to degenerate into the priest. The man who speaks for God is always prone to slip down into the man who performs ceremonies for God. The altitudes on which the prophet of the Lord must live are so lofty that poor, frail human nature, finding it exhausting to breathe the difficult air, seeks the first opportunity to come down. But every time the prophet degenerates into a priest, a new darkness falls upon the world. There were great prophets in Israel in Elijah's day and in Isaiah's day and in Haggai's day, but little by little the light of prophecy died down, the men who spoke for God became interested in the incense and burnt offerings, and when the last of the prophets departed, darkness fell on Palestine.

The Christian church began in a blaze of glory, in the glory that burst from a sermon. For a season the church had great preachers— Tertullians and Chrysostoms, Augustines and Ambroses—but gradually the prophetic fire died down; instead of the preacher, there was only the priest, and the world was in darkness again. The Reformation was ushered in by a mighty preacher—Martin Luther —a man educated to be a priest, but who, by the grace of God, grew to the stature of a preacher. So long as Luther and Calvin and Latimer and Knox, and the mighty men who came after them, kept the pulpit fires burning, the world rolled more and more into light, and it was daybreak everywhere. But when the preachers slid down into pedants, there was darkness once more on the earth.

England in the eighteenth century was dead, and it was a preacher —John Wesley—who raised the dead and ushered in a new epoch of Christian history. Has not America had the same experience? Did we not start with Cotton and Hooker and Shepherd and Eliot and the Mathers, and did not the people who sat in the shadow of great hardships see a wonderful light? And when the light faded, it was because the great preachers were dead; and there was no life and no light in New England till an Englishman, George Whitefield, and an American, Jonathan Edwards, stood in the pulpit, like annointed princes of God, and spoke once more to the people, in burning accents, the message of redemption. The bones in the valley of death have always taken to themselves flesh and stood erect on their feet, and the water has always gushed out of the rock, and new heavens have always bent over a new earth whenever and wherever a man has appeared who was able to convert the pulpit into a throne.

4. If this is the great danger of the Christian church, then we know what is its great need. The churches, from the Atlantic to the Pacific, are crying out for preachers. It is a question often debated whether there is a call for more ministers; but however that may be, there is no doubt that there is an ever-increasing demand for more preachers. Why do churches with fifty or one hundred applicants for their pulpit wait for months and sometimes for years before they can find the man they want? It is sometimes because in the whole crowd of applicants there is not one man who knows how to preach. No man who knows how to preach with grace and power need stand idle in the market place a single hour. Churches are scouring the country in search of such a man, and he cannot escape if he would. Throughout my entire ministerial career I have been receiving almost every month, and sometimes every week, letters from church committees asking, "Do you know a man whom you can recommend to us for our pulpit?" And the churches which ask such a question are, as a rule, the large and influential churches at the center of great populations, where strength and ability are needed and where weaklings can avail nothing.

Church committees, when the time comes to select a minister, simply stand dumfounded and baffled, unable sometimes for months to find a man with the ability and training sufficient to make him a power in the pulpit. The great universities and the great railroads and the great banks and the great business houses and the great industrial enterprises find it easier to secure capable men to carry on their work than do our important churches in securing men equal to the demands of the modern pulpit. The age demands men of power. And unless we can get men for the pulpit as brainy and competent, as versatile and resourceful, as virile and effective, as the great captains of industry and the merchant princes, the church will be handicapped in her labor and the ungodly will have fresh occasion to blaspheme.

There are more great openings in the Christian church for men of genuine ability than in other department of our modern world. But only strong men are equal to the problem. The work of the preacher is today more difficult by far than it was in the days of our fathers, and it is growing more arduous and taxing all the time. It will be more difficult in twenty years from now than it is today. The world is growing increasingly luxurious. Wealth is piling itself up in glittering heaps. The world has never been so comfortable and cozy as it is now, and it will be still more comfortable a quarter of a century further on. With life on earth increasingly delightful, it will be increasingly difficult to lift men's eyes to the glory of the things which are invisible and eternal. John Bunyan's man with the muck rake would not look up because he was engaged in raking together sticks and straws; but the man to whom we preach is raking gold and precious stones; and who is strong enough to lift his eyes to the celestial crown? Life is increasingly crowded. There never have been so many papers and books, and songs and concerts, and entertainments and lectures and plays, and clubs and societies and social duties as now. Never have there been so many things to play at or to work with; never, so many ways to make money and to lose money; never so many teachers who are ready to entertain, instruct, or inspire.

The minister is in a crowd, and he must make room for himself or he is lost. The cities are growing all the time, their populations becoming more heterogeneous, their problems more complicated, their interests more multifarious, their burdens heavier, their needs more urgent, and their perils more alarming. The art of living together is a great and fine art, and to teach men how to do this requires a saint and a sage. The evils of our day are all monsters, and only a Hercules in whose heart is the spirit of Christ can face them and vanquish them. The level of culture is rising year by year. Streams of young people pour out of our universities, academies, and schools, and the graduates of these schools have a taste which must not be offended and powers of thinking which must not be ignored. Bunglers in language and blunderbusses in the art of thinking cannot expect to catch and hold the attention of the rising generation. The man who is to preach the unsearchable riches of Christ to cultivated congregations must be a man of native force and superb equipment.

5. What an opportunity is thus afforded to the theological seminary for making itself a factor in the civilization of our century! Its supreme work is the training of preachers. It is first of all a school of the prophets. Whatever else it may do, it must do this, or it fails to do the one thing essential. That it should be even suspected of being negligent in pursuing its supreme work is little less than a calamity. The seminaries have for two decades been the target for unlimited criticism. Sometimes the criticism has been discriminating, and at other times it has degenerated into almost brutal abuse. The arraignment has been varied in the mouth of different accusers. Sometimes it has been the professors who have been cudgeled, sometimes it has been the curriculum which has been denounced, sometimes scornful things have been said of the caliber of the men who have presented themselves as students. But whatever the form of the criticism, the root of it runs down into the fact that our seminaries for some reason or other do not seem to be able to supply the churches with preachers. The graduates are in many cases fine scholars, linguistic experts, church specialists, good for professors' chairs and for the work of research, but not effective in the pulpit as preachers of the word.

It is surprising how stoutly and stubbornly the churches insist upon preachers knowing how to preach. They will forgive almost everything else, but they will not forgive inability to preach. They have a wholesome reverence for learning, but they would rather have a man with no diploma who can preach than a man with two diplomas who cannot preach. They believe in experience, and acknowledge its value; but they would rather have a man with no experience who can preach than a man with years of experience who has lost the gift of presenting truth in ways which lift and strengthen. In all this the churches may be stiff-necked and unreasonable, but it is a frame of mind which is not likely to be changed. And if I were the president of a theological seminary, I should listen to what the spirit is saying through the churches, and should set my house in order for the training of preachers. Every professor in the faculty should be chosen with an eye on the question, Will he fit men to preach? and every study in the curriculum should be there only on condition that it assisted men to preach. I should have courses in theology, for theology is the queen of the sciences, and without theology a preacher is not equipped for his work.

But along with theology I should multiply the courses of study which deal with the problems of presenting thought in such ways as shall reach the reason and the emotions and influence the will. The science of logic, and the science of debate, and the science of rhetoric, and the science of elocution, should all have high places, higher than have been given them hitherto. And in addition to the regular professors I should want every month some recognized pulpit leader to come into personal touch with my students, and also some great criminal lawyer who has proved indisputably by his triumphs that he can by an argument influence the thoughts and decisions of men.

There should be no stronger argument or mightier appeal heard anywhere than that which goes forth from the Christian pulpit. That men should Sunday after Sunday stand in Christian pulpits, ignorant of the fundamental rules of thinking and utterly incompetent to use the English language with either grace or power, is a scandal of such huge dimensions that every seminary in the land ought to consecrate itself afresh to the great task of putting an end to the scandal, and training up a race of preachers who shall be able to clothe in fitting form the heavenly message intrusted to their lips.

6. Here then, brethren, is a wide door and effectual, and I appeal to you to go in. Whatever else you want to be, take a vow that you will first of all be preachers. It is a tragic thing to be a feeble and ineffective preacher. To speak for half an hour on the Lord's Day to a company of intelligent and hungry-hearted people and create no atmosphere, make no impression, lift no soul nearer heaven —this is something of which a man ought to be ashamed and for which he ought to repent in sackcloth and ashes. You have no right to disgrace yourself and degrade the pulpit by a sermon which does nothing. If you cannot start at a definite point and move onward with steadfast foot toward a well-defined goal, and stop there when you have once arrived, you do not have sufficient mental discipline to warrant you to think that God has called you to be a preacher. You cannot afford to do a stupid and ineffective thing in the pulpit. You owe it to your brother ministers to do your best. If you preach poorly, you make it harder for all your brethren to gain a hearing. You owe it to your profession to contribute your best in order that your profession may be advanced.

All of us suffer from the boobies and blunderers who have gone before us. It has become a proverb "dull as a sermon," "prosaic as a parson," and there is a prejudice in the public mind against preaching which would have been less intense and more readily removed had it not been for the sickly twaddle and the unctuous exhortation which has so often been palmed off under the name of preaching. If you by your slipshod preaching create a bias against the pulpit, you not only fail to enter the kingdom of power yourself, but you prevent others from going in. Your failure involves not only yourself, but it subtracts from the influence of preachers everywhere. For the sake of your brethren in the ministry, aim to preach as well as you can. And for the sake of the people to whom you as a messenger are sent, you ought to be willing never to do less than your best.

Men and women judge Christianity largely from sermons. If you make your sermons dull, then religion becomes dull also. If you present Christ in such a way that he does not attract, then you help men to fix themselves in unbelief. The worship of God will become to men a tedious and irksome thing unless you can fill it with life drawn from the fountains of your own heart. You never know what damage you do by the preaching of a weak and worthless sermon. And in all your congregation there are no ears so sensitive and so critical as are the ears of a boy. You may have a church in which there is no millionaire, no professor, no author or painter or orator or scholar, no man or woman of cultivation or social prestige, but you will never be the pastor of a church in which there is not a boy, and that boy ought to be your salvation. On entering your pulpit, say to yourself, "There is a lad here," and for his sake, if not for your own, you must preach well. How many thousands of men are hopelessly estranged from the Christian church and her services because in the days of their boyhood they listened to sermons which were shallow and cheap, only the final Judgment will declare. A boy's impressions are deep, and when once made, no subsequent preacher is likely to efface them.

Sir Walter Scott was all through his life biased against the evangelical branch of the Christian church because, when a boy, he had listened to the ranting of a number of ignorant and bigoted evangelists. Augustine was the son of a Christian mother, but his mother prayed for him thirty years apparently in vain. Her son was interested in philosophy and the philosophers, and one of them, Faustus, had a mighty influence over him. The church had no attraction for him. Her music and her ceremonies did not appeal to him. Her officiating priests were not so interesting as the philosophers. But by and by Augustine found his way to Milan and in the cathedral there, behold, a man! Ambrose. Like a prophet of the Lord he stood there in the pulpit, expounding the Scriptures in tones which fell on human hearts like flakes of fire. Augustine listened, pondered, began to read the Scriptures. The old familiar words of Jesus and the apostles began to open, unsuspected meanings came into view, and thus through the personality of a preacher, Augustine found his way to God. He lived to become one of the giants of the church of Christ, and of all men born of women since the days of Saul of Tarsus, not one has surpassed him in the width of his influence or in the enduring splendor of his fame. He was saved to the Christian church by a man in the pulpit.

What future saint of God may sit in boys' clothing in your congregation you cannot know; but the fact that somewhere among your hearers there may be a boy who by his faith may transform the life of cities or the policy of state should lead you to make unceasing efforts to make yourself the most effective preacher which a man of your native gifts and acquired graces can in the Providence of God become.

How can you do it? Only by having faith. In preaching, as in every other form of Christian service, the secret of our power is faith. If a man has faith as a grain of mustard seed, he can perform wonders both in the pulpit and out of it. No one can preach well who does not believe in preaching. He must believe that it is a divine institution and that it is accompanied by supernatural power. He must grasp St. Paul's deep-rooted conviction that it has pleased God to save the world by the foolishness of preaching.

The voice for which the preacher is to listen always is the Master's voice, saying, "Go preach the gospel"; and hearing this, the voices of the world will not disconcert nor make afraid. The world is always doing its best to discourage preachers. The Devil would rather have a minister do anything else than preach a sermon. He will persuade him if possible not to preach at all, and if he fails in this, he will coax him to preach poorly. There is nothing that the powers of darkness fear and hate like the light which bursts from a genuinely Christian sermon. The world is filled with voices pleading with men not to preach. They say that the days for preaching are gone forever, that the printing press is lifeless, it is made of iron and steel, and nothing without a throbbing heart can soothe and heal the hearts of men. So long as the hearts are human, and so long as tongues know how to speak, the hungry heart will listen to a tongue which has learned the story of Jesus and His love. The day of preaching has not gone; it has only fairly begun. The great days of the pulpit are in front of us, and the world is groaning and travailing in pain together until now, waiting for the coming of new sons of pulpit power.

The world keeps twitting the minister on the loss of his professional prestige. He is no longer on a pedestal. He is not now the most conspicuous personage in all the town. And to all this the answer is, What of it? He never belonged upon a pedestal. That was not his place. The world gave and the world has taken away, and the minister is where he was at the beginning—a servant of the Lord. Jesus was not on a pedestal, and it is enough for the disciple to be as his Master and the servant, as his Lord. No man looms up today in any of the kingdoms of life as men loomed several decades ago. There is no statesman so conspicuous as Daniel Webster, no editor so famous as Horace Greeley, no merchant so much talked of as A. T. Stewart, and nowhere in the world is there a teacher who had the reputation once possessed by Gamaliel.

But to be conspicuous is not so great as to be useful, and has the time now arrived when the minister can be of no service to men? Is no one needed to comfort women in the agony over the grave of their first-born, to encourage men who, harassed by business cares, know not how to endure, to strengthen young men who are fighting with passions fiercer than the beasts of Ephesus, and to brace the trembling hearts of those who are passing into the valley where the deep shadows lie? What right has a minister to covet a pedestal? Let him stand on the ground by the side of his brethren!

Listen not to the world and listen not to the despondent voices of your own discouraged heart. Often you will be tempted to accept the view that men are little more than animals, and that the prevailing forces in their life are sordid and materialistic. There are eloquent descriptions of the world, representing it as a world in which faith is dying and aspiration, dead, inhabited by men who have lost out of their hearts the hopes of nobler times and who are asphyxiated in an atmosphere filled with spiritual poison. The man who doubts the dignity and divinity of human nature cannot preach. Banish every doubt concerning man as you would banish doubt concerning God. Meet men always on high ground. Speak to them as though they were indeed the sons of God. Have faith in God, and also have faith in man. Go out to meet men on the lofty levels on which Jesus walked in the upper chamber and in the Sermon on the Mount, and you will never lack an audience, and never speak in vain.

Pay no attention to your heart when it mourns over the fact that there are no results. Appearances are usually deceiving, and never so deceiving as in the field in which the preacher does his work. Little is said about sermons to the preacher. Few of his parishioners ever take the trouble to thank him for any of his sermonic work. They come, listen, and go home—silent on the sermon and on what it has accomplished for their soul. Moreover, the results cannot easily be seen. The preacher strains his eyes to find them, but they are invisible. Men seem to remain just what they were in spite of all his labor. But a minister should walk by faith and not by sight. If men do not praise him for his sermons, let him seek the honor which comes from God only. If he cannot see the results of his work, let him remember that spiritual harvests are slow in coming, and that his will grow golden in some far-off autumn sun.

Lyman Beecher, preaching on the sovereignty of God, did not know that young Wendell Phillips was in his congregation; nor did he know that after the benediction Wendell Phillips hurried to his room, threw himself on his knees, and dedicated himself for life to the service of the King. Newman Hall did not know that during one of his sermons a poor, obscure seamstress was converted by his words. It was at the end of twenty years that she sent him a bouquet as a token of gratitude for the peace of God which had come to her through him. The humble preacher in Ecclefechan never dreamed that little Tommy Carlyle would some day be one of England's foremost men of letters, and would say, referring to the early sermons, "The mark of that man is on me!" No man ever knows what he is accomplishing when he works with ideas and human souls. It is enough to know that he who works with truth and life never works without results, and that he who works with God works with one who has said, ". . . my word . . . shall not return unto me void, but it shall accomplish that which I please, and it shall prosper in the thing whereto I sent it."

Be of good cheer, therefore, and remember you stand in the line of a great succession. Think often of the giants who have preceded you in this work. Read what they did, and revel in their triumphs.

Surrounded by so great a cloud of witnesses who have received their crowns, you will offer a more steadfast testimony and abound in the work of the Lord till the end of the day. It is well to remember also the saying of a Puritan preacher Thomas Goodwin: "God had only one Son, and He made Him a minister."

14

Building the Brotherhood

Brotherhood is St. Peter's name for the church. The conception of the church held by the leader of the Twelve and the man to whom our Lord first promised the keys of the Kingdom is deserving of sustained attention. That members of the church are brothers, St. Peter everywhere takes for granted. "Be ye all like-minded, compassionate, loving as brothers, tender-hearted, humble-minded"—this sums up his idea of the disposition which church members should have toward one another. He has many bits of advice to give his converts, but this is chief: "Above all things be fervent in your love among yourselves. Honor all men. Love the brotherhood."

St. John holds the same conception. To him the church is a band of brothers, and the first duty of church members is loving one another. There is little else that the beloved apostle cares to write. "He that loveth his brother abideth in the light. . . ." "We know that we have passed out of death into life, because we love the brethren." ". . . we ought to lay down our lives for the brethren." "This is his commandment, "That we should believe on the name of his Son Jesus Christ, and love one another. . . ." "Beloved, let us love one another. . . ." ". . . God so loved us, we also ought to love one another." "If a man say, I love God, and hateth his brother, he is a liar: for he that loveth not his brother whom he hath seen, cannot love God whom he hath not seen? And this commandment have we from him, That he who loveth God love his brother also."

With St. John's writings before us, it is easy to believe the tradition that when he was old, unable any longer to walk, the young men in the church in Ephesus were wont to carry him before the people to whom he repeated again and again, "Little children, love one another." When they asked him why he said this so many times, his reply was, "Because it is the Lord's precept, and if only it be done, it is enough."

St. Paul was not in the upper chamber when the Twelve received the new commandment, but his conception of the church is identical with that of John and Peter. To Paul the church is a brotherhood. "Concerning love of the brethren," Paul writes to the church in Thessalonica, "ye have no need that one write unto you, for ye yourselves are taught of God to love one another. And for indeed ye do it toward all the brethren which are in all Macedonia: but we exhort you, brethren, that ye abound more and more." This is his exhortation to all Christians and he gives expression to it again and again, "In love of the brethren be tenderly affectioned one to another; in honour preferring one another." It is only as Christians are rooted and grounded in love that they are able ". . . to apprehend with all the saints what is the breadth, and length, and depth, and height; And to know the love of Christ, which passeth knowledge. . . ." In his first letter to the Corinthians, Paul's conception of love breaks into language of unsurpassed and unforgettable splendor. He declares what love is, how it acts, feels, thinks, and what victories it wins. Without it, no matter what else we possess, we have nothing. This was written to the church which was most deficient in that which is the distinctive treasure of a Christian church. Unless a church is a brotherhood, a company of men and women whose sympathies and purposes are intertwined and whose lives are interlaced and blended, we may call it a Christian church, but it does not bear in the body of its life the marks of the Lord Jesus.

Whence did these three preachers get their conception of the church? They preached only what they received. It was Jesus's habit to remind His disciples that He was their Master and that all they were brethren. The crowning period of His life was devoted almost exclusively to the task of knitting together the hearts of the men who were to constitute the nucleus of His church. How heavy this burden lay upon His heart is seen in His behavior and words in the upper chamber. All along the way that day, there had been outbreaks of temper on the part of the Twelve, and the old spirit of ill will crops out again as they take their places round the table. The feast cannot go on. Christ can hold no festival except where hearts are sweet. He takes a basin and a towel and proceeds to bathe the disciples' feet, not because He cares about the dust on their feet, but because He is pained by the estrangement of their hearts. This done, He announces a commandment which is to take precedence over all the instructions which He has hitherto given them. "A new commandment I give unto you, That ye love one another; as I have loved you, that ye also love one another. By this shall all men know that ye are my disciples, if ye have love one to another."

This is indeed startling teaching. Let all who would preach the gospel read, mark, learn, and inwardly digest it. The distinctive note of the Christian life is here proclaimed to be love for one's fellow Christians. A man proves himself a Christian, not by loving men in general, but by loving his brethren in Christ. The first and inevitable fruit of an instructed Christian heart is love for one's brother Christians. This is a truth which our Lord labored unceasingly to make clear to His disciples.

The things which are uppermost in one's mind are likely to come out in one's prayers. They are sure to emerge in the prayers which one offers in the presence of death. Listen then to the last prayer of Jesus. He prays that His disciples may be one. He prays for it again and again. It is the one longing which throbs through His whole prayer. The outside world passes for a season out of His thought. The nations and their needs sink below the horizon. He thinks only of His church, of the men who are there in His presence, and of the multitudes who will believe on Him through their word. He can conceive of no higher blessing for them than communion of spirit, comradeship in heart, union in love. "That they all may be one; even as thou, Father, art in me, and I in thee, that they also may be one in us: that the world may believe that thou didst send me."

Fellowship, then, is to be the proof of the divine power of Jesus, evidence to the world that He came from heaven. The world is not to be convinced and converted by reasoning or philosophy or eloquence, but by the love of Christians for one another. "The glory which thou hast given me I have given them; that they may be one, even as we are one: I in them, and thou in me, that they may be perfected into one: and that the world may know that thou didst send me, and lovedst them, even as thou lovedst me." This is amazing doctrine. It sounds novel even now. Christ declares his mission to be the binding of men together by indissoluble bonds. It is by the brotherliness of those who believe in Jesus that the hard heart of the world is to be softened and the truthfulness of Jesus's words established. The world is to be brought to God by Christians loving one another.

It is incontrovertible that, according to the New Testament, the men who were baptized into the spirit of Jesus looked upon the church from the begining as a brotherhood or family. The vocabulary and customs of home life were carried over into the church. The church was known as the household of faith, the family of God. Christians called one another, not "Christians," but "brethren," and after the fashion of Eastern lands, they greeted one another with a kiss. In their assemblies they gathered round a common table, enjoying a love-feast together. The Sacrament of the Lord's Supper was linked to the dinner table, the central social institution in the home. The church's most sacred ceremony was a reminder that believers belong to one another. The church was a communion of brothers. High in the list of graces stood the grace of hospitality. Christians when they traveled were never to find themselves away from home. All congregations of believers were to be bound together by sacred and spiritual ties, and thus was the Lord's prayer to be fulfilled. A favorite name for "church" in the early Christian centuries was "brotherhood." Alas, that it was ever lost!

When we close the New Testament and look around us, we find ourselves in a different world. There is a change in the atmosphere which is chilling. The Roman Catholic idea of the church is not the idea of Peter. Her definition of the church as phrased by Cardinal Bellarmine is: "The one and true church is the congregation of men united by the profession of the same Christian faith and the communion of the same sacraments under the rule of the legitimate pastors, and especially the one vicar of Christ upon earth." Everything mentioned in this definition is external. Love has no stated place at all. In Roman Catholic practice the church is essentially a heirarchy, the officials being exalted far above the laity, constituting a class apart, while the rank and file of the Lord's followers, often reduced to the level of mere spectators, come to God only through the hierarchy. How different Christian history would have been if from the fourth to the sixteenth centuries the men who claimed to sit in Peter's chair had followed Peter, and had said to all priests: "Tend the flock of God, exercising the oversight, not of constraint, but willingly, according unto God; nor yet for filthy lucre, but of a ready mind; neither as lording it over the charge allotted to you, but making yourselves ensamples to the flock," and to all congregations, "Love as brethren, have fervent love among yourselves, love the brotherhood."

Nor has Protestantism ever read with unclouded eye what the New Testament says about the church. The definition formulated by the Anglican Church and adopted by the Protestant Episcopal and Methodist Episcopal churches reads thus: "The visible church of Christ is a congregation of faithful men, in the which the pure word of God is preached, and the sacraments be duly administered according to Christ's ordinance, in all those things that of necessity are requisite to the same."

The Westminster Confession says: "The Catholic or universal church, which is invisible, consists of the whole number of the elect that have been, are, or shall be gathered into one, under Christ, the head thereof; and is the spouse, the body, the fulness of him that filleth all in all. The visible church, which is also catholic or universal under the gospel, consists of all those throughout the world, that profess the true religion, and of their children; and is the kingdom of the Lord Jesus Christ, the house and family of God, out of which there is no ordinary possibility of salvation."

These definitions reappear with minor variations in most of the creeds of Protestant christendom. The two features of the church which Protestants have made conspicuous are the preaching of the word and the administration of the sacraments. But preaching is not sufficient to make a church, nor is the proper administration of the sacraments. That a definition of the church should have in it no reference to what the Head of the church counts fundamental is indeed calamitous. When did Jesus magnify sacraments and sermons, passing by the obligations and ministries of love? The alleged "one vicar of Christ upon earth" does not make a church, nor does a bishop, nor a preacher, nor a man who baptizes, nor an official who offers a prayer over the bread and the wine. A church is a brotherhood, a school for training in fellowship, a home for the cultivation of the social virtues and the human graces, a society in which men are bound together in sympathy and holy service by a common allegiance to the Son of God. It is a congregation of faithful men, ever striving to learn and live the new commandment, looking unto Jesus for power to understand and practice the law of love.

The new commandment is the standard by which all churches

must be measured, and in the light of this standard the church universal knows herself to be poor and blind and naked. Many city churches are made up of people who do not even know one another, and who do not want to know one another. Too many village churches are composed of people who know one another, and are sorry that they do. The very thing which the New Testament asserts to be the one thing needful, and without which the world cannot be won for Christ, is the thing which is today least abundant. To create an ampler and a warmer fellowship inside the church of Jesus is the first work for which preachers are ordained, and yet many of them, instead of staying at home and attending to their business, have gone scampering off in wild crusades against the distant Saracens, wasting their strength in frenzied efforts to reconstruct by a furious blowing of trumpets the economic and social order.

There are many congregations, let us be thankful, in which the new commandment is understood and honored, and it is these congregations which constitute the hope of Christendom. They hold in their hand the key which unlocks all the doors. They possess the secret for which the world is waiting. No churches, let us hope, are altogether devoid of the love for which the Master and His apostles pleaded. Even in congregations which seem paralyzed or dead, there is usually at the center a little circle of loyal and devoted believers, whose hearts have been fused by the Holy Spirit, and whose lives have been blended by fellowship in Christian work and prayer. To extend this circle of lovers, whether it be larger or smaller, and endow it with a fuller measure of wisdom and power is, in my judgment, the distinctive and crucial work of the Christian minister. It is the work which the Master did, and He says, "Follow me!"

There are probably few important sentences in the Gospels used so seldom by Christian ministers as texts for sermons as is the golden sentence of our Lord: "Love one another, even as I have loved you." It seems to be a difficult sentence to find, and even more difficult to understand. It is often made to mean something different from what it teaches. A common interpretation makes it equivalent to "love all men everywhere." But such an exposition empties it of its content, and robs it of its power to accomplish the work which Jesus had in mind. He is not exhorting here to a vague humanitarianism or a wholesale philanthropy. He is not proclaiming the brotherhood of man. He is not thinking of men in general. He is speaking to members of His church, and telling them how to live together so as to convince the world that He is what He claims to be. Victory for His cause is to be achieved by their love for one another. It is no ordinary love which is called for, but love fashioned after His own, and lifted to its white intensity and heavenly temper. A Christian owes something to a fellow Christian which he owes to no other human being, his first duty is to his fellow believers, his first obligation is to his Christian brethren, his first concern is with his comrades in Christ.

It is by Christian loving one another after the sacrificial manner of Jesus that other men are to become Christians. Love is the law of the church. Love is the badge of discipleship. Love is the chief evangelist and head worker. Love is the power which overcomes. It is not love for the community or love for humanity, but love for one's fellow Christians by which the door of the world's heart is to be opened. The teaching was plain, and the early Christian caught it. The secret of the progress of the early church lies revealed in the exclamation of the pagan crowd: "Behold how these Christians love one another!"

The primary work of a preacher, then, is the cultivation by word and deed of the spirit of Christlike brotherliness among the members of his own church. Many ministers shrink from this work as something narrowing and unworthy. The very statement that such is a minister's work sounds like heresy and arouses antagonism and revulsion in many hearts. Such teaching seems like harking back to the Dark Ages. The brotherhood of man and not the brotherhood of Christians is the doctrine which our century is ready to hear.

All men are our brothers. A man who is up to date will make no distinctions, but will love everybody alike. Let a preacher, therefore, exhort his people continually to love humanity, being careful to lay no special emphasis, as a New Testament writer mistakenly did, upon those who belong to the household of faith.

It is just here that many a minister makes his greatest mistake. In his eagerness to be broad, he becomes narrow. In ignoring limitations prescribed by the Lord of life, he becomes feeble. By trying to do too much, he achieves nothing. In his liberality, he wipes out distinctions which cannot be repudiated without loss. In his zeal to rise above boundaries, he loses himself in the clouds. Nothing is more essential to a preacher in our day than an understanding of the function and power of limitations. It is only as a man is willing to confine himself within narrow limits that he can do any mighty work. Men all round us are frittering away their lives because of their vagueness. Sermons in appalling numbers amount to little because of their generalities. Definiteness in thought and action is the thing above all things for the twentieth-century preacher to cultivate. Concentration is the supreme prudence of ministerial life.

It is easy to declaim eloquently about the brotherhood of man, but much that is said upon that subject is vapid and futile. The air is full of talk about brotherhood, but brotherhood does not come by poetic quotations and rhapsodical orating. Brotherhood is a spiritual creation, the work of men who have been re-created in Christ. It is a fellowship of souls based upon a fellowship with God's only-begotten Son. The redemption of the world is carried onward by the binding of Christian hearts and lives together. To Paul, fellowship was everything. His letters were full of it because his heart was overflowing. To get the members of the local church closer together, and the churches of each region closer together, and the churches of the Jewish and Gentile worlds closer together—this was the object of his labors and prayers. Christianity to him is fellowship in the Lord. Without fellowship, faith is empty, hope is darkened, love is starved. It is through the communion of saints that this world and all worlds are to see what God is and what He is able to do.

Do not be afraid, then, to preach boldly the doctrine of the new commandment. Preach it just as the Lord himself taught it. Count it your joy to train the members of your church in the fine art of living together. It is the most difficult of all the arts, and the church is the school ordained of God for perfecting men in this art. You are not doing a narrow work when you teach the members of your church the range and wealth of Christian fellowship.

The church is the world in miniature. In it exist all the forces and relationships, the entanglements and evils, which the world as a whole presents. There is not a world evil which can be anywhere so effectively attacked as within the church of Christ. There is not an industrial or social or racial problem which can be dealt with outside so profoundly as inside the Christian brotherhood. When you straighten out the tangled relations of your church members to one another, you are contributing to the solution of social problems everywhere. When you soften class antipathies and racial antagonisms within your congregation, you are helping to solve the most baffling of the world complications. When you induce all sorts and conditions of men to live together as brethren in your own church communion, you are hastening the day when men the wide world over shall be brothers.

Humanity is in the making, and the church is the institution in which society is molded into nobler forms and fitted for finer issues. When Paul built a slave into the brotherhood at Colossae, he signed the death warrant for slavery in England and America. When Jesus induced twelve men differing from one another widely in temperament, idea, and social standing to sit down together in an upper chamber in Jerusalem, He contributed to the solution of the social problem in every city throughout the world. It is impossible to kindle a fire on your church hearth without the world feeling the warmth of it. But you cannot kindle a fire unless you bring the fagots together. The minister's first business is to get his people together. Let him preach to his church; and his church, when converted, will preach to the world. Let him kindle the church, and the church will illumine the community. The lamp of the town is the church. If the lamp of the church is darkness, how great is that darkness!

The minister who gives himself to the training of a church in Christian fellowship is not dwarfing the affections or curtailing the range of the sympathies of his people. He is creating the very capacities and powers by means of which Christ's large wish for the world can be most speedily fulfilled. Affections are most surely enriched and strengthened only when cultivated in narrow fields. It is the man who loves his own wife as he loves no other woman who comes to take a chivalric attitude to all women everywhere. By his love for one woman, he grows into a widening appreciation of the dignity and beauty of womanhood. It is the father who loves his own children as he loves no others whose affections go out furthest toward all boys and girls and who is swiftest to gather them into the round tower of his heart. Men who are most faithful to their own homes are the men to be first counted on for the defense and maintenance of the interests of all homes. It is the man who has come into fellowship with his brother men in his own church who is most likely to come into right relations with men who have no connection with organized Christianity.

Love, when once kindled, travels far, but it must first be kindled.

The church of Jesus is established for the express purpose of kindling the fire of love. Sermons are a part of the fuel by which the fire is nourished. Pastoral work also feeds and safeguards the holy flame. The wise preacher is always striving to bring the members of his church into a richer fellowship. The weakness of the modern church lies in its dwarfed affections. The shame of present-day Christianity is its stunted sympathies. The church is rich in money, ideas, apparatus, numbers, but poor in love. This is in part the fault of preachers. Too many of them fail to cultivate the affections. They do not understand how to open the heart. They are interested in problems and what they call the "Kingdom," but they are not sufficiently interested in the group of people of whom they are the appointed religious teachers. They neglect the work of interlacing lives, of binding men into bundles, of twining purposes and sympathies together for the advancement of Christ's glory. There are congregations which have scant sympathy with the outside world, because their members have meager sympathy with one another.

If sympathy is cultivated inside the church, it spills over into the outside world. There are churches which have no interest in the struggles and hopes of wage earners, largely because there is no interest among the members of those churches in one another. Christian love is expressed in the hymnbook, but does not exist in the hearts of the people who sing the hymns; and not loving the man by his side, it is impossible for the loveless church member to love the man who is far away. When love is kindled in the hearts of church members for one another, it is a fire which burns its way to the end of the world. Not a little of the indifference of many Christians to the work of foreign missions is due to their atrophied social sympathies. Their social nature has become enfeebled, and by neglecting their obligations to their fellow townsmen, they find it impossible to respond to the claims of unknown men on the other side of the globe. Their lack of the spirit of brotherly affection incapacitates them also for the worship of God. Their worship is mechanical and unsatisfying.

The secret of this was told long ago by a man who laid it down as axiomatic that if a man does not love his brother whom he has seen, he cannot love God whom he has not seen. It is the very quintessence of the Christian teaching that we can know God only through man, that we come to God only through man, and that we worship God best by loving men. Many a preacher has tried to put warmth into the worship of his church, and all in vain, because he did not know that the source of warmth is human fellowship, and that the place to begin working for an enrichment of the devotional spirit is not among his books, elaborating arguments going to prove that men ought to delight in the worship of God, but in the social meeting where church members come to know one another. Christians who are interested in one another invariably become more interested in God. Loving men is the only way to grow in the grace of loving God. Unless a church is socialized, how can it be expected to feel an interest in social movements? A set of people who are not interested in one another will not be likely in the house of prayer to worship God with glad and exultant hearts, or in the field of Christian service to work effectively for the advancement of the Kingdom. The preacher's first work is the building of a brotherhood. Out of this, when once created, all sorts of reviving streams will flow.

These are good times for preachers to ponder the meaning of the new commandment and to train their people in the practice of it. Men are thinking as never before of solidarity and organic life and corporate responsibilities. In the commercial world there is an amazing revelation of the power of co-operation; in the industrial world, a growing apprehension of the possibilities of collectivism; in the new psychology, a deepened insight into the relation of personality to society. There is a world-wide movement called socialism. In all the kingdoms of life there is a new vision of the meaning of social relationships and the miracle-working power of combinations. In the whole trend of the world's thought, the Spirit of God is saying something to the churches, and the preacher who has ears to hear will receive a revelation. We are living in a social age, and the question at the front is the social question. Man's social nature is unprecedentedly alive and is clamoring for a satisfaction which cannot be denied it. Men are massing themselves in cities, not chiefly because they are most needed there, but because they find in city life gratification for their social cravings. Men hunger for companionship. They have discovered that it is not good for them to live alone. Solitude is unendurable, isolation is death.

As soon as men come together, they organize, gather themselves into groups, form fraternities, unions, leagues, clubs. Men live by fellowship. It is only when hearts and hands come together that existence passes into life. The multiplication of societies, therefore, goes on increasingly. This is a fact of which every alert preacher is bound to take notice. Many a preacher has already observed it to his consternation. He has found the unions and lodges, granges and clubs, swallowing up the men of the community, leaving for the church only women and children. In bitterness of spirit he has cried out against these secular organizations, denouncing them as enemies of the church of God. But all such denunciation is futile. One cannot change the movement of the tides. Man is a social animal. God made him such. Men are made for fellowship, and if they do not find it in the church of God, they will seek it where it may be found.

The wise preacher will waste no time in hurling thunderbolts at rival organizations, but will set to work with both hands to strengthen the church where the church today is weakest. His ambition will be to make his church the warmest and most effective brotherhood in all the town. No stranger member shall go unbefriended. No invalid shall be unvisited. No needy person shall be unassisted. No bewildered soul shall go unadvised. No home of mourning shall be neglected. No act of needed mercy shall be omitted. The church shall be a home. Men cannot live by sermons alone, but by every word which proceeds out of the mouth of God. One of God's choice words is *fellowship,* and unless a church offers fellowship, it is doomed. Worship without fellowship is contrary to nature. The worship in the New Testament is carried on by brothers. Men cannot love a church if all it offers is the privilege of listening to sermons and paying pew rent.

It is the comradeship of college life which makes men love their college. Their devotion to their alma mater springs out of the friendships formed during their student days. The abstract truths taught by learned professors will not account for that undying affection which many a man feels for his college. His heart is warm because it is bound up with other hearts. A man's love for his church depends in large measure upon the relationship established between himself and his fellow members. The friendships formed in church life and work are among the most sacred and enduring into which the soul of man can come. Unless a man enters into the social life of the church, he is practically not a member of it at all. Listening to a preacher speak on religious topics every Sunday does not make one a church member, even though his name is written on the church roll. Fellowship is of the essence of church membership, and to cultivate and enrich the fellowship is the primary task of the Christian preacher.

A sharp distinction ought to be made between a church and an audience. It is to be regretted that he have come to rank churches by the size of their nominal membership, and to judge preachers by the number of persons who listen to their sermons. A superficial man is consequently tempted to work, not for a church, but for an audience. An audience, however, is not worth working for. An audience is a set of unrelated people drawn together by a short-lived attraction, an agglomeration of individuals finding themselves together for a brief time. It is a fortuitous concourse of human atoms, scattering as soon as a certain performance is ended. It is a pile of leaves to be blown away by the wind, a handful of sand lacking consistency and cohesion, a number of human filings drawn into position by a pulpit magnet, and which will drop away as soon as the magnet is removed. An audience is a gathering; a church is a fellowship. An audience is a collection; a church is an organism. An audience is a heap of stones; a church is a temple. Preachers are ordained, not to attract an audience, but to build a church. Coarse and ambitious and worldly men, if richly gifted, can draw audiences. Only a disciple of the Lord can build a church. It is not uncommon for a supposedly mighty church to wilt like Jonah's gourd as soon as the man in the pulpit vanishes. The structure was of hay and wood and stubble, and it disappeared in the fire of God's swift judgment day.

It is because so many churches are audiences, rather than brotherhoods, that thousands of Christians on changing their place of residence drop out of church connections altogether. Their old church membership meant nothing to them, and therefore membership in another church has no attraction for them. When they joined the church, it was the minister who welcomed them. The church took no note of their advent. When death visited their home, it was the pastor who offered condolence. The church was not grieved by the bereavement. When a financial crisis swept the little fortune away, leaving the world dark, it was the preacher who spoke a sympathetic word; but the church cared for none of these things. When the hour for departure arrived, it was the head official of the church who said, "Good-by," but the brotherhood had nothing whatever to say. This is the tragedy which goes on in hundreds of parishes, and so long as it continues, many preachers must preach to dwindling congregations and the church must limp like a giant, not with a wounded heel, but with a broken leg. A man who has been starved in one church is not likely to connect himself with another. When he makes for himself a new home, he will identify himself with a society which offers him comradeship and furnishes an atmosphere in which his soul can live.

The problem of developing new converts is even more perplexing than that of retaining the allegiance of old ones. It is easier to convert men than it is to educate them. The converts are many, but the developed workers are few. In a season of spiritual awakening ten seem to be healed, but when the preacher goes in search of them, he cries in bewilderment, "Where are the nine?" Only a small proportion of those who start the Christian life ever reach spiritual maturity. One of the reasons is a deadly environment. The atmosphere is so cold that the young convert is fatally chilled. He gasps for a few months and then expires. There are many congregations in which church obligations are so little known and practiced that it is only the exceptional convert who survives the early stages of Christian discipleship. The atmosphere of the church has in it no life-giving qualities. The church is not a brotherhood, and when a new recruit starts to follow Jesus, he is not cheered by brotherly voices or guided by fraternal hands. In the darkness of the first days, there is no one to do what Ananias did for Saul when he laid his warm hand on the trembling convert's head, saying, "Brother Saul, receive thy sight."

It is often the touch of a brother's hand which opens the heavens to the beginning Christian. In successful church work the voice of the preacher must be supplemented by the welcoming hand of a brother. The preacher is never sufficient when he stands alone. Peter was mighty on the day of Pentecost, because one hundred and twenty—the entire brotherhood—stood with him. The Bible is not enough to make men strong. Human hands and hearts are needed. The revelation which came through holy men of old must be completed by a revelation coming through men now living. The human hand has a power which even the Scriptures do not possess. There is something in a human heart which completes the power of Almighty God in the work of saving men. Eloquence is a force, but affection is a force still more potent. Social intercourse is a means of grace as truly as are prayer and the sacraments, and is of equal rank with these. Warmth is as essential as light in the growing of souls. The preacher may furnish light, but the bulk of the heat must be supplied by the brotherhood. The finest and deepest powers of the soul are called into play only by social contact. Every point of contact—or, as Paul puts it, "every joint"—is a channel of divine grace.

It is at the points where Christian lives touch that there springs up the life by which the church is nourished and made capable for her work. God's grace flows through social bonds. We are held in our place by personal attachments. We save one another. This is why Paul is always exhorting his converts to subject themselves one to another. He is not satisfied at times with his figure of a temple. He supplements it with his figure of the body. Church members are even closer together than the stones of a temple wall. They are knit together like the parts of an organism. Each organ exists for the life and prosperity of the whole. Each is needed by all. The whole is dependent on each. The preacher is impotent without the assistance of the brotherhood. His words will never catch fire unless the brotherhood creates the atmosphere in which gospel truths blaze. He cannot, unassisted, hold his converts. It is impossible for him, single-handed, to keep his spiritual children from falling. His success in conserving the fruits of his labors will be measured by his ability to build and maintain a compact and conquering brotherhood. Many a sermon must be preached on the duties which Christians owe to one another. Many an hour must be devoted to the difficult and delicate work of linking the lives of the new converts into the lives of those who have traveled farther along the perilous and glorious way.

Building the brotherhood, this is our work, and work more taxing and baffling, God has never given to mortals. It brought the Son of God to the cross, and every man who attempts the same work must drink of a like cup and be baptized with a similar baptism. Not until a minister strives to build a brotherhood does he realize how unsocial human nature is, how narrow and how cold. Not till then does he discover what havoc sin has wrought, and what low and crude conceptions of the obligations of Christian disciple-ship lodge in many a Christian heart. It is only then that human nature begins to reveal its deeper ugliness and that many interior littlenesses and meannesses come trooping into the light. Even the Lord himself could not get twelve men to sit together at a table on the last night of His life on earth without an exhibition of petty irritation and wounded vanity which cast a deeper shadow over His already breaking heart.

It is comparatively easy for most Christians to give money. Some of them will give it generously. It is not difficult to persuade certain of the elect to engage in Christian work. Work among the submerged has in many places become even fashionable. But for church members to be brotherly with one another, this is indeed difficult, in many quarters, apparently impossible. Men teach boys in mission schools who cannot be induced to show an interest in their younger brethren in their own church. Women work for women in a settlement or mission who will not recognize women of a different social station in their own church family. Men make contributions for carrying the gospel into foreign lands who act like heathen in their home church. To the amazement of the young preacher, social estrangements flourish inside the company of the sanctified. Class antagonisms do not soften under the most fervent preaching of the gospel. Racial lines remain straight and fixed, and all the rivalries and enmities, vanities and prejudices, of which the world is full, grow rank inside the garden of the Lord. Possibly it is for this reason that certain preachers devote so much attention to sinners outside their congregations. A man finds relief in striking at a distant octopus who has been discomfited by some unregenerate pigmy within his reach. The sinners inside his parish are so helpless that in sheer desperation the defeated preacher gives his attention to the great outside world, whose tragedies it is easy to portray, whose colossal culprits it is harmless to castigate, and concerning whose reconstruction it is refreshing to give advice.

But the servant of the Master must not follow the things which are easy. Let him take hold of the things which are hard. Let him lay both hands on his church. He may find that his church is after all only an audience, and that its members need to be fused into a body which the Lord can use. It may be that the older people are not interested in the young people and that they eye each other across a chasm which widens and deepens with the years. Possibly employers have steadfastly held aloof from wage earners, and the rich men have never shown friendliness for the men who are poor. It may be that the new members have been allowed to continue strangers, and that older members have sat for years within six feet of each other without even so much as a look of mutual recognition. Possibly there are men who quarreled ten years ago, and who have doggedly resisted every suggestion of reconciliation. They do not speak in the church or on the street, and this ill will festering in their hearts poisons the atmosphere of the whole church.

Here is a problem more urgent for the minister than any of the disputes between labor and capital. It may be that members of the church are estranged from one another by differences in doctrinal opinion. An orthodox brother thinks that his orthodoxy gives him a right to malign those who differ from him, and in defending the truth he tramples the new commandment under his feet. To train Christian men to love one another who differ from one another theologically is a task more formidable than converting the toughest of the publicans and the trickiest of the sinners. But Jesus is explicit on this point. Worship must wait on reconciliation. Get right with your brother, says the Lord of love, before you set up your altar. It may be that some Pharaoh has grown up in the midst of the congregation who lords it over both the minister and the saints. He has made trouble for years, and, unless suppressed, he will make trouble for years to come. Such a man must be dealt with. His sin is as destructive to the life of the church as habitual drunkenness or flagrant lust. Unbrotherly conduct in a church member always makes him a fit subject for church discipline, and the minister is not doing his duty who allows the church to be torn and harassed by an ungodly despot who has set up his throne in the parish. Nothing worth while could go on in the upper chamber until Judas was got rid of, and so in many a church the communion should not be celebrated again until the confirmed mischief-maker has been cast out. Patience and mercy are always in order, but there are certain transgressors who are apparently incorrigible, and their way ought to be made hard.

These are the arduous and cardinal things which a minister has to do. It is easy to denounce sins in general, and still easier to unfold beautiful ideas, but to induce different classes of church members to live and work together as Christians—this is the most stupendous and heart-breaking labor to which a minister of the gospel can set himself. The church of Christ if not a brotherhood is a failure. To make it a brotherhood—this is the hope and despair of the minister, this is his cross and his crown. To build all types of humanity into this brotherhood is an aim never to be lost sight of.

Churches organized along social lines are breeders of mischief. A church made up of people of but one social grade is a church doomed to a blasted spiritual experience. A church of the rich is not a church after the ideal of Jesus, neither is a church of the poor. It is only when the rich and the poor sit down together that they come to believe that the Lord is the Maker of them all. A church exists for the express purpose of knitting together the lives of those whom the forces of the world have driven asunder. The rich and the poor are to come together at the feet of Him Who, once rich, for man's sake became poor. The laborer and the capitalist are to join hands in front of the Cross. The cultivated man and the man without schooling are to learn each other's worth in Christian service. The foreigners are to be no more aliens, but full members of the family of God. Brotherhood is what the world is clamoring for, and it is an example of brotherhood which the Christian church must give. The church is the laboratory in which experiments in brotherliness are to be conducted first and farthest. The church is the factory in which men are to be converted into brothers. A man with a brotherly heart is a form of power which the industrial and commercial worlds are waiting for. That church is doing humanity the largest service which develops within itself the highest potencies of love.

Let preachers, then, create in their churches by their preaching the spirit of love, and the churches will pass it on. The world will never listen to sermons on sympathy and good will until these exist in heavenly abundance inside the church. What is the use of preachers trying to give the world a theory of something which the church itself does not practice? No man can preach love effectively over the body of a loveless church. Our immediate task is not to Christianize the world, but to Christianize the church. The church progressively Christianized will gradually Christianize society. God cuts our piece of work small in order that we may do it well. The task, though limited, is dynamic and far-reaching. The church, if leaven, will leaven the whole lump. Our first business is not with the lump, but with the leaven. He is the greatest preacher who so frames and utters the thoughts of God as to bind together the largest number of Christian hearts in closest fellowship for Christlike service.

III

CONVERSATIONS

15

What Is the Matter?

No, I have no objection to telling you what I conceive to be the radical defect in much of the preaching of our time. It is lack of spiritual passion. The tone of authority is faint. Too much of the preaching is like that of the Scribes. Clergymen are numerous, but prophets are few.

Here lies the trouble. Only a prophet can achieve genuine success in these hurried and fascinating days. Time was when a scholar could do it. When books were expensive, and locked up in the libraries of the elite, a man versed in book-lore could find a Sunday audience eager to listen to the information which he was willing to impart. Those days are gone. Before the rise of the daily paper, the preacher could be an editor, and make his sermons running commentaries on current events. That sort of preaching was once counted successful. It is a failure now. Before the multiplication of lecture platforms and music halls and art galleries, and other sources of intellectual entertainment and aesthetic gratification, fine music from the organ loft and exquisite essays from the pulpit seemed to satisfy all reasonable demands. But music, while it may still have charms to soothe the savage beast, is not conspicuously successful in attracting non-churchgoers into the house of God. And much of the finest literary work displayed at present in American pulpits seems to be hopelessly lost on this unkempt and stiff-necked generation. Even the pulpit reformer does not wear his crown long. He has had his day, like the editor-preacher and the rest. By striking one special evil hard, he may cause the world to resound for a season with the echoes of his blows, and may even succeed in chipping off a fragment of some false custom or established wrong; but unless a preacher is a great deal more than a reformer, he cannot long hold the attention of an intelligent congregation, or hope to build an enduring Christian church. In short, the poor preacher has been ousted from the snug position of editor, lecturer, essayist, reformer; and there is nothing left him now but the arduous vocation of a prophet.

And this has been his true place from the beginning. His other positions were either usurped or thrust upon him by the exigencies of the times. The printing press has pushed him up at last into his proper sphere. If he attempts now to compete with other men in their fields of labor, he invites the failure which he deserves. The position of a minister is unique. His mission is momentous. His work, while fitting into the labors of all other servants of the Lord, is different from theirs. The moment he forsakes the task appointed him and attempts to share the work and honors of other men, swift retribution follows in his track. Woe to the preacher who in these modern days shrinks the wrestlings and agonies of the prophet, and attempts to perform the duties assigned to others!

And yet this is the very thing which many preachers are doing. Notwithstanding the discussion *ad nauseam* through the week in the daily press of every happening and event, there are preachers who have the temerity to expect people to come to the church on the Lord's Day to hear the old newspaper straw threshed over again. And notwithstanding every center table groans with periodicals and magazines edited with consummate ability, and filled with articles written in many cases by the pen of genius, there are ministers who dabble on the Lord's Day in literary discussion and philosophical speculation, and then wonder why the blessing of the Almighty does not rest upon their labors. There is an itch abroad just now to work reforms. Everything is being overhauled, from systems of theology to boards of aldermen. The social order is rotten, the industrial system is accursed, the ecclesiastical regime is ripe for burning—so men assert. There is a hubbub of discordant voices, each voice screaming out a panacea, and promising the golden age; and in this fury for readjustment and reconstruction, too many pulpits, I am inclined to think, waste their time and strength. It is a proof of Christ's matchless greatness that he stood in the presence of the Roman Empire and never struck it. His work was to strike the heart. By striking the hearts of peasants, he overturned the Empire. He says to his heralds, "Follow me!"

Unless a sermon is different from all other forms of address, the world today does not care to hear it. If tired men and women are to be expected to attend public worship Sunday morning, the atmosphere of the house of God must be made different from that which these people breathe through the week. The late R. H. Hutton, in one of his essays, says that Walter Bagehot once asked him to hear one of the afternoon sermons of the chaplain of Lincoln's Inn, Frederick D. Maurice. Bagehot assured Hutton that he would feel that something different went on there from that which went on in an ordinary church or chapel service, that there was a sense of "something religious" in the air which was not to be found elsewhere. Bagehot's word was fulfilled. Hutton heard and saw and felt that day things which lived in his memory through life. He heard a prophet. Maurice spoke for God. The intense and thrilling tones, the pathetic emphasis, the passionate trust, the burning exultation, the atmosphere of reverence and devotion, awed and subdued the worshipers. The church became indeed a holy place. The words of the service seemed put into the preacher's mouth, "while he, with his whole soul bent on their wonderful drift, uttered them as an awe-struck but thankful envoy tells the tale of danger and deliverance."

It is this "something religious" which one misses in too many of our American churches and in too much of our modern preaching. Bright things, true things, helpful things, are said in abundance, but the spiritual passion is lacking. The service smacks of time and not of eternity. The atmosphere of the sermon is not that of Sinai or Calvary, but that of the professor's room or the sanctum of the editor. The intellect is instructed, the emotions are touched, but the conscience is not stirred, nor is the will compelled to appear before the judgment throne and render its decision. The old tone of the "Thus saith the Lord" of the Hebrew prophets is lacking. Men are everywhere hungering and waiting for it, but in many churches they have thus far waited for it in vain.

16

Thoughtlessness

It causes a deal of mischief in the church of God. It is not an inhospitable disposition but thoughtlessness which leads many church members to neglect strangers who come to worship with them. Let us hope it is the same distemper which glues men sometimes to the end of their pew, so that late-comers are obliged to clamber in over their knees. It is not malice but heedlessness which impels a layman to rummage under his pew for overshoes and umbrella during the singing of the closing hymn. What is it but absent-mindedness that starts belated pew-holders up the aisle during the singing of the anthem? Not lack of mind but lack of thought is responsible for the conduct of the woman who disturbs her neighbors through prayer and Scripture reading by her incessant whispering. And what but paralysis of the organ of thought can account for the fact that a congregation of courteous people will sometimes turn their backs at the close of service upon a minister who has preached in exchange with the pastor without a word of greeting or thanks? Today, as in the days of Isaiah, the Almighty has just cause to complain, "My people doth not consider."

Thoughtlessness is one of the demons which every minister soon learns to fear. For instance, if some good brother seizes him while on the way to the pulpit and pours into his ears the latest gossip, it is not considered ministerial to say to such a man, "Get thee behind me, Satan." Though oppressed and afflicted, he must not open his mouth. Or some nervous saint may keep turning over the pages of the hymn-book straight through the preaching of the sermon, not knowing that the constant turning of pages may be to a sensitive man as distracting as the buzzing of a full-fledged sawmill. Or at the close of the service someone may rush forward and drag him from the pulpit stairs into a subject a thousand miles away from the sermon. This is "the most unkindest cut of all." To labor hard to bring a congregation into the central glory of a truth, and then have some one dash forward at the earliest opportunity—presumptively to render thanks for the help he has received, but in reality to ventilate his mind on some subject totally foreign to the day, or to propound a curious conundrum which has no conceivable relation to anything which has been said—is inexpressibly galling and disheartening. After a preacher has struck with all his might on the heart-chords of a congregation, and then discovers that in at least one of his apparently most attentive listeners there is no hint of a response, he instinctively looks around for Elijah's juniper tree. Why God allows the Devil to play such pranks on ministers in the very hour of their exhaustion is not yet revealed. It may be to bring them more completely into the fellowship of the suffering of His Son. At the close of one of Jesus's sermons on the sin against the Holy Ghost, a preoccupied egotist shouted out, "Master, speak to my brother, that he divide the inheritance with me." It would be hazardous to say that the Son of Man ever lost his temper; but if there is a trace of impatience visible anywhere in His recorded sayings, it is in the answer which He gave to this exasperating and incorrigible sinner.

But a dash of cold water at the close of a sermon is not so fatal as an interruption in the midst of sermon-building. It is difficult for the average man to realize the value of uninterrupted time. He himself does not get a day without interruptions, nor does he want it. A minister, however, if he is to do his best work, must have at least a part of certain days absolutely free from all intrusion. "But I want to see him only a minute," pleads the importunate inquirer, not knowing what he asks. He who thinks that only a minute is a trifle does not know the nature of the mind, and has probably done no sustained and constructive thinking. "Only a minute" may ruin the work of a day. In a minute an express train can be thrown from the track, but to place it again on the rails requires the arduous labor of hours. The mind in its highest operations moves more swiftly than the limited express, and the interruption of only a minute may hurl the train of thought down an embankment and stop all progress indefinitely. In the hot hours of sermonic creation, when the mental furnace is seething and the molten thought is ready to be poured into words, an outsider who asks for a minute not only checks the momentum of the mental process, but chills the glow of the emotions, and introduces into the mind a foreign substance which is not easily cast out. In those hours when your pastor goes into the mountain to commune with God, do not let the Devil tempt you to ring his doorbell.

This seems all foolishness to some of you. You know ministers who are not so cranky. They are open at all times to their people. They say so with swelling pride. Morning, afternoon, and night the latchstring is out, and whosoever will, may come. But it must be borne in mind that there are preachers and preachers. Some are carpenters and others are poets. Some men build sermons as carpenters build houses—they manufacture them. They cut out the material piece by piece, join the pieces together, and sandpaper and varnish them at their leisure. They can drop their work at any moment as easily as the carpenter drops his hammer. The poet-preacher is a different man. His sermons are not made; they grow. Sermons come to him as poems do, in rare and luminous hours, which hours, when they come, must be seized and used. Some days are opaque. No light streams through. And then there comes

> One of the charmed days
> When the genius of God doth flow.

Mind and heart are ready. In a few hours the work of weeks bursts into blossom, an argument is forged, a truth is unfolded, a vision is worked out into speech which will make glad many hearts.

As a rule, the preachers who see people at all hours through the week do not see many people at the hour of service on Sunday. If your minister lacks the will power to protect himself from people who steal his time, you ought to buy him a large-mouthed bulldog, which shall serve as a sort of flaming sword to guard the study door.

17

Ways of Killing a Sermon

A layman may, with a little practice, develop amazing dexterity in counteracting the influence of his pastor. After the preacher has kindled by his sermon a fire in many hearts, a layman may, if industrious and enterprising, extinguish the fire in all the people near him. It is a critical season in the week—the brief period immediately succeeding the benediction. In those few moments a layman can, if he will, do infinite mischief. He can turns his back on the stranger that stands nearest him, and show by his conduct that the pastor's sermon on brotherliness is a mere theory, not intended to be reduced to practice, at least in that church. Or, if he chooses to be talkative, he can smother the sermon in his conversation. He can plunge into a discussion of the music. That theme is very fascinating and fatal. He can say, "How did you enjoy the music? How did you like the soprano?" or "What did you think of the bass?" Such questions are exceedingly effective in the mouth of an expert sermon-killer.

A dozen members of the church propounding such questions to everyone they meet convert the house of God into a concert hall, and train people to look upon public worship as a performance to be measured by the aesthetic gratification which it affords to the congregation. Many a minister, after pouring out his very life to convict men of their sins or to lift them to the level of some arduous duty, has been cut to the heart by hearing his best people discussing in the aisles the excellences or defects of the anthem and passing judgment on the voices of the singers.

But the question concerning music is not a whit more demoralizing than the question heard even more frequently, "How did you like the sermon?"

Asking that question has become a habit which it will probably take centuries to eradicate. It is a demon which can be cast out only by prayer and fasting. Even the saints are addicted to the use of it. When strangers come to the church, the first question at the close of the service often is, "How did you like the sermon?" No wonder spiritual results of preaching are so meager. What can be expected from preaching unless laymen realize that they are to follow up the work of persuasion by driving home the word set forth by the preacher? Sermons are not toys to be played with, or pretty pieces of rhetoric on which every member of the congregation is expected to pass judgment. To ask, How did you like the sermon? is to drag it down to the level of a crazy quilt, or a piece of crochetwork. A sermon is not an exquisite bit of literary bric-a-brac, to be chattered over and judged by the technical rules of art. It is not a dumpling into which every self-constituted critic is invited to stick his fork that he may praise or condemn the cook. A sermon is a solemn warning, a bugle call to duty, a burning condemnation, an earnest stroke against a giant wrong, or exhortation to high endeavor, the illumination of a majestic truth. What a question for an earnest Christian to ask inside the house of God: "How did you like it?"

Sermons are preached, not to be liked, but to be accepted and lived. Suppose, pray, you did not like the sermon! What of it? Suppose that scapegrace who sat with you in the pew went away disgusted! When the arrow goes in, curses often come out. John the Baptist, Jesus of Nazareth, Peter, and John were not anxious that their sermons should be liked. Why should you be so solicitous concerning the opinion of the critics? How did you like the sermon? Such a question injures the one who asks it, and debauches the person who answers it. It trains men to measure sermons by false standards, and to seek for entertainment rather than for truth.

No wonder so many ministers have been spoiled, and are today preaching sermons full of everything else but the gospel. They itch to catch the crowd, and cater for applause, because they have been ruined by churches which have trained them to think of the sermon as something to be admired, eulogized, exulted over. A true preacher speaks for God, and whether the people like the message or not is the very last of all questions to be considered. No church can have conversions in it whose leading members ask the unconverted, How did you like the sermon? When a man is wrestling with problems of life and destiny, it is an insult to throw at him such a frivolous inquiry. It calls him off from a decision unspeakably momentous, invites him to pose as a critic, and requests him to pass judgment on the instrument which in the providence of God is being used for his regeneration. Many an aroused soul has been hurled from a serious mood of conviction into the mood of a trifler by, How did you like the sermon?

It is impossible for earnest men to do anything in the pulpit unless they are seconded by earnest men in the pews. Of what avail are passions and solemnity and burning earnestness in the preacher if the sermon is followed up by a swarm of triflers propounding idle questions? Holy impressions are easily dissipated. It does not take much to strangle newborn aspirations. One silly interrogation may crush a rising impulse toward God. The church should carry on and complete the work begun by the preacher. All conversation at the close of the service should deepen and fasten the impression of the hour. The church should be a trumpet through which the voice of the preacher gains volume and power. But if the trumpet gives an uncertain voice, who shall prepare himself for war? If the preacher cries, "In God's name, act!" and the saints stand around and ask, "How do you like that?" who of the unconverted will prepare himself for the marriage supper of the Lamb?

The crucial question is not, Did you like it? but, Did it help you? Did it comfort you? Did it give you new visions of duty? Did it bring you nearer to the Lord? The parable of the sower has an abiding significance. Those birds which devour seeds are like the poor: they are always with us. In our days such birds have no feathers, but in instinct they are true to the nature of the bird which Jesus saw; and one of their favorite methods of rendering vain the work of the Sower is asking, How did you like the sermon?

18

Criticizing the Minister

It is a difficult task, but there are times when it must be done. By criticism I do not mean that aimless detraction in which undeveloped church members occasionally indulge, but the brave and open disapprobation of a minister's conduct, or the condemning judgment of his work. Ministers are not infallible. Like other mortals, they fall into ruts. They sometimes allow idiosyncrasies to become so pronounced as to narrow their influence and cripple their power. Alas for a man who is placed beyond the reach of intelligent and discriminating criticism! There is scarcely any limit to the number of foolish things a minister may be guilty of. He may come to church meetings habitually late, or he may sniffle at the close of every paragraph, or he may whoop like a wild Indian in delivering tame ideas, or he may practice elocutionary slides in his prayers, or he may make faces which frighten the children, or he may stare at the wall instead of looking at the people while preaching his sermons, or he may make the church a place in which to rehearse the chapters of his next book, or he may refer in every sermon to his trip to the Holy Land, or he may make missions or some other equally good theme his hobby, and ride it straight through the year, or he may allow his voice to drop into inaudibility at the close of every important sentence, or he may repeat old sermons so frequently that even people with a poor memory find him out, or he may go gadding over the country shining at all sorts of celebrations while his people sit in darkness at home, or he may keep on for years mispronouncing a half-dozen common words to the disgust of every high-school girl in the congregation, or—— What does your minister do?

"Oh, if he would only quit that!" is the distressed cry of many a long-suffering saint who wants to cure his pastor of a bad habit and does not know how to go about it.

What can be done? The providential remedy is a wife, but the remedy is not always sufficient. Some men do not marry, and some wives do not know how to criticize. Some women are adepts in criticism; but their husbands, being stiff-necked and rebellious, refuse to hearken to their strictures and admonitions. It is not uncommon for both the minister and his wife to tumble into the same ditch. What can you do? Will you write him an anonymous letter? Never! It is the work of a coward and a sneak. A minister who values his time will not read anonymous letters. Life is too short to waste it in reading communications whose writers are ashamed to own them. If a minister is foolish enough to read an anonymous fault-finding letter, he is almost sure to think it the production of some crank or knave, and consequently its appeal does not lead him to repentance. Do not write such letters. If you know something you are convinced that your pastor ought to know, stand up and say it to him like a man. "I withstood him to the face," says Paul, in describing the way in which he rebuked Peter. Paul knew how to censure as well as how to praise.

The object of Christian criticism is to edify. To edify is to build up. A man is not built up by criticism which he never hears. Consequently it is foolish to criticize a minister behind his back. Such disparagement may offer an outlet for one's bad humor, but it does not redound to the glory of God.

If the talk is carried on in the presence of children, it becomes a tenfold greater sin. What deeper wound can a parent inflict upon his child than to render the minister of religion ridiculous to him by laughing at his mannerisms or depreciating his intelligence or his piety! Children are easily prejudiced, and their hearts can be readily closed. They are naturally trustful and receptive, their affections are fresh, and their confidence in adults is unbounded. They give their hearts readily to those who are placed over them, and it is in their docility of heart that there lies the possibility of education and culture. To criticize in their presence those whose business it is to mold them destroys in them the very capacity which it is the duty of parents to safeguard and develop. The more deeply a child loves his pastor or teacher, the more he will learn from him. How can a boy be helped by a minister whom his father picks to pieces every Sunday? How can the life of a girl be molded by a man whose methods and attainments are constantly sneered at by her mother? Many parents have lamented in later life that their children did not join the church, not knowing how to account for such conduct, when the reason was that the children lost confidence in the church on account of the conversations they heard at the dinner table. No matter how limited in wisdom and goodness the minister may be, it is wicked to criticize him in the presence of boys and girls. The office of the minister of Christ is sacred, and the child-heart should be trained to reverence the office by being taught to honor the man who fills it.

Whenever, therefore, you want to censure your pastor, follow the directions given by the Lord in the eighteenth chapter of St. Matthew's Gospel. The minister is your brother, and if he has trespassed against you by actions which offend, go and tell him his fault between you and him alone. If he is willing to hear you, you have done both him and the church an invaluable service. But if he will not hear you, then take with you one or two more, that he may know your criticism is not a personal crotchet, but the sober judgment of representative members of the church. If he shall neglect to hear them, tell it unto the church. A minister too touchy and stubborn to listen to the counsel of his best people is a fit subject for church discipline. If he insists on acting like a heathen, he ought to be treated like one. Many a clergyman has injured his influence for years by some oddity of behavior or crudity of character which might have been corrected in a day had a few sane and substantial laymen been brave enough to call his attention to the thing wherein he gave offense.

19

The Minister's Wife

I knew you would want to talk about her—people always do. I do not blame you. I cannot refrain from saying a word about her myself. Since a man and his wife are one, no revelation of a minister would be complete which ignored or slighted the mistress of the manse.

Yes, she has a hard time, but not so hard as some of you imagine. Her tribulations have been greatly overestimated. When she has a harder time than other women, it is frequently her own fault. A parson's wife has unique opportunities for blundering. When such opportunities are numberless, it is a rare woman who is able to turn her back upon them all. Many a minister's wife makes herself wretched by attempting the impossible. It is impossible, for instance, to please everybody; and woe to the mortal foolish enough to attempt it. The chief end of woman is not to please people, but to do her duty. A failure to learn this has wrecked the happiness of many hearts. Or she may attempt to keep pace with her husband in pastoral calling. A woman who takes upon herself the pastoral work of a large parish need not be surprised to find herself, sooner or later, in a nervine hospital. God punishes women who break His law in a foolish ambition to satisfy public expectations. Or she may try to walk in the footsteps of her predecessor. This is a gratuitous method of self-immolation. No two women have the same nature, and it is foolish to wear one's self out in trying to do things simply because somebody else did them. Or she may allow the good women of the parish to place her on the twelve thrones of Israel—a proceeding which invariably invites disaster. Uneasy lies the head that wears twelve crowns! It is much better, as a rule, for a minister's wife to let other women sit on the thrones, while she takes her place among the loyal workers who engage in obscure and unofficial labors. Because a woman is married to a minister, it does not follow that she must be the president of every organization in the parish or preside at every public meeting which women may hold. No minister's wife should bear any more parish burdens than her own good sense tells her she ought to carry. To carry them simply because some good and officious sister thinks she ought to do it is consummate foolishness.

Much depends upon the way a minister's wife uses her tongue. It is not necessary for her to talk about her ideas of what a church has a right to expect of her. People will find out her ideas from her conduct. Ministers frequently start antagonisms on entering a parish by blowing a trumpet at the gate announcing to the faithful what they propose to do. If they would quietly do what they propose to do, and say nothing about it, there would be less friction and more progress. A minister's wife who blows a trumpet on entering the town, publishing what she will do and what she will not do, inevitably stirs up opposition which she will never be able to overcome. If she intends to perform marvelous feats, her intention should be kept a profound secret; if she proposes to shake off most of the burdens which the wives of clergymen usually carry, she should be exceedingly meek and say nothing. The people of the parish will allow a minister's wife to do practically what she pleases if she does not challenge their criticism by shouting from the housetop what she considers her privileges and rights. It is remarkable how sensible most Christians are if they are not provoked to act the fool. Just a spark of folly in the pastor or his wife will often kindle a conflagration of foolishness which no one can extinguish. Whenever you hear a clergyman or his life laying down in public the limits of their obligations and the extent of their duties, look out for a squall. If a minister and his wife offend not in tongue, the same are a perfect couple.

But the minister's wife is not always to blame. There are women in every parish who are adepts in the art of making the wife of the minister uncomfortable. They can call on her at all hours of the day, upsetting her plans and interrupting her work. They can everlastingly urge her to call on them. If she accepted every invitation to call, there would be no time left for anything else. They can repeat to her all the dismal stories afloat in the parish. They can insist upon her taking the leadership in every good cause, whether God created her for leadership or not. They can give her advice without being asked for it. They can say uncharitable things, and make damaging comparisons, and—

it would take a woman to enumerate all the things which women can do.

Let her alone. If she has children and wants to stay at home with them, let her do it. It is her right to do it. If she prefers to give her time to her husband, helping him in his correspondence and bearing the burden of household cares, let her do it. There are other kinds of Christian work besides work done at sewing bees and missionary meetings. It is work enough for any woman just taking care of a minister. If she is timid and retiring, let her alone. What right have you to haul her out in public places when every fiber of her being revolts against it? If she wants to dress plainly or superbly, let her alone. If her husband is satisfied, you ought to be. If, on the other hand, she insists on running everything—from her own kitchen up to the missionary convention—forgive her. Some women are made that way; they cannot help it. If she has an unbridled tongue, and persists in saying things which ought to be left unsaid, do not repeat them. A woman who rehearses through the parish the foolish remarks of injudicious women is more blameworthy than the women who first spoke them. If she has poor taste in dress and slight tact in conversation and scant ability in housekeeping, you cannot cure her by talking. Minister's wives are very much like their husbands—they are not perfect. They could, no doubt, have been created perfect, but God made them to match the men. It is not to be expected a woman should be your ideal minister's wife. It is sufficient that she be the ideal of her husband.

20

Impatience

But it is possible to be too bold. All virtues when pushed too far degenerate into vices. Excessive boldness is recklessness, and recklessness wrecks a church. Some ministers are so afraid of being cowards, they make themselves a nuisance by marching always on the warpath. They count a Sunday lost on which they do not preach a new crusade. Denunciation is their forte, and to scalp a hoary-headed sin is the aim of every sermon. But the human heart cannot live on anathemas. In the economy of preaching, as in that of nature, thunderbolts have their place; but in the pulpit, as in nature, there must be abundant sun and seasons filled with bloom and holy calm. The twenty-sixth chapter of Matthew's Gospel must be followed by the fourteenth chapter of John's. A man may be courageous when not trampling abominations under his feet. One may mistake an undue development of the red Indian in him for a manifestation of saving grace. Spunk is good, but the servant of the Lord must be something more than fighting cock or bulldog. Evils cannot be battered into dust by the ceaseless lashings of vociferous tongues: they are disintegrated by the atmosphere created by the unfolding of great ideas. Ministers must be patient.

When William Pitt declared that the quality most essential for a successful prime minister is patience, he gave utterance to words which contain a hint for every man whose business it is to work with men. No man, either in church or state, can carry beneficent enterprises to their consummation who lacks a patient spirit. Probably no other single sin works such havoc in the Christian church as the impatience of her ministers.

It is characteristic of average human nature to move but slowly toward those goals upon which Christ bids men set their eyes. It is likewise human to cling to customs old and tried, rather than to enter upon paths which are new. It is a minister's work to lead, not simply one man, but a company of men, from one position to another, and then another, along that upward and difficult road; and unless his spirit is held in firm restraint, he will not be able to brook delays or endure the oppositions and retrogressions which are sure to come.

A leader of men must be patient with them. Even the malcontents and the cranks must not be snubbed or squelched. Some ministers cannot endure the presence of even one man whose heart is not with them, and proceed forthwith to harry him out of the parish. Unless this man is gotten rid of, there can be no peace in the ministerial bosom. But in rooting out the offender, what damage may be wrought! The tares always grow close to the wheat, and one cannot be uprooted without damaging the other. If a preacher is only patient, Death may come to his assistance, and remove the tare without touching the wheat. A beautiful, indispensable friend is Death! He saves preachers from despair when they see certain parishioners flourish like a green bay tree.

If men's sins are to be patiently endured, much more worthy of gentle consideration are their stupidities and frailties. It is the province of the preacher to see the New Jerusalem hovering in the air, but he ought not to break the skulls of the saints in his haste to get the fair city squarely located on the earth. Every man who sees visions and dreams dreams cannot but yearn to have his parish far different from what it is, and to change whatever seems to hinder the free development of church life along the lines of largest usefulness is certainly a laudable ambition. But in making changes, a minister should ponder Josh Billings' counsel to young men, "If you want to get along quick, go slow." Because a thing is good, it does not follow the parish must have it before sunset. That the preacher wants it is not sufficient reason why the parish should bow sweetly and instantly to his will. Things which are accepted willingly are the only things which a minister can establish in his parish to the edification of his people. Whatever is forced upon them, even though excellent in itself, causes an irritation which offsets whatever service it might have been expected to render. The momentary gratification which comes to a man who succeeds in having his way is poor compensation when it is secured at the sacrifice of the sympathy and good will of the people. A minister ought to learn how to stand and wait. If a man is convinced in his own mind that a certain step is advantageous for his people, and his people will not let him take it, let him not lie down and turn his face to the wall, watering his couch with his tears, neither let him stride stormfully across his people's wishes doing the thing of which they disapprove, but let him be resolute and patient.

> Men's souls are narrow; let them grow,
> My brothers, we must wait.

A congregation is composed of pupils in various stages of development, and the wise preacher remembers this in the preparation of his sermons. The congregation is a flock of sheep. Many sheep can walk but slowly, some of the lambs must be carried, while an occasional old ram must be dealt with with discretion. It is the business of the shepherd to be ahead of his sheep, but he must not be so far in advance as to be out of sight. If he gets too far ahead, a sense of superiority may take possession of him, and this may pass into a feeling of contempt. New-found truth, says Carlyle, like new-got gold, burns the pockets until it is spent. The clerical miner who has been digging gold all week coins it and throws it down before his people on Sunday with an air which says, "If you do not accept this, you are benighted!"

Ministers should imitate the Holy Spirit and guide men into the truth. Too many of them try to take their hearers into truth on the jump. If a man has advanced ideas, he must give his people time to catch up with them. Many a good man, in his eagerness to display his emancipation from the past, has by his headlong impetuosity closed the hearts of his best people, and rendered impossible the achievement of that which was dearest to his heart.

Brethren, study the life of Jesus for the high art of reticence and reserve. "I have many things to say unto you but you cannot bear them now"; so he said, and says. The mind cannot be forced. New truth cannot be hammered into the heart, even by a man fresh from the seminary. Old interpretations are sloughed off and new conceptions find entrance into the mind only as the affections are enriched and the life is enlarged. This work is done by the Holy Spirit, and like all the work of God, it is carried on by processes which require time for their completion. If a man is willing to speak out in love the truth which has become certain to his soul, and has sense enough to abstain from scornful words of bygone teachers and traditional teachings, he can ordinarily preach what his people need without the slightest danger of precipitating an ecclesiastical earthquake.

Patience, then, is the queen of the ministerial virtues. Like the farmer, the preacher is engaged in a work which demands the exercise of all the powers of long-suffering, diligence, and protracted wakefulness and waiting. It is noteworthy that our Lord saw in the slow and stately operations of nature a revelation of the processes of spiritual growth, and to nature we must go for rare disclosures of the secrets of successful spiritual labor. To his disciples then and now and always the Son of God makes this declaration, "In your patience ye shall win your souls."

21

The Value of a Target

But let no man rail at the soil till he has examined his soul. Obstacles without are as nothing compared with hindrances within. Men sometimes disparage their parish when they ought to be cudgeling themselves. "I have a hard field!" The good man sighs, and on his sigh, as on a rug, lies down. The self-complacence of some men is colossal.

It is easier to lose one's way in the ministry than in any other calling. Many a man gropes hither and thither like a traveler lost in a fog. The vastness of the world in which the minister moves renders it easy for him to be vague. Theology itself is a boundless science, but it is only one of many which closely touch the preacher's work. In the library, as on the ocean, one is lost without a compass.

The details of administrative labor are multitudinous, and a man, unless clear-headed, will be swamped. A minister's work is of a routine character, and routine always tends to reduce the vitality of a propelling purpose. When the community expects a man to pray at stated seasons every week whether he is in the spirit of prayer or not, and at fixed intervals to give a discourse whether or not he has received a message, and to keep up his clocklike regularity straight onward through the years, it is not difficult to see that the exercises which began as means to lofty ends may at last become ends in themselves. The prayer which once was winged with a definite aim may become a spoke in a revolving wheel from whose turning neither the preacher nor anyone else expects results. The sermon which once thrilled with a burning purpose may dwindle into a display of verbal handiwork or a string of meaningless commonplaces with which to tie up a service. Even men who work prodigiously on their sermons may forget the end for which sermons ought to be prepared. To no one is sermon production easy, to many it is exhausting toil; and so intent sometimes does the worker become in the unfolding of his idea as to lose sight entirely of the work which the idea is meant to accomplish. The arrow is carefully and ingeniously fashioned and then shot at random into the air. The bullet is molded at great pains, but no target is visible to the marksman's eye. Preaching, which is, if rightly done, the most exacting and purposeful of all forms of labor, may easily become the most desultory and purposeless of all.

This lack of aim works havoc in a parish. The man without a goal seldom gets anywhere. The leader who knows not whither he wishes to go will land his followers in the ditch. A man is effective in the ministry, other things being equal, in proportion to the clearness of his purpose and the definiteness of his aim. This lack of intention reveals itself in the sermon. An aimless sermon breaks down the interest of a congregation and sends it home disheartened and confused. Men say to one another, "I do not know what he was driving at"—one of the saddest wails which ever escapes the lips of church attendants. Unless a man can make the purpose of his sermon stand out broad as a barn door, he ought to go into some work for which the Lord has fitted him. The very mission of the pulpit is to fire men's hearts and set them moving out to battle; but if the trumpet gives an uncertain sound, who will prepare himself for the conflict? Laymen frequently stand nonplussed at the close of a sermon, not knowing what they ought to think or what they ought to do.

This target-blindness also discloses itself in parish administration. If a minister has nothing definite in his mind, he is likely to organize a new society. There may be no need of it in the parish, and its creation may absorb vitality needed for the development of organizations already in existence; but to the clouded vision of a man without an aim a new society is always a thing to be desired, partly because it gives him opportunity to appear to be doing something when he is doing nothing and partly because a community is always ready to mistake the multiplication of wheels for an increased speed in the progress of the Lord's chariot. Probably half the organizations now in existence would never have cumbered the ground had it not been for the idle and fussy brains of men and women who care more for the manipulation of machinery than for the accomplishment of spiritual ends. Those whose heart is set on the attainment of definite results do not want to be weighted with unnecessary paraphernalia, and desire as little machinery as possible.

A clear-cut aim is the preacher's life preserver. A preacher without a purpose is worse off than a man without a country. The frequent pondering of a purpose braces the heart and energizes the will. No question should be oftener on the preacher's lips than, "To what purpose is this?" That is the question with which he should begin every sermon. On the first page he should write in clean, terse Saxon the precise work which this particular sermon is intended to do; and on the last page he should write his honest answer to the question: "Is this sermon so constructed as to be likely to accomplish the result for which it has been written?" The first and last pages of the sermon need not be given to the people, although if a minister has not the gift of clothing thought in garments of light, let him help his people by telling them frankly at the beginning just what his sermon aims to do, and at the close let him condense into one compact and memorable sentence the gist of all he has tried to say.

To what purpose? That is an improving question for men who lead in prayer. It is a knife which prunes away superfluous petitions. There would probably be fewer skeptics in regard to prayer if ministers had not prayed so abominably. The man who goes into the pulpit to dawdle aimlessly through a long series of meaningless and unrelated petitions is taking God's name in vain.

If a clergyman has lost his purpose, let him seek for it as for rubies and fine gold. When he finds it, let him use it day by day. Let no meeting be held, no society organized, no new enterprise launched, no campaign entered upon, no sermon preached, no prayer offered without a sharp and serious pondering of the question, For what purpose is this? There will be a new consternation in the ranks of the army of the Prince of Darkness when a larger number of the captains of the Lord's host come to realize more fully the necessity of keeping one's eyes on the target.

22

Building the Tower

A church likes to feel itself in the grip of a man who knows not only where he is going but also by what stages the goal can in all probability best be reached. Wretched indeed is the predicament of a congregation whose leader is a man with a higglety-pigglety mind and with no ascertainable ambition but to keep the sermonic mill grinding through the year.

A minister should live and move and have his being within the four corners of a far-reaching, constructive purpose. All his work should be done with an eye single to some one glorious end. Marvelous is the transfiguring power of a purpose held firmly in the preacher's mind. Language cuts with a keener edge. Ideas burn with a hotter flame. Sermons, no longer isolated and unrelated, become confederates in a holy cause, joining hand in hand to pull down the strongholds of evil and lift men to the upper heights. Some men's sermons are only bushwhackers fighting a desultory and bewildered skirmish, other men's sermons sweep through the year like a well-disciplined battalion going forth to fight the battles of the Lord. To one preacher sermons are variegated beads loosely strung together on Sabbatic thread; to another, they are constituent parts of an organic and growing whole. It is only when the sermons become connected chapters of a continuous story, the aim of which is clearly in the preacher's mind, that the heart-life of a congregation is symmetrically developed and the parish built up foursquare in righteousness.

Ministers of Christ are church builders, and the architectonic gift is one of the most valuable of the gifts bestowed by the Eternal Spirit. A preacher should have the instinct and skill of the builder. What materials and in what quantity and in what proportions and at what times and in what places—these are questions as important in spiritual church building as in the erection of structures of brick and steel; but they are questions which in many a parish are slighted or ignored. The Master said that any man about to build a tower ought first to calculate the cost. This preliminary investigation and estimate is an indispensable part of the work. The preacher is a tower builder, but not every preacher seems to be aware of the fact. The most patent fact to some men is that two new sermons must be gotten ready every week. Like avenging furies, these sermons drive their victims through the days and nights, and whether they will carry on and complete the work which preceding sermons have begun or prepare the way like John the Baptists for other sermons not yet arrived is a question for whose consideration the hurried hours allow no opportunity. A man thus harassed may become so absorbed in the work of preparing bricks and mortar for his tower that no time is left for the consideration of its architectural proportions or for a thought concerning the eternal laws in obedience to which all lasting structures must be built.

This lack of forethought and design is painfully apparent in many men whose gifts are conspicuous and whose success might be increased a hundredfold if they should form the habit of building the months and years into a plan. Such a habit systematizes the study and thought of the preacher and gives him a poise and power not otherwise obtainable.

It is the misfortune of many men that they fear to take hold of large things. Their texts and themes and outlooks and projects and problems are too small to develop themselves or inspire a congregation. A man may tempt himself by setting before him a block of five or ten years and saying to himself, "By the help of God I will carve out of this huge block of time the loveliest and greatest piece of work of which my powers are capable." By fixing his eyes, not on next Sunday, but on a Sunday ten years away, he will walk with a new tread under a new heaven and across a new earth.

Lift up your eyes then, Brethren, and take in the years which are to be. Every preacher ought to see clearly at least one year ahead of him. If he can see five, it is still better. If he blinds his eyes in the dust of the immediate present and allows life to become a haggard scramble for two new sermons for the coming Sabbath, he not only stunts his own intellectual development but dwarfs the spiritual stature of his church.

Every preacher should have a church year. This is well-nigh

indispensable. If he does not like the one laid down in the books of the churches which retain the traditions of the fathers, let him make one of his own. If he does not map out his Scripture lessons in advance, he will find himself reading the same passages again and again, passing over large sections of Holy Writ which his people need. It is only by painstaking planning that a minister can secure variety in his pulpit themes. Unless he takes time to recall his sermons of last year and to organize into a schedule the sermons of the coming year, he will almost invariably cultivate some narrow field to which his own tastes incline him, ignoring wide domains of revelation which are never neglected save at the sacrifice of health and growth. He will fail also to present truth in its true proportions. There are certain facts of the Christian revelation which ought to be presented to a congregaton every year. There are a few principles of conduct so central to Christianity and so vital to spiritual health that no year should pass without the preacher bringing to their unfoldment the united strength of all his powers. Without prearrangement these vital matters will be slurred or crowded completely out.

Not only are the phases of truth manifold, but the methods of presentation are almost numberless. These should be employed in such a way as to give variety and refreshment. Some preachers are intolerably monotonous because they invariably appeal to the same faculties and deal always with the same type of doctrine. If they would sit down at the beginning of each year and make a careful diagnosis of the spiritual condition of their people, the tempers to be nourished, the errors to be choked, the truths to be enthroned, the vices to be starved, the virtues to be cultivated, and then map out the year as a general outlines a campaign, appointing a definite number of sermons for the accomplishment of each particular design and arranging the sermons in a sequence which will secure both continuity and momentum—and at the same time allow relaxation both to the preacher and the hearer by calling into exercise new combinations of faculties by the presentation of diverse but related realms of truth—he will not only find himself doing his work with increased facility and joy, but he will see the spiritual life of his parish passing under his hand into those forms of beauty and power which he beheld first in vision and which by the co-operation of God are now embodied in the life of humanity to the glory of His blessed name.

23

Selfishness

The crowning glory of the character of Jesus was His unselfishness. "For their sakes I sanctify myself." In this golden sentence of His high-priestly prayer is expressed the disposition which shaped His conduct from Nazareth to Golgotha. If it is essential that the servant be as his master and the disciple as his Lord, then to every minister of Christ there comes the call to sanctify himself for the sake of his congregation. It is for his people that the true preacher lives and labors. To serve them is his cardinal ambition, his consummate joy. By serving them, he serves God. God and the people cannot be separated in the preacher's work. Thick-witted men occasionally get the notion that they can glorify God by preaching theology and at the same time scorn their congregation. By proclaiming in the pulpit unpalatable ideas in offensive ways, they pride themselves on serving God no matter how they hurt God's people. Indeed, a man may become so wrong-headed as to think that the further he gets from his people, the nearer he is to the Almighty. But if a man loves not his congregation whom he has seen, how can he love God whom he has not seen? If a minister says he loves God, and in his heart slights or despises his people, he is not only a liar but a murderer of the spiritual life of his parish.

This neglect of the people on the part of the minister is more common than one likes to acknowledge. Selfishness may crop out in a man's vocabulary. Because a minister is familiar with the language of German philosophers and Scotch metaphysicians, he may thoughtlessly use this dialect in addressing businessmen and farmers, servant girls and mechanics, uncaring whether they understand him or not. The man with the unselfish heart sanctifies his language for the sake of his people. He trims his sentences and simplifies his periods until his thought stands out, radiant and compelling, before every attentive mind. He makes himself of no reputation and takes upon him the form of a servant and is made in the likeness of a man. By humbling himself and becoming obedient to the law of the Cross, God highly exalts him by giving him access to the hearts of his hearers. A man of sympathy instinctively thinks of the limitations and needs of those with whom he deals. Paul always carried in his mind's eye the faces of the unlearned and the unbelieving. He insisted that a church service ought to be shaped with these people in mind. If they could not understand what was going on, they could take no part in the service and might think Christians out of their heads. He was hotly vehement in his denunciation of the selfishness which uses language that edifies the speaker but does not enlighten the hearers. In a burst of magnificent earnestness he says, ". . . in the church I had rather speak five words with my understanding, that by my voice I might teach others also, than ten thousand words in an unknown tongue." Would that this Pauline common sense were abundant in all our pulpits!

The choice of themes often bears witness to this same deep-seated sin. The true preacher lives for his people. To build them up is his supreme delight. For their sakes he shapes his reading and directs the main currents of his thought. Their aptitudes and attainments, their conscious wants and their unconscious needs, stand before him day and night like so many angels of the Lord, sent to tell him of what sort his sermons ought to be. But not every minister listens to these angels. Personal tastes are often followed, favorite lines of study are pursued with no consideration of the parish needs. Literary ambitions are cultivated and scholastic inclinations gratified in wicked disregard of everybody but the preacher himself. Such a man becomes a specialist, and while cultivating his speciality, his people pay the bills. They come to the house of God on the Lord's day hungry for bread, and instead of bread, they receive a discussion of a tangled problem in sociology, or the elaboration of a distinction which struck the peacher's fancy in his reading of the last new volume on ethics. It is advantageous and right for the preacher to have favorite studies and to set aside particular domains of learning for special cultivation, but over the gateway of this garden the words should be written, "For their sakes I sanctify myself," that both on entering and coming out of the garden he may be reminded of the obligation which surpasses all others and be saved from the selfishness which favorite studies so insidiously induce.

To persuade a clergyman to forsake his parish the Devil counts his greatest victory. If he can beguile him to scamper over the country, giving his strength and time to miscellaneous audiences while his own people remain at home, unshepherded and untrained, he wins a triumph over which the nether world rejoices. An English writer of note has said that the Devil in our day comes to ministers disguised as a railway train. He might have added that if a Pullman sleeper cannot catch a man, the printing press may. The prophet of the Lord may be seized with a mania for writing books. These books may have little relation to the gospel or to the needs of his congregation, but the chapters of these books may be worked off on unsuspecting and defenseless saints as sermons. It has happened more than once that a preacher has allowed his pulpit ministration to be determined largely by the demands of his publisher. A man who perpetrates the chapters of his next book on his people, not because his people need these chapters, but because his publisher can use them, may excuse himself by saying that in his books he can serve a larger audience than could be assembled inside his church walls. But the average layman who has not debauched his conscience by any such sophistical argumentation will say that the man who receives a salary from one set of people for time and strength which he habitually gives to others, and who uses the pulpit simply as a source of supplies while engaged in a work other than that which he has promised to perform, is a shirk and a scamp, even though he is a Doctor of Divinity and pursues his rascality for the avowed glory of God.

A minister owes much to his community, denomination, and country. The man who steadfastly stays at home refusing to turn a wheel or lift a burden outside his own little parish is the victim of a selfishness as loathsome as any of those above mentioned. Upon the Lord's wide work a minister must look with sympathetic eyes, and to many companies of brethren he must give himself, as occasion offers, with generosity and gladness. But he belongs first of all to his parish. The field in which he works is the world, and his church is the force with which he cultivates the field. To develop and consolidate this force and use it with increasing efficiency in subduing the world, this must be his supreme ambition, his constant study, his incessant care. To love his brethren over whom he has been appointed teacher and shepherd, this is the beginning and end of the whole matter. ". . . let us not love in word, neither in tongue; but in deed and in truth."

24

Autocracy

A witty New Englander has given the world a fascinating sketch of the Autocrat of the Breakfast Table, but no one has yet given us a full length portrait of the Autocrat of the Communion Table. The Communion Table is used in this connection as a symbol of clerical prerogative. No one can touch it but a minister. Not even lay officials can take the bread and wine until they have passed through clerical hands. There is here a distinguishing distinction which lifts the minister above his brethren; and all distinctions, however justifiable and necessary, have a tendency to feed the pope which comes into the world with every man.

The environment of a clergyman contains abundant nutriment for the nourishment of the papal proclivities of human nature. Not only is there a gulf between clergy and laity worn broad and deep in popular thought by the teaching of a thousand years, but a minister's work is of such a nature as constantly to give him the sense of importance and authority. Does he not speak for God? Is he not a successor of the apostles? Has not a sacred change been entrusted to his keeping? The very dignity of his work gives him a lofty-mindedness which easily passes into pride and makes him exceeding jealous of all outside interference.

Moreover, in his preaching, no one is allowed to contradict him. No matter what he says, the congregation sits dumb and acquiescing. Bitter protests may rise in the hearers' hearts, but they fall back dead, strangled in the silence. If laymen were allowed today the privileges they enjoyed in the time of Jesus, and could say to ministers, as they said to Him, right in the midst of the sermon, "You are crazy! What do you mean by this?" church decorum would be badly mangled, but the minister would be saved from a temptation which, like a beast, now crouches at his door. The practice of presenting to

234

people instruction on a variety of subjects without fear of open contradiction is apt to beget in any man who is not constantly on his guard a temper which Shakespeare takes off in the lines:

> I am Sir Oracle,
> And when I ope my lips, let no dog bark!

It is this immunity from contradiction on the Lord's day which renders many a minister so difficult to live with through the week. He cannot suffer opposition at any point in the entire circle of church administration. To differ from him is spiritual treason, to oppose him in any of his movements is to be a son of Belial.

It is this stripe of man who wants to run a church. He is sure to meet a layman who wants to run it too. And then—! But a church cannot be run by anybody except to its destruction. A church is an organism, and like all organisms, it refuses to be run. It will grow if carefully nourished and guided, but to run it is to wreck it. It is as delicate as a lily and as dependent on the law of freedom. The earth does not run the lily. It holds the lily tenderly by its roots and then gives it largest liberty to unfold in obedience to that mystic genius with which the lily is endowed. A church must receive nourishment from the preacher, but it is not for him to determine the shape of each petal or the precise length of its stem. Or to change the figure, a church is a family, and a family cannot be run. Some men try to do it, and the result is a tragedy which shows itself in the face of the wife and the disposition of the children. One can run a hotel but not a home. That home is happiest in which there is least visible constraint and most spontaneity and affection. A machine may be run, but not a household; a business enterprise, but not a church.

Some men now in the ministry were evidently intended for engineers or managers of railroads and trusts. They cannot free themselves from the conviction that the church is a machine which they are to run along a track of their own devising, to the destruction of every obstreperous layman who gets in their way. A church is a family, and wise is the minister who is content to let it grow. It is for him to create the atmosphere in which the lovely things of the spirit shall come to their best estate. From him must come much of the energy by which the church fulfils the law of its being, but he will often do most when to onlookers he seems to be doing least.

Happy is the man who has the faculty of so inspiring his church with the spirit of freedom and service that while he himself stands in the background, the church apparently moves of itself into enlarging circles of spiritual culture and achievement.

It is a fatal blunder for a minister to make the Decalogue and his own wishes equally binding on the consciences of his people. A preacher ought to prize with all diligence the men who differ from him and make use of their gifts up to the level of his opportunity. Every church ought to have in it men of all types of disposition and temper and opinion and culture and politics and theology. No one type ought to be suppressed in the interest of a deadening uniformity or for the purpose of securing universal harmony with the preacher. It is the business of a minister to make his church roomy. He must be the friend of the radical and of the conservative, of the orthodox and the heretic, of the zealous and the phlegmatic, of the sane and the crotchety, of the popular and the friendless, of the man who is with him and the man also who is against him, making himself all things to all men that he may do them good. For him to drive out the men who do not agree with his theology or politics, or refuse to fall in with his favorite enterprizes, is to rob the church of its virility and originality and cripple it hopelessly in the work it aims to do.

A minister must learn to labor and submit. Cromwell's dictum is worth remembering, "In yielding there is wisdom." Even a good man is not infallible, and the stars will not fall from heaven though the preacher fails to get his way. The things which a church ought to have will come to us, not by pushing, but by waiting. Horace Bushnell late in life said that could he live his life over again, he would never push. The fable of the sun and wind making a wager as to their ability to compel a traveler to remove his cloak is not without significance for the man who would deal successfully with men. The minister who, in order to induce his people to throw off habits or notions which he does not like, converts himself into a cold northeaster, filling Sunday mornings with his icy blasts, will not succeed in the thing which he aims at and may possibly blow himself out of the pulpit.

25

Discontent

When Paul assured the Philippians that he had learned in whatever state he was therewith to be content, he confessed a higher state of grace than many of the successors of the apostles have yet attained. Discontent may be said to be one of the prevailing sins of the ministerial world. How prevalent it is, the public does not fully know, for ministers who are discontented do not shout their dissatisfaction from the housetop. They write it in bulky letters and send it in sealed packages to their ministerial brethren. The number of preachers now wishing a change of pastorate cannot be accurately computed, but if all the facts were known, the world would be astounded. Men in the East, fretted by the stereotyped customs of fossilized communities, look with longing toward the West, with dreams of the blessedness that must belong to ministers who can take a forward step without cracking their skull against a precedent. Toilers in the West, sick of the unchartered freedom of a population disinclined to submit to yokes either of God or men, wish themselves in the East, where church-going is an established custom and life runs smoothly in channels made for it by the fathers. Preachers in rural places look with hungry eyes toward the city, where pulpit gifts and graces meet with grateful appreciation; and preachers in one city look toward another city, where the mountains have been apparently leveled and the ways of the Lord have been made straight. Of a host of clergymen it may be said, as one has written of the patriarchs, that they are strangers and pilgrims on the earth, and declare plainly that they seek a country.

In justice to the clergy it must be said that ambition is not generally the inciting cause of this restlessness. The popular impression that the average clergyman stands on tiptoe, eager to heed the beckoning of the first parish which offers a larger salary or a softer bed of roses, is as malicious as it is false. The explanation of the desire to escape from one parish to another may usually be found in the fact that ministers, like other mortals, do not like to be uncomfortable, and one sees fewer brambles in a garden which some other man has cultivated than in the garden in which one works himself. Every parish has in it men and women with whom it is difficult to live, and every church has problems which are a burden to the heart. Some men are so constituted that they cannot carry heavy burdens or face circumstances which prick like thorns. Their first impulse on the sight of any difficulty is to run.

A man never knows a parish until he gets fairly settled in it. The years bring out the skeletons as the night brings out the stars. A few church skeletons are as terrible to a timid clergyman as graveyard ghosts to a small boy after dark. He may find to his dismay ancient quarrels which have been smoldering several generations and which at his first important movement blaze out in a conflagration which threatens to burn up the church. He may find a set of rogues in his official board, or a good-sized Pharaoh in the broad aisle. The church may be tied hand and foot by the pagan notions of a heathen clique, or the choir may be in a state of ferment sufficient to drive the spirit of devotion from every service. Grayheaded men with antique ideas may frown down every suggested step of progress, captious critics may carp at this theology, rhetoric, or necktie. Euodias and Syntyche may heat the atmosphere to torrid temperatures because they cannot be of the same mind in the Lord, prominent pew-holders may give up their pews and disgruntled workers may resign their offices—in short, the church may have so many devils in it as to lead the unhappy preacher to question whether by any amount of prayer and fasting on his part the unhallowed brood can be cast out. A man in such circumstances may honestly wonder whether he is the one who is intended to redeem Israel or whether this particular parish ought not to look for another.

There are times when the trouble is the outcome of an evident misfit. When this is the case, the minister should promptly shake the dust from his shoes, for there are other towns and cities in which the gospel must be preached. But a minister should not too hastily conclude that because things are not altogether pleasant, the Lord has need of him elsewhere. Unless the signs of an irreparable misfit are numerous and unmistakable, the minister ought to set his hand resolutely to the plow and not look back until the furrow has been finished. It is not becoming in a prophet to run at the sight of trials. It shows fickleness of heart to accept a church and then drop it in the first fit of despondency. If he accepts the care of a parish in need of a surgical operation, let him perform it and give the wounds time to heal before he turns the patient over to a new practitioner.

Honorable men will not toy with churches. There is something of the sacredness of marriage in the pastoral relation, and when once entered on, it is for better or for worse. Short pastorates are unfortunate both for pastors and people. They develop in clergymen and laymen dispositions hurtful to spiritual growth. If a man knows he has but a short time in a parish, he is tempted to do the things which are easiest and cheapest. He will not enter deeply into the hearts of his people, but will be in danger of looking upon all laymen as so many pawns to be manipulated in an interesting game of ecclesiastical chess. It is the long pastorate which draws on the fountains which are deepest and which builds up in congregation and pastor those elements of character in which the New Testament exults and rejoices. A man who expects to live with the same people through many years will have every incentive to be sane and industrious, far-sighted and true. He will not hesitate to enter upon schemes of education and training which can be completed only in long periods of time; and his life, blending more and more with the life of his people, will grow richer and fuller unto the perfect day.

Be content wherever you are, my brother, and whether you abound or are in want, be not hasty to take up arms against a sea of troubles and attempt to end them by running away. For in that change of place what dreams may come and rough awakenings who knows! It may be your present parish is obscure, but blessed is the man with grace sufficient to grow in the shade. It is said that the chief reason why the sugar maple makes up a great part of the native forests of New England is that the maple is willing to grow in the shade. It is taking precedence of all other trees because a young maple is always in training, ready to take the place of any tree which may die. Go to the maple, young preacher, consider her ways and be wise. In a few years the great trees of the clerical forest will lie low, and your final place will depend in large measure on your present willingness to grow in the shade.

26

Near to Men, Near to God

It is not good for a man to live alone. He belongs to humanity, and only in close relation with his fellows does he realize the life for which he was created. The highest virtues and sweetest graces grow only in an atmosphere made warm by human fellowship. Isolation, like a blighting frost, nips spiritual aspirations in the bud. A man may be a pagan alone; he cannot be a Christian. It is where two or three are together that Christianity promises a life which is divine.

A preacher of Christianity must live as close as possible to men. Isolation to him is fatal. If he has a disposition which shrinks from the society of others, his disposition must be born again. Young men in whom the literary instinct is strong and the literary ambition, stronger still, sometimes enter the ministry determined to be strong— as they say—in the pulpit, and suppose that it is by the constant poring over learned volumes that pulpit greatness can be achieved. Shutting themselves up in their study, they proceed to dig in a dozen different fields of learning, leaving untouched the very field in which the pearl of great price is hid. It is with reluctance that they lay aside their books to go among the people, and every hour given to parochial visitation is bitterly begrudged. Among their books they are serene and happy; among God's children they are restless and forlorn. By pampering this disposition, a man may come at last to have a horror of entering the homes of his people and may secretly despise the very souls he is sent into the world to love.

Knowing men is the preacher's first and most important business. To know them he must be with them. It is not enough to know man, he must know men. He can study man in his library, but he must study men in his parish. It is one thing to know human nature as portrayed in books and another thing to know it at first hand. Europe in books is not more different from the Europe which the tourist sees and hears and feels than is the man whom we read about different from the man whom we meet in the streets. It is the man in the street whom the preacher must know, and if he does not know him, no other sort of knowledge will make him a successful preacher. There are two volumes to which a preacher must give his days and nights, his Bible and his parish. A knowledge of the second is not a whit less important than is a mastery of the first.

According to the New Testament the minister is a servant. His rank in the Kingdom is determined by his proficiency in service. A man who desires to be "great" in the pulpit must be first of all a minister, and if he has an ambition to be chief, he must be the servant of all. If a preacher really deserves to serve his people, he will not count time lost which is spent in their company. The closer he comes to them, the larger his opportunity to give them what they need. What they are fearing and hoping, feeling and thinking, enjoying and suffering, loving and hating, reading and dreaming—all this can become known to him only as he comes into contact with them, and to know these things is more important than to know nine-tenths of all the books can teach. It is because men love to luxuriate in the "quiet air of delightful studies," and "to suck the sweets of sweet philosophy," or are ambitious to shine as oratorical or literary stars, that they come to underestimate the value of pastoral visitation and place a knowledge of books above the love of men.

But it is for the preacher's own advantage that communion with his people may be most strongly urged. He needs the people even more than they need him. As a preacher he is maimed unless he has warm and tender sympathies, and how are these to be maintained unless he lives close to men? Men who aim to keep the Godward side of their soul open while the manward side remains shut aim at the impossible. It is the fundamental doctrine of the New Testament that we approach God only through humanity. According to Jesus right relations with man precede all the forms of worship. According to John we know we have passed from death to life only when we love the brethren. If the world is to know that men are Christ's disciples because they love one another, then a minister's self-denying affection for his people is the one supreme test of his right to be counted a faithful servant of the Lord.

From his parish he will glean ideas and also gather nutriment with which to feed all his powers of feeling. One half day spent close to ordinary mortals will give a man more clear and helpful thoughts than can be found in the last learned book, no matter who the author. Men are better any day than books. They are written all over by the finger of God, and happy the man who can read this living revelation edited down to date.

If a pastor neglects his people for his books, he pays dearly for his sins. Not only does he lose that keenness of sensibility and tenderness of sympathy which give sparkle and warmth to the sermon, but like a man who has lost his way, he wanders in a realm of ideas foreign to the lives of his people. His vocabulary will sound like that of a man from far-off regions. By his mouth he is condemned. He may try to induce his congregation to believe that he cares for it, but the tell-tale words with which he builds his sermons will cry out against him. Worst of all, he will have in his own heart a hunger which is never satisfied, and will find the satisfactions of the ministry grow less with the increasing years.

The joy of life lies in one's relations with his fellowmen. If a minister is not taking his people deeper into his heart, and if he is not constantly growing deeper into theirs, his life will grow increasingly monotonous and he will be likely to be one of the notorious one hundred who apply for every vacant pulpit. To sit in one's study grinding out great ideas, that to a young man seems the road to pulpit greatness; but in later years he learns that pulpit greatness is not the knack of playing with ideas but the power of expressing a loving message in familiar words and throwing around it an atmosphere of fire. In short, it is the gospel of love which the preacher is most in need of. Not until he loves is he truly born of God. "In the government of nations," said Cromwell, "that which is to be looked after is the affection of the people"; and no less is true in the government and leadership of churches. A recluse may by unusual gifts of speaking win a short-lived admiration by extraordinary pulpit feats, but it is the man who sincerely loves his people and who is sincerely loved by them who most surely molds their temper and turns their feet into the way of life.

27

Unconscious Decay

It is the nature of many of the most vital and transforming of the spiritual processes to take place below the reach of consciousness. A man growing better does not measure the stages of his progress, nor does a man becoming worse realize the headway of his descent. There are things which are hidden from the vision of both saints and sinners. Their eyes are holden so they cannot see them. Thus Moses after his long communion with the Eternal came down from the mountain with a glory on his face, but "Moses wist not that . . . his face shone." What was evident to others was concealed from him. Likewise, Samson after that the Spirit of the Lord had departed from him "wist not that the Lord was departed." This awful fact did not break upon him until by the failure of doing things which formerly he had done with ease, he found himself impotent and humiliated in the presence of his foes.

The processes of life and death run on today, held in the grip of laws established at the beginning, and many a Moses illumines his people with a glory of which he himself does not dream, while many a Samson, with great deeds behind him, still marches boldly against the Philistines, not realizing that the spirit of the Lord goes with him now no more.

It is for this reason that many of the professional apostles of the so-called higher life do not win the confidence of the discerning. They talk too much. The man who says, "Look at me, see how my face shines!" closes our ears to his argument for holiness by the imprudence of his vainglorious invitation. Self-consciousness and lofty spiritual attainments do not go together. Men who live nearest to the heart of God do not prate of their visions nor boast of the light in their face.

We cannot fail to be suspicious likewise of the Samsons who lose the power of conquering but in their weakness go on boasting as if they were still able to carry off the gates of Gaza. Because a man is once a preacher, it does not follow that he is always a preacher. A man may lose his heavenly credentials although he continues to write "Reverend" in front of his name. The descent to Sheol is easy, and for the minister, as for all mortals, the way is always open. It is not closed on Sundays, and no broader entrance opens into it than from the pulpit platform. It is the truth even as Father John has written it, "our old man is constantly present with us, tempting us, snaring us, corrupting us, destroying us." The deterioration of spiritual life in men ordained to preach the gospel is one of the saddest of all the mysteries of sin. Like Judas, men for a while cast out devils and then fall by a devil themselves.

Always some one besetting sin lies at the root of the tragedy. The wages of sin is death in all circumstances and generations. Ministers escape exposure longer than most men because their sins are in general sins of the spirit rather than of the flesh, and hence bring only spiritual retribution. They who sow to the flesh reap corruption. Gluttony and drunkenness and licentiousness—these sins are evident going before to judgment; but these are not the sins which entrap and slay the leaders of the church. Ministers, with rare exceptions, fall by the hands of enemies no less fatal but far more insidious and respectable—pride, selfishness, envy, covetousness, laziness, ambition, these and a host of others. The sinner is not exposed to sudden and spectacular ruin, he dies piecemeal. Unconscious of the progress of the processes of moral disintegration, he suffers as the paralytic suffers by a progressive loss of sensibility and power. Who does not know ministers of the gospel who once were favored and mighty men and of whom the world now says, "How are the mighty fallen!" They are still in the pulpit, but their usefulness has ended. Their sermons are sounding brass and worse. Their prayers are useless as the prayers of the priests of Baal. What they say has no influence on their congregation, for their voice has lost the subtle and commanding accent of spiritual veracity. When one comes to know these men in the privacy of their own personal life the cause of the decay of spiritual power becomes clear. They are ministers, but they are not good men. They are petty or niggardly or stingy or lazy or censorious or pretentious or pessimistic or sour. The light and joy have gone out of their own soul and therefore power has gone out of their preaching. Their failure in the pulpit is to them a mystery, but it is not a mystery to any one who knows them and understands the conditions of spiritual power.

The deadline, then, is a terrible reality which ministers of all ages need fear and shun. Some men die earlier, others die later, the date is determined by the rate of progress of their sin. Only a man genuinely good can be a minister of power to the end of the day. All others are sooner or later overtaken and overwhelmed.

Nothing is more tragic than the spectacle of a minister who began his career with men eager to hear him, preaching at last to a world unresponsive to his message. The world to such a man is an insoluble enigma. Why he should fail while other men succeed is a tormenting problem. He compares himself with his successful brethren and in no whit does he seem to fall behind the chief of them. He has gone through college, and completed a seminary course, and read shelves of books and studied elocution under a dozen teachers, and therefore why should he not succeed? He frames his diplomas and reads over his ordination papers. These are regular and valid, and therefore wide doors of usefulness ought to open. He compares his sermons with those of men to whom the world seem glad to listen, and in illustrations, ideas, rhetorical finish, logical force, homiletical art, his sermons are fully equal and in many points superior to all. He picks up the name of a favored preacher and says, "Why should his name be sounded more than mine? Speak them, mine doth become the mouth as well. Weigh them, mine is as heavy. Now in the name of all the gods at once, upon what meat doth this our Chrysostom feed that he is grown so great!"

Poor man, he has left out of consideration the one thing essential —the Spirit of God. It is not by rhetorical might nor by logical power but by the breath of the Spirit that congregations are swayed and the gates of the Kingdom thrown open. And this only a good man can have. Sermons are like salt; they have a color and texture and weight, but all these are as nothing unless there goes along with them a savor. If the sermons have lost their savor, no matter what may be their rhetoric or logic or thought, they are good for nothing but to be trodden under foot of men. For ministers then as well as for laymen, the words of the Hebrew preacher have abiding significance.

Fear God, and keep his commandments: for this is the whole duty of man.

28

To Fathers

"I write unto to you, fathers, because . . ." I JOHN 2:13

The apostle wrote to fathers who were interested in Jesus Christ. They had a rich store of spiritual experience, and could therefore appreciate the significance of what he had to say. I purpose writing to a larger company of fathers, not only to those who are confessed followers of the Son of God, but also to many who are without spiritual experience, and who care little for the cause of organized Christianity.

It is often assumed that religion is chiefly intended for women. They are the so-called weaker sex, and religion is supposed to be one of their indispensable supports. It is counted axiomatic in certain quarters that women are naturally more religious than men, probably because they outnumber the men in the churches and are foremost in all forms of church work. Let a man attend to business, and the woman look after the religious interests of the home: this seems to be a division of labor which commends itself to the sound judgment of multitudes of sensible men. It brings a certain sense of relief to many a man to feel that piety is not his forte, and that his religious obligations can be successfully shifted to the shoulders of his wife.

There is no sanction for this, however, in the Bible. The Bible does not seem to be conscious of any native lack of religious capacity in the male sex. It everywhere assumes that men as well as women are naturally religious, and it holds them both alike to a strict accountability for the way in which they perform their religious duties. Religion, according to the prophets and apostles, is not exclusively a feminine affair. It belongs also to men. The Bible was written by men, and it has a message level to men's deeds. Jesus of Nazareth preached chiefly to men, and it was on the shoulders of twelve men that He laid the burden of bringing the world to God.

RELIGIOUS SHIRKERS

It is an extraordinary fact that so many American men should be willing to shirk their religious obligations. They do it habitually, and many of them, without compunction. Religion to them is merely an elective, and they pass it by without sense of loss. In the days of courtship they may be found in the church, but after the wedding day they attend church less frequently, and by and by drop out altogether. This constitutes for many a woman her first serious domestic problem. She does not know what her duty is. She loves the church, and she also loves her husband. If he prefers to stay at home, she is likely to stay with him. In this way many a woman crucifies her spiritual inclinations and sinks down into the indifference of a worldly life.

The tragedy deepens when children come into the home. The bringing up of a child is a colossal task. Both father and mother are needed for the work. Each has something to contribute which the other cannot give. If either contribution is withheld, the character of the child is marred. The religious education of a child is the most important feature of his bringing up. What he thinks of God and his relationship to God is of more moment than anything he can learn out of the books at school. No matter how extensive his intellectual culture, his nature is stunted unless his heart has been trained to reverence and adoration and his spirit has been disciplined to obedience to the will and ways of God.

If a child does not receive a religious education in his home, where is he likely to obtain it? If his own father is not interested in this sort of education, or if he rolls the responsibility of imparting religious knowledge upon the shoulders of somebody else, he is recreant to the highest of all parental duties, and must stand condemned before the judgment bar of God.

It is not uncommon for a man to leave the religious education of his children entirely to his wife. This is often done even in cases where the man is professedly religious. A believer himself in the Christian revelation, he makes no effort to impart his faith to his children. It is the mother who teaches the children to pray, who trains them in the reading of the Bible, who encourages them to go to church, and who manifests a solicitude in the development of their religious life. It is a long and difficult, and oftentimes a discouraging, task, even when both father and mother work together at it; but it becomes far more baffling and disheartening when the woman is left to work at it alone. For the example of the father often counts for more, at least with boys, than the precepts of the mother.

THE FATHER'S EXAMPLE

In the earlier years, children can be controlled by their mother; but by and by there comes a time when they begin to note the conduct of the father. No eyes are keener than the eyes of a child. He sees everything the father does; he reflects on what the father does not do. His logic is inexorable. He argues his way to conclusions which cannot be shaken.

If his father does not pray, prayer must be unnecessary. Grown men surely know what is needed. If his father never reads the Bible, then the Big Book can be dispensed with. Fathers know what books are worth reading. If he does not go to church, then church attendance is a pastime and not a duty, for men so old and wise as Father is would not neglect church if church were of value to them. If he never talks of God or Christ or the Holy Spirit, if he shows no interest in the Bible or church or Christian work, the inference is clear and certain that religion is not a vital part of human life. The reasoning of a child is unanswerable. It is not what children are told from time to time but what they see in the lives of their parents from day to day which makes the deepest impression on their characters. A man can pull down by his conduct all that the saintliest woman can build up by her instruction.

But to the Christian fathers also I write. You, too, are in need of admonition. I write only the things which you already know. But repetition is wholesome, and it is a good thing to stir the mind up by way of remembrance. A man in his home may feel secure from the cold-eyed scrutiny of the world, but if he have children, he is subjected to a gaze almost as piercing as the eyes of God. Is there anything which escapes the eyes of a child? Who is quicker to note inconsistencies, and to detect hypocrisies? A man's piety is no better than that which he displays at home. In every home the judgment seat is set, and he who sits upon it is a little child. A failure to measure up to one's professions is always humiliating, but it becomes altogether galling in the presence of children who look up to us and trust us.

HYPOCRISY'S COST

Hypocrisy is always ruinous, but nowhere does it work such frightful havoc as in the home. If the children see that religion is a coat put on at church and taken off as soon as the front door is shut, then all religion is made to seem to them a show or sham, and they lose confidence in the world's foundations.

One of the mysteries of sin is that many men are better in public than they are within ther homes. In the presence of strangers they are courteous, considerate, and obliging, whereas in the home they are selfish, heedless, and boorish. Conduct of which they would be incapable in the presence of business comrades they are addicted to in the presence of their children. Foolish explosions of temper, of which they would be ashamed should a passing stranger glance in and see it, cause them no remorse because they are witnessed by no one but their children.

Church attendance is important, but still more important is what takes place in the home before and after the hour of public worship. Family prayers are beneficial, provided they are offered in an atmosphere which is kept clean and sweet by the daily practice of the Christian virtues. Christianity never seems so revolting as when its ceremonies are stuck into a life that is habitually pagan. It is the example of the father which the boys copy, and not his professed principles. Many a father has found it impossible to continue his warnings against tobacco with a cigar or pipe in his mouth. It is useless to caution a boy against the insidious danger of alcohol so long as wine is served daily on the table. The reason so much parental instruction comes to nothing is because it is not backed up by a course of consistent living.

Whatever grown folks may be, children are genuine and true. They speak out bluntly the thing that is in them, and allow their feelings to express themselves completely in their acts. If the parents are playing a part, the children are certain to know it. If in the realm of religion father and mother are actors, the very name of religion becomes revolting to the unspoiled youthful heart.

Now in his home a man shows his innermost self in the way he treats his wife. If he is a coarse-grained, selfish boor, his boorishness will come out in his conduct toward her. If he is a Christian gentleman, he will have daily opportunities to prove it in his attitude to her.

Of all the tyrants on earth a tyrannical husband is the most despicable. A man who lords it over a woman, keeping her painfully conscious of her daily dependence on him, holding all the money in his hand, and doling it out to her in reluctant pittances as though she were a beggar, insulting her by disparaging remarks in the presence of her children, is a man who deserves the whipping post.

In the treatment of his children, also, the man's innermost soul stands revealed. There are men who do not know how to deal with children, and then make no honest effort to learn. Their entire course of parental conduct is a blunder. In some cases they simply ignore their children, making no effort to enter into companionship with them. In other cases they recognize their existence, but only by way of occasional reprimand or condemnation. If their children do well, no word of commendation is ever forthcoming.

The highest distinction ever conferred upon fatherhood was conferred by Jesus of Nazareth. When He went in search of a word by which to name the character of the Eternal, He chose the word "Father." This word, in His judgment, more nearly adequately expresses the nature of the Infinite than any other word in human speech. God is our Father, immeasurably wiser and nobler and more loving than any earthly father can be, and yet fatherhood as we know it is the best obtainable symbol by which to picture to our imagination the disposition of God. Fatherhood in the Hebrew race had been so cleansed and ennobled by a long line of faithful and loving fathers that Jesus could take the word "Father" as the best possible word for suggesting the attitude and character of God. When we are worried about things that are essential to us, we are to remember that our "Father" is fully conscious of our needs. When we go down into the valley of the shadow, we are to comfort ourselves with the thought that we are in our "Father's house" and that it contains many rooms. Earthly fatherhood gives us insight into the fatherhood of God.

Every man, therefore, who by his life adds luster to the idea of fatherhood, makes it easier for mankind to believe in God. The more beautiful earthly fatherhood becomes, the more attractive seems the fatherhood of God. No sadder letters ever come to a minister than those written by persons who confess that they find no comfort in thinking of God as their Father, because of the distressing experiences they had in their childhood home. Their father was unfaithful, or cruel, or repulsive, and through him the name "father" has become so stained and degraded that it seems a profanation to apply it to the Creator of mankind. The memories of the early years are so bitter and depressing that even the Lord's Prayer is marred for them by the introduction of the word "father." What greater wrong can a man commit on earth than to live such a life before his children, that in after years they shudder at the very thought of calling God their Father?

ST. PAUL'S EXHORTATION

Let us listen, then, again to Paul's noble exhortation: "Husbands, love your wives, even as Christ also loved the church, and gave himself for it; . . . fathers, provoke not your children to wrath: but nurture them in the chastening and admonition of the Lord." Husbands still need to be reminded that the spirit of self-sacrifice lies at the heart of love. Fathers need to be told again that the child can be so often found fault with that he loses hope of being able to do better.

It is not the mother alone who is to be patient and kind and forbearing. This is the duty of the father, also. He is to crucify his overbearing manner and his irascible disposition, and become the affectionate companion of his sons and daughters. He must do more than this. He must bring them up, not simply in the knowledge of arts and sciences, but in the things of the spirit. He must join with his wife in the work of shaping the religious conceptions and purposes of his children. He must educate them in the chastening and admonition which the Son of God prescribes.

What is the greatest fortune a man can leave his children? A bag of gold? No. An honorable man? No. The best of fortunes is a parental example which makes it easy to believe in the fatherly goodness of God. The crowning achievement of a man upon earth is to make the word "father" so rich in memories and associations that it brings God nearer to his children and opens for them the gates of heaven.

29

To Mothers

". . . all her household are clothed with scarlet." PROVERBS 31:21

The man who made the collection of proverbs contained in our Bible included in his volume a sketch of the ideal woman. She is a wife and mother. The Hebrew mind never questioned the fact that married life is the normal life for men and women on this earth, and that a home is incomplete without children. A woman's highest career—so the Hebrew was convinced—lies in the home. She comes to the fullest realization of herself in motherhood. Her supreme work is caring for her family. Her chief jewels are her sons and daughters. The richest contributions she makes to the world are the immortal beings she molds and trains.

This is not only the Hebrew view, it is the human, universal, everlasting view. Whenever this conception is repudiated, the life of society is bound in shallows and in miseries.

The outstanding feature of the woman who looks out on us from the book of Proverbs is her efficiency as a homemaker. It is she by whom the family is nourished. She spreads the table in the presence of her husband and children:

"She giveth . . . food to her household."

She not only feeds her family, she clothes it. She protects it from the weather. She keeps in mind not only its comfort but also its appearance. She makes it brightly beautiful. Her children are a feast to the eyes:

". . . all her household are clothed with scarlet."

In clothing her children, she does not neglect her own appearance. Having dressed her daughters in scarlet, she does not array herself in drab. She also is beautiful to look at:

"Her clothing is fine linen and purple."

But dress alone does not make a woman. Her adorning must not be "the outward adorning of braiding the hair, and of wearing jewels of gold, or of putting on apparel." She must be adorned with the graces of a lovely heart, and her crowning beauty lies in her disposition:

"Strength and dignity are her clothing."

Weakness is not an essential element of womanhood. To be feminine does not mean to be feeble. A woman's strength must possess charm. It must have in it the suggestion of royalty, the distinctive grace of queenliness. Her soul is calm. She is not agitated by constant fears, nor consumed by petty worries. She faces life with a courageous heart:

"She laugheth at the time to come."

She is neither frivolous nor sarcastic. Her conversation is seasoned with salt. It gives life fresh tonic. She does not talk an infinite deal of nothing, nor does she habitually occupy her mind with trifles. She is as gracious as she is sensible. She does not use words which stab and cut. She is gentle in her speech, and genial and generous in her judgments.

"She openeth her mouth with wisdom; and the law of kindness is on her tongue."

Industriousness is one of her shining virtues. She is never idle. She looks after her home with a fidelity which never fails. Early and late she gives herself to her calling:

"She riseth . . . while it is yet night, . . . her lamp goes not out by night."

She has a great work to do, and she does not shirk it. She constantly studies the comfort and happiness of the little kingdom of which she is the anointed queen:

"She looketh well to the ways of her household, and eateth not the bread of idleness."

But her horizon is not formed by the four walls of her home. She owes a debt to the outside world, and pays it. She is not unmindful of the great poverty which lies beyond her door. Her heart goes out in sympathy to those who need her, and her hands give help to those who cannot help themselves:

"She stretcheth out her hand to the poor; Yea, she reacheth forth her hands to the needy."

The result of it all is that she wins and holds the hearts of her husband and children. She sways them by what she does, and still more by what she is. She is a true woman, and does a true woman's work, and great is her reward:

"Her children rise up, and call her blessed; her husband also, and he praiseth her."

Nor is her praise confined to those who are nearest to her. Poets and orators, philosophers and sages, unite in eulogizing her. The heart of mankind exclaims:

"Give her of the fruit of her hands; and let her works praise her in the gates."

THE IDEAL PORTRAIT

What page of the Bible might a woman more profitably keep before her than this page of the ancient book of Proverbs! Centuries have passed since the portrait was painted, but the colors have not faded, and the world, gazing on it, still exclaims, "This is ideal!"

Fierce is the light which beats upon the modern home. The gaze of the world is fixed upon it. It has been discovered by the scientific students of social problems that nearly all our woes flow from defective homes. Our thorns and thistles are rooted in the family. Our tragedies are largely created by fathers and mothers unequal to their task. It is because family life is what it is that social life is what it is. It is because parents are what they are that children in thousands of instances fall far short of the world's expectations. Fathers are notoriously delinquent, and mothers are by no means guiltless.

Housekeeping is a fine and difficult art, and demands a large and trained intelligence. Thousands of mothers are distressingly ignorant. They do not know the elementary laws of health. They know nothing whatever of hygiene. No wonder they are semi-invalids and bequeath their infirmities to their children. They do not know how to cook, or sew, or keep house. They can do all these things bunglingly, but not superbly. Their ignorance of things psychological matches their ignorance of things physical. They understand neither the body nor the mind of a growing child. They do not know how to feed children, or how to manage them, or how to train them. Such ignorance is unpardonable. We live in a day of schools and books. Information on every department of a woman's work is abundant and within easy reach. If a homemaker remains ignorant, it is due to intellectual sloth or lack of ambition to fit herself for the work to which she is called.

KNOWLEDGE AND LOVE

But knowledge is not enough. A mother may understand all mysteries and all knowledge, but if she has not love, she is nothing. Strange to say, some mothers seem to be deficient in love. At least their love is not the sort which enables them to lay down their life for others. It is a divine law that only as one loses himself is it possible for him to find himself. Not a few mothers are afraid to lose themselves. They have lofty notions of their social or artistic or literary gifts, and strong ambitions to develop these to the utmost. They begrudge every moment they give to their children. They hand them over to governesses and nurses, and at the earliest possible moment send them off to boarding school. In this way they rob themselves of that enrichment of affection and discipline of spirit which God has provided for mothers who faithfully perform their duties. They lose also the highest raptures which a mother's heart can know.

Mothers who are unwilling to be bothered by their children cannot expect their children to know or love them. If in the morning a mother refuses to rise up and serve her sons and daughters, she will find in the afternoon that they will not rise up and call her blessed. Many a mother reaches the end of life with a lonely and hungry heart because, when she was young, she was too busy to knit the hearts of her children to her.

It is important that a mother should keep first things first. For instance, the children are first and the house second. The house was built for the children, and not the children created for the house. If the carpets are more precious than the little feet which scamper over them, then later on the children are likely to be in the street. Some women's thoughts seem to revolve everlastingly around a dustpan and a mop.

First the body, and then the raiment. If the dress is put first, then the health is certain to suffer. The joy of living fades out as soon as life becomes a constant struggle with milliners and dressmakers.

First, the life, and then the meat. If the serving of victuals is given precedence over the things of the spirit, then life is in danger of becoming a haggard worry over silver spoons and dishes, tablecloths and napkins.

First God, and then man. If man is placed first, then the child forms the fatal habit of listening to men rather than to God. A child's attitude to the Eternal is determined in most cases largely by the attitude of his mother. If God is a real power in her life, the children all know it.

CHRISTIAN IN NAME ONLY

There are many mothers who are Christian only in name. Their attitude to life is altogether worldly. Conventionality is their God. They take their standards not from the New Testament, but from society. Their conception of work is pagan, and their idea of marriage is that of a heathen. In the presence of their daughters, they constantly rank men according to their wealth. They speak enthusiastically of "a good match" when the bridegroom is a fop or a roué, and declare that a girl has "done well," when she has bound herself to a man whom it is certain she can never love.

When the secret causes of the innumerable domestic tragedies of our time are laid bare, who knows but that foolish mothers will be found to be the chief culprits? They will stand condemned at the judgment because they never taught their daughters what marriage is. They gave them false ideas of men. They never trained them in the rudiments of household work. Many a woman, amid the heartache of later years, remembers with bitter resentment her mother's inexcusable and tragic neglect.

A mother has a mighty influence in shaping the views not only of her daughters, but also of her sons. One of the reasons why Europe is today deluged with blood is because the mothers of Christendom have been recreant to their duty. They have been hoodwinked by the sophistries of men into the notion that war is something inevitable, and even glorious. War is, in fact, an ancient atrocity which would have been long ago banished from Christendom had Christian women only been true to their finest instincts.

Men will never hate war as it deserves to be hated until mothers breathe into their children an inextinguishable abhorrence of the inhuman abomination of settling disputes by butchering men. The time has come for women to cease to condone or to tolerate such savagery. For ages they have suffered in silence and have been content to bind up the wounds of the poor bodies which cruel war has mangled, but a new day is dawning.

A GREAT SOUL, A NOBLE HEART

But more important than anything that the mother does or says, is what she is. She must be a great soul, alert in intellect, noble of heart. Her outlook must be wide and her sympathies generous and warm. To do her best work in the home, a woman needs to keep her eyes on the world. It is possible to devote one's self too exclusively to household cares. The woman who does this degenerates into a drudge. A drudge is never interesting either to herself or to anyone else. The grinding routine of the days will, unless guarded against, leave the spirit jaded. The endless monotony of commonplace duties is deadening to the higher powers of the soul. Every mother, therefore, needs the influence of the church. To the church the field is always the world. No other institution so liberalizes and broadens the mind. The church stands for service, and it is not service done in a corner, but service carried to the ends of the world. A wise woman is never too busy to take an active interest in movements looking toward the uplift of mankind.

Many a woman is today discontented and unhappy for no other reason than that the range of her interests is too contracted. The most vitalizing and charming women in the land are mothers who have taken some great and noble cause into their hearts.

This, then, is essential to the ideal mother; she must be vital, glad, and strong. She must clothe her family with scarlet, and to do this she must herself be clothed with scarlet. She must be radiant. She must wage uncompromising war against worry and fear. These are two demons to be rigorously faced and irretrievably overwhelmed. She must not allow herself to become so cumbered with many cares that she becomes peevish. There is nothing so destructive to the happiness of the home as a fretful and complaining woman. A woman is certain to become morbid and petulant unless she breathes the atmosphere of a large and varied world. She needs multiplied interests and a wide horizon to keep her brave and bright and true. When Paul wanted the Corinthians to give money to the needy Christians in Palestine, he got them to thinking first of the Resurrection of the Son of God and the life eternal. The Hebrew poet made no mistake when he combined in the ideal woman loyalty to home duties and fidelity to outside obligations. The ideal homemaker is the ideal philanthropist. She dresses her family with scarlet, and she reaches forth both hands to the great world which needs her.

30

To Boys and Girls

". . . one mightier than I. . . ." MARK 1:7

. . . "one mightier than I. . . ." This is what John the Baptist said of Jesus of Nazareth. John was one of the mightiest of men who ever lived, but he knew he was not so powerful as Jesus. Jesus's birthday falls in December. Nearly everybody is now thinking of that day. It is a pity to think of the day without thinking of the man. No Christmas is rightly spent on which we do not think at least for a minute or two of what this man Jesus said and did. No man ever lived a life so beautiful as His. No man ever spoke words so wise as His. No man has so many things to teach us as He. His name is above every name, for He is the holiest of the mighty, and the mightiest of the holy.

It is not enough to know about Him. We ought to try to be like Him. By this is not meant that we ought to dress as He dressed, or to do all things which He did, but that we should have His disposition and think of God and people as He thought. This is by no means easy. We cannot become like Him without trying, and trying hard, and trying all the time. It is so hard to be like Him that some never try at all. Others try and fail, and are so discouraged that they do not try any more. But still others, when they fail, try again. Trying again is the secret of success in all hard undertakings. Never allow yourself to be conquered by failures. No one can finally fail who perseveres. A Christian is one who keeps on trying to be like Jesus. Every boy and girl, then, can be a Christian. It is not necessary to wait until one is grown up before he begins to try to be like Jesus. As soon as one makes up his mind to do this, and begins to do it, he has a right to call himself a Christian.

THE MOST VALUABLE BOOK IN THE WORLD

To become like Jesus, one must know what kind of person He was, and to know this, one should read the Gospels. The Gospels are four short accounts of Jesus's life, and form the first part of the New Testament. The New Testament is a book which every boy and girl should own. It is the most valuable book in all the world. It has in it many jewels, but its richest treasure is the story of the life of Jesus. This story ought to be read again and again. To be ignorant of the life of Jesus is not only a pity but a disgrace. A big boy or girl living in a Christian land who does not know what Jesus said and did ought to feel ashamed. Everyone is poor, no matter what else he owns, if he does not own a copy of the New Testament.

According to the Gospels Jesus was a wonderful man, and the most wonderful thing about Him was His strength. It was His power which caused His fellowmen to stare and wonder. He was so strong that He drew great crowds to Him as though He were a magnet. He did things which no one else could do. Even His words had something in them not to be found in the words of any other teacher. They drove men to do things they had never done before. Even the glance of His eyes was wonderful. One night when some men came to arrest Him, He simply turned His eyes on them, and they were so frightened, they fell backward to the ground. He was so mighty that men obeyed Him just as though He were a king, and they loved Him so dearly that they were willing to die for His sake. He had more than the strength of a giant, for no giant of the story books was ever able so to bend the human will and control the human heart as He did.

It does us good to be with those who are true and strong. Some of their soul seems to pass into us. Looking at what they do makes us want to do likewise, and the sight of their example gives us courage. The worst thing about us is our weakness. A large part of the misery of the world is due to feebleness. The weakest thing about us is our will. We resolve to do something, and do not do it. We make a plan, and fail to carry it out. We are not able to control ourself. Even our tongue often runs away with us. We have a temper, and become its slave. An appetite overpowers us. We form a foolish habit, and have not strength enough to break it. Our companions follow a silly custom, and we are too timid to cast it off. If we were not so weak, we could always do our duty and live up to what we know is right, and obey that little voice within us which is known as conscience. Our only hope of living a life that is simple, brave, and true is in keeping our eyes on One who is mightier than we are.

REAL STRENGTH

Every boy and girl wants to be physically strong. Not to be able to play as other boys and girls play is counted a great misfortune. But there are greater misfortunes than this. One may have strong muscles, and a weak will. He may have good legs, and a feeble conscience. His body may be vigorous, and his heart faint. One may be strong as an animal, and feeble as a human being. Many a little invalid is really stronger than his robust companions. No one ought to be thought strong who cannot hold his tongue, or curb his temper, or speak the truth.

Some people have queer notions of Jesus, and of what it means to live a Christian life. They think that Jesus was an innocent, sweet-natured dreamer Who did not understand the world and Who was too soft to stand up like a man. To be a Christian—so these people think—is to be flabby and weak. Many boys do not want to be a Christian because they are not sure that one can be a Christian and still be manly. They think that to be brave, one must be a soldier and learn to kill, that to be a hero, one must do big things in the public square.

But Jesus was heroic, and the things He did called for a greater amount of courage than He would have needed to lead Caesar's army. Everything He did was hard, and called for an amount of strength which no one of us possesses. The reason why many persons never become Christians is that they are weak, and the reason there are not more good Christians in the world is that men have not the strength to do the things which Jesus commands His followers to do. Jesus was the bravest, truest, manliest man who ever lived, and as soon as you begin to try to live His life, you find that He is mightier than you are.

For instance, Jesus never hated anyone. He had cruel enemies, but He never hated them. Bad men tried to do Him harm, and in return, He was their friend. To return good for evil is hard. If you do not believe it, try it. To hate requires no effort. To get even with a person who does us wrong is as pleasant as eating Christmas pie. Tit for tat is a game we all like to play. We like it because it is so easy. But Jesus did the difficult thing. He loved His enemies, and did good to those who persecuted Him. When men drove nails through His hands and feet, He asked God to forgive them.

Because He tried to do good to those who wronged Him, it was not possible for Him to fight. He never used His fists, or carried a club, or threw stones. He was too manly. Even when He was struck, He did not strike back. To strike back is easy, and not to strike back is hard. To hold the tongue is more difficult than to speak. To use harsh speech when people make us angry is easier than to give a soft answer. To hold back the fist takes more strength when one is provoked than to make use of it. To fight is the easiest thing a boy can do. But Jesus never fought. He was too strong.

THE GREATEST COURAGE

Because He never fought, we are not to think that He never resisted evil. He hated cruelty and falsehood and injustice, and fought them with all His might. He was never afraid to rebuke meanness, no matter where He found it. He did not hesitate to denounce dishonesty in its every form. He never kept still, as many persons do, when lies were spoken in His presence, and He condemned the big men of His country so severely that they seized Him and put Him to death. If we are ever to become able to do good to those who do us harm, and to help those who try to hurt us, and to resist wrong of every kind, we must look to One who is mightier than we.

Jesus was not afraid of what others said about Him. He did not change His plans because someone opposed Him. He was strong enough to stand alone. Few of us are. We go with the crowd. This is easy. When we do things which we suspect are not right, we quiet our conscience by saying, "They all do it." We are afraid to be different from others. We do not want to pay the cost. We do not like to be made fun of, and it hurts us to have people dislike us. A boy who is dared by another boy to do a thing is likely to do it because he does not want to be considered a coward. But if the thing is either foolish or wrong, then the boy who does it is a coward, for he is afraid of another boy. Jesus was never afraid of anybody. He could do anything which He believed it was right for Him to do. He dared to be Himself. He believed that it is better to die than to be afraid to do what one knows is right. I do not see how we can ever be strong enough to do our duty unless we get strength from Someone who is mightier than we are.

Jesus was humble. This does not mean that He felt like a worm, for He never did. It does not mean that He cringed and lay down for everyone to trample on Him. To be humble is to be willing to perform lowly duties. In this sense, Jesus was humble. He liked to think of Himself as a servant. On the last night of His life, He took a towel and a basin of water, and bathed the feet of the men who were going out to preach His message. He did not feel that this was a humiliation. He did not think it was beneath His dignity. Nothing was beneath His dignity which needed to be done. Many of us are too vain to be useful. We hold our heads too high. We like to be despots and have others do our bidding. There is no hope for any of us unless we get help from One who is mightier than we are.

Of all the virtues, Jesus liked obedience best. He thought that without obedience, it is impossible to make progress in life. He often talked about this to His friends. He knew from experience that it is only by obeying God that we are able to learn what next God wants us to do. Disobedience brings darkness, so that one does not know where to go or what to do. He said one day that doing God's will was the food He lived on, and at the end of His life he was able to say what no other man has ever been able to say, that He always did the things which God wanted Him to do.

WHAT OBEDIENCE MEANS

Now, obedience is not a virtue which boys and girls as a rule admire. They think it a nuisance to be compelled to do what someone else wants them to do. They long to grow up so that they shall not be obliged to obey any more. Some of them disobey just as often as they can, for they think that obedience is a form of weakness, and that it is manly and noble to do always just what one pleases. But this is an error. It is disobedience which is easy, and it is obedience which is hard. Obedience is bending the will to a will higher than one's own. To do this requires strength. Anybody can be willful, and follow his own impulses; but only he who is strong can obey. Obedience lights up a home like a lamp. Disobedience darkens and chills like a November fog. Boys and girls who want to take lessons in the art of obedience must look to One who is mightier than they.

Because Jesus was gentle and tender, we must not imagine He was soft. Because He was kind and forgiving, it does not follow He was weak. When men tried to induce Him to do wrong, He was as unyielding as rock, and when He was faced by His foes, He was as bold as a lion. He was the strongest man who has ever lived upon our earth. He never faltered; never ran away. He never told a lie. He never knew what it was to be afraid. No king on earth was powerful enough to hold Him back from doing what He felt He ought to do, and not all the armies of the Roman Empire could have forced Him to do a thing of which His conscience disapproved. He was tempted just as we are, but He never yielded. He went out of this world a conqueror.

This is why the world cannot forget Him. He is the hero of our race. We can never let Him go. We need Him. We are weak, but He is mighty. To look at Him makes us braver. To think of Him adds to our strength. He is mightier than we, and He has promised to help us with His strength. We ought to ask for it every day, especially on Christmas. A great man once declared that He could do all things through Christ who strengthened him. Through Him we also can conquer.

To Grown-Up Sons

"Why do ye . . . transgress the commandment of God because of your tradition?" MATTHEW 15:3

Hot indignation burns in the words. Jesus here strikes at one of the most contemptible of all sins—a son's neglect of his parents. It is an eternal law that children shall honor their father and their mother; but, like all other laws of God, it is easily evaded. Men invent excuses for ridding themselves of their filial obligations. They say they have no time, or that they are too poor, or that their parents are unworthy, or that they are attending to matters of greater importance. In Palestine there had grown up a custom of escaping the performance of filial duty under the guise of fidelity to religion. No matter how needy they might be, the son could free himself of obligation to support them by pronouncing over his money the pious words: "This is dedicated to the Lord!"

Such conduct stirred the heart of Jesus to indignation. To Him the filial relation is infinitely sacred. His heart was sensitive to all the laws of God, especially to the law: "Honor thy father, and thy mother." On the Cross in His dying hour, it was the welfare of His widowed mother which lay heavy on His heart, and He could not go out of the world until He had provided for her support. In this, as in all things else, He is forever the great example.

But among His countrymen there had grown up the pernicious notion that a man can be true to God and at the same time unfaithful to his parents. The Temple was given an iniquitous precedence. Its needs were allowed to overtop the needs of a man's father and mother. A man could be considered good, even though he trampled on the fifth commandment. Against all this the soul of Jesus stood up in vehement protest. These were His crushing words to the religious teachers of His day: "You have made void the word of God because of your tradition!"

There are in the world many mischievous traditions which have a tendency to dull the edge of the law of God, and one of them is the tradition that as soon as a boy is grown up, he has a right to do as he pleases. Every boy, perhaps, at some time or other in his boyhood, ponders the tradition with delight, and longs for the happy day when he shall be delivered from the yoke of parental authority and live a life that is free.

Under the inspiration of this tradition many a boy, when full grown, proceeds forthwith to set at naught the law of God. Exulting in this newfound liberty, the young man now proclaims in attitude and action that he is at liberty to do what he will.

A LIFE-LONG OBLIGATION

It is true that to every man there comes at last the day when he must decide all the great questions of life for himself. When he was a child, he bore the yoke as a child; but when he becomes a man, many of the restraints of childhood are laid aside. Parents have no longer the right to command as they once did, and the youth becomes the architect of his own fortune.

But whatever else a grown-up son may be released from, he never outgrows the obligation of honoring his parents. So long as they live, he owes them a reverence which he owes to no one else. However busy he may be, he owes them some of his time. Whatever may be his attainments, and however exalted his position, the law of God holds him to filial veneration and love.

If the son, having become a man, continues to live under the parental roof, he must not forget that he is in his father's house, and that at many points his father's wish should be considered law. No son in the twenties or thirties or forties is justified because of his age in recklessly disregarding the expressed wishes of his parents, and in declaring by his conduct that he will exercise his legal right of doing what he pleases. Attention to the parental voice is beautiful in sons of whatever age. Considerateness is always lovely, especially when shown to one's parents. Boorishness is never so ugly as when manifested by grown sons to their father or mother. Little boys can be boisterous and rude without lacerating the hearts of their parents, but when boys become men, they cannot speak harshly to their father or mother without having their words hurt worse than a stab or a blow. A grown son who acts the boor in the home of his parents is a barbarian, however polite he may be in society.

When the son leaves his father's house to make a home of his own, he should take heed lest the bonds which bind him to his parents may be weakened. A wise man has reminded us that we ought to keep our friendships in repair, and what friendship is better worth attention than the friendship between parents and their children? By occasional visits and by regular correspondence a son should keep his heart warm toward the old folks at home. In the list of duties which a man owes to his parents, the practice of writing letters should have a prominent place. Other letters may be postponed, but not this one. Others may be cut short, but never this one. This is the one which is most eagerly awaited and thoroughly enjoyed, and the one which the world can least afford to lose. The time is surely coming when there will be no one at home to read these letters, and until that day arrives, let the correspondence go on without interruption. Boys in college often grow negligent at this point. The college tradition in regard to the importance of study and recreation is allowed to set aside the law of God. It is not so important that a lesson in science or mathematics should be mastered or that a game of football may be won as it is that a hungry-hearted mother should be satisfied by her son. Big boys do not know the loneliness which mothers feel in those awful years when for the first time there is a vacant place at the table and no familiar footfall in the hall at evening because their sons have entered college. It is a solemn time for parents when they realize that the home life has been broken and can never be the same again. There is nothing which will so light up the gloom as a loving letter.

If a son is careless in writing home during his college years, the habit is not likely to be broken. The years become increasingly crowded as we go on in life, and the one excuse which covers all sorts of sin is, "I have no time."

Many a son is for a season faithful in his home correspondence; but after marriage and the increase of his business cares, he allows his letters to become more and more infrequent, and the parents, as they go down into that valley which runs out toward the sunset, are deprived of one of the supports which God has planned for them.

Some sons do not write at all. They have gone far from home.

Their parents do not know where they are. There are fathers and mothers who never go to bed without wondering whether their son is alive or not, and never enter upon a new day without hoping that possibly this may be the day on which the long-expected letter shall arrive. What greater cruelty does this world present than this? If these lines should perchance fall under the eye of some prodigal who for years has subjected his father and mother to a lingering torture by his failure to let them know where he is, may the Spirit of God touch his heart, and prompt him to send the long-delayed message. There would be rejoicing today in a thousand homes if prodigal sons would only pay one of their debts.

UNREASONABLE PARENTS

Some of the most puzzling problems which men must face are created by the attitude of their parents, and not a few of the most distressing tragedies in human life spring out of tangled parental and filial relations. A tragedy is not necessarily the product of conscious sin. It may be the creation of ignorance, or carelessless, or mistaken notions. If sons are sometimes a burden to their parents, so do parents sometimes tax the patience and good nature of their sons. Fathers and mothers are not always reasonable, and make demands which no son, however devoted, can comply with.

For instance, who is going to decide what a boy's life work shall be? Parents sometimes insist that this is a part of their parental prerogative. They attempt to drive their sons into callings for which they have no taste and no native aptitude. Many a man is today unhappy and defeated because his self-willed father forced him into a business which he despised. There is a point beyond which no parent should go in attempting to control the career of a son. It is fitting that the father should give the boy the benefit of his counsel, and urge upon him considerations which in his judgment are of weight; but having done this, there is no more which he can rightfully do. Every youth must decide for himself what shall be his calling. He may make a mistake, but he is not so likely to blunder as his father. No son dishonors his parents by insisting on his right to choose his life work.

Nor is it within the province of parents to select for their son a wife. Many parents are incorrigibly wrong-headed at this point. They assume the right to dictate to their son which girl he ought to fall in love with. This is a form of tyranny which must be unflinchingly resisted. It is for every man to decide for himself who his life partner shall be. The fact that a man is younger than his parents is not proof that they are wiser than he, when it comes to the choosing of a wife. A youth may, indeed, choose the wrong woman, but he is not so likely to err as his parents. Instinct is often wiser than experience, and a man in the twenties is better fitted to settle certain questions than are men twice or three times his age. It is he and not his parents who are going to live with the bride, and after they have given their advice and had it rejected, they should have the good sense forever afterward to hold their peace. It is distressing to a loyal-hearted son to go contrary in his matrimonial affairs to the expressed wish of his father or mother, but this is a cross which many a son is called to bear. It is not his fault that he bears it. It is laid on him by his crotchety and dictatorial parents.